The Complete Aeschylus

The Complete Aeschylus
by Aeschylus

Wilder Publications, LLC.
PO Box 3005
Radford VA 24143-3005

ISBN 13: 978-1-5154-2591-5

Table of Contents:

Agamemnon

Dramatis Personae:
A WATCHMAN
A HERALD
CHORUS of Argive Elders, faithful to AGAMEMNON
AGAMEMNON son of Atreus and King of Argos and Mycenae; Commander-in-Chief of the Greek armies in the War against Troy.
AEGISTHUS son of Thyestes, cousin and blood-enemy to Agamemnon lover to Clytemnestra.
CLYTEMNESTRA daughter of Tyndareus, sister of Helen; wife to Agamemnon.
CASSANDRA daughter of Priam, King of Troy, a prophetess; now slave to Agamemnon.

The Scene is the Palace of Atreus at Mycenae. In front of the Palace stand statues of the gods, and altars prepared for sacrifices.

A WATCHMAN
I pray the gods to quit me of my toils,
To close the watch I keep, this livelong year;
For as a watch-dog lying, not at rest,
Propped on one arm, upon the palace-roof
Of Atreus' race, too long, too well I know
The starry conclave of the midnight sky,
Too well, the splendours of the firmament,
The lords of light, whose kingly aspect shows—
What time they set or climb the sky in turn—
The year's divisions, bringing frost or fire.
        And now, as ever, am I set to mark
When shall stream up the glow of signal-flame,
The bale-fire bright, and tell its Trojan tale—
Troy town is ta'en: such issue holds in hope
She in whose woman's breast beats heart of man.
        Thus upon mine unrestful couch I lie,

Bathed with the dews of night, unvisited
By dreams—ah me!—for in the place of sleep
Stands Fear as my familiar, and repels
The soft repose that would mine eyelids seal.
And if at whiles, for the lost balm of sleep,
I medicine my soul with melody
Of trill or song—anon to tears I turn,
Wailing the woe that broods upon this home,
Not now by honour guided as of old.

    But now at last fair fall the welcome hour
That sets me free, whene'er the thick night glow
With beacon-fire of hope deferred no more.
All hail!

    [A beacon-light is seen reddening the distant sky.

    Fire of the night, that brings my spirit day,
Shedding on Argos light, and dance, and song,
Greetings to fortune, hail!

    Let my loud summons ring within the ears
Of Agamemnon's queen, that she anon
Start from her couch and with a shrill voice cry
A joyous welcome to the beacon-blaze,
For Ilion's fall; such fiery message gleams
From yon high flame; and I, before the rest,
Will foot the lightsome measure of our joy;
For I can say, My master's dice fell fair—
Behold! the triple sice, the lucky flame!
Now be my lot to clasp, in loyal love,
The hand of him restored, who rules our home:
Home—but I say no more: upon my tongue
Treads hard the ox o' the adage.

                Had it voice,
The home itself might soothliest tell its tale;
I, of set will, speak words the wise may learn,
To others, nought remember nor discern.

    [Exit. The chorus of old men of Mycenae enter, each leaning on a staff.
During their song Clytemnestra appears in the background, kindling the
altars.

CHORUS

    Ten livelong years have rolled away,

Since the twin lords of sceptred sway,
By Zeus endowed with pride of place,
The doughty chiefs of Atreus' race,
  Went forth of yore,
To plead with Priam, face to face,
  Before the judgment-seat of War!
   A thousand ships from Argive land
Put forth to bear the martial band,
That with a spirit stern and strong
Went out to right the kingdom's wrong—
Pealed, as they went, the battle-song,
  Wild as the vultures' cry;
When o'er the eyrie, soaring high,
In wild bereavèd agony,
Around, around, in airy rings,
They wheel with oarage of their wings,
But not the eyas-brood behold,
That called them to the nest of old;
But let Apollo from the sky,
Or Pan, or Zeus, but hear the cry,
The exile cry, the wail forlorn,
Of birds from whom their home is torn—
On those who wrought the rapine fell,
Heaven sends the vengeful fiends of hell.
  Even so doth Zeus, the jealous lord
And guardian of the hearth and board,
Speed Atreus' sons, in vengeful ire,
'Gainst Paris—sends them forth on fire,
Her to buy back, in war and blood,
Whom one did wed but many woo'd!
And many, many, by his will,
The last embrace of foes shall feel,
And many a knee in dust be bowed,
And splintered spears on shields ring loud,
  Of Trojan and of Greek, before
  That iron bridal-feast be o'er!
  But as he willed 'tis ordered all,
  And woes, by heaven ordained, must fall—
  Unsoothed by tears or spilth of wine

Poured forth too late, the wrath divine
Glares vengeance on the flameless shrine.
    And we in gray dishonoured eld,
Feeble of frame, unfit were held
To join the warrior array
That then went forth unto the fray:
And here at home we tarry, fain
Our feeble footsteps to sustain,
Each on his staff—so strength doth wane,
And turns to childishness again.
For while the sap of youth is green,
And, yet unripened, leaps within,
The young are weakly as the old,
And each alike unmeet to hold
The vantage post of war!
And ah! when flower and fruit are o'er,
  And on life's tree the leaves are sere,
  Age wendeth propped its journey drear,
As forceless as a child, as light
And fleeting as a dream of night
Lost in the garish day!
    But thou, O child of Tyndareus,
  Queen Clytemnestra, speak! and say
  What messenger of joy to-day
Hath won thine ear? what welcome news,
That thus in sacrificial wise
E'en to the city's boundaries
Thou biddest altar-fires arise?
Each god who doth our city guard,
And keeps o'er Argos watch and ward
  From heaven above, from earth below—
The mighty lords who rule the skies,
The market's lesser deities,
  To each and all the altars glow,
Piled for the sacrifice!
And here and there, anear, afar,
Streams skyward many a beacon-star,
Conjur'd and charm'd and kindled well
By pure oil's soft and guileless spell,

Hid now no more
Within the palace' secret store.
  O queen, we pray thee, whatsoe'er,
  Known unto thee, were well revealed,
That thou wilt trust it to our ear,
  And bid our anxious heart be healed!
That waneth now unto despair—
Now, waxing to a presage fair,
Dawns, from the altar, Hope—to scare
From our rent hearts the vulture Care.
  List! for the power is mine, to chant on high
  The chiefs' emprise, the strength that omens gave!
List! on my soul breathes yet a harmony,
  From realms of ageless powers, and strong to save!
  How brother kings, twin lords of one command,
  Led forth the youth of Hellas in their flower,
Urged on their way, with vengeful spear and brand,
  By warrior-birds, that watched the parting hour.
  Go forth to Troy, the eagles seemed to cry—
And the sea-kings obeyed the sky-kings' word,
When on the right they soared across the sky,
  And one was black, one bore a white tail barred.
  High o'er the palace were they seen to soar,
  Then lit in sight of all, and rent and tare,
Far from the fields that she should range no more,
  Big with her unborn brood, a mother-hare.
  And one beheld, the soldier-prophet true,
  And the two chiefs, unlike of soul and will,
In the twy-coloured eagles straight he knew,
  And spake the omen forth, for good and ill.
  (Ah woe and well-a-day! but be the issue fair!)
  Go forth, he cried, _and Priam's town shall fall.
  Yet long the time shall be; and flock and herd,
The people's wealth, that roam before the wall.
  Shall force hew down, when Fate shall give the word.
  But O beware! lest wrath in Heaven abide,
  To dim the glowing battle-forge once more,
And mar the mighty curb of Trojan pride,
  The steel of vengeance, welded as for war!

For virgin Artemis bears jealous hate
Against the royal house, the eagle-pair,
Who rend the unborn brood, insatiate—
  Yea, loathes their banquet on the quivering hare._
  (Ah woe and well-a-day! but be the issue fair!)
  _For well she loves—the goddess kind and mild—
  The tender new-born cubs of lions bold,
Too weak to range—and well the sucking child
  Of every beast that roams by wood and wold.
  So to the Lord of Heaven she prayeth still,
  "Nay. if it must be, be the omen true!
Yet do the visioned eagles presage ill;
  The end be well, but crossed with evil too!"
  Healer Apollo! be her wrath controll'd,
  Nor weave the long delay of thwarting gales,
To war against the Danaans and withhold
  From the free ocean-waves their eager sails!
  She craves, alas! to see a second life
  Shed forth, a curst unhallowed sacrifice—
'Twixt wedded souls, artificer of strife,
  And hate that knows not fear, and fell device.
  At home there tarries like a lurking snake,
  Biding its time, a wrath unreconciled,_
A wily watcher, passionate to slake,
  In blood, resentment for a murdered child.
  Such was the mighty warning, pealed of yore—
  Amid good tidings, such the word of fear,
What time the fateful eagles hovered o'er
  The kings, and Calchas read the omen clear.
  (In strains like his, once more,
Sing woe and well-a-day! but be the issue fair!)
    Zeus—if to The Unknown
  That name of many names seem good—
Zeus, upon Thee I call.
  Thro' the mind's every road
I passed, but vain are all,
  Save that which names thee Zeus, the Highest One,
  Were it but mine to cast away the load,
The weary load, that weighs my spirit down.

He that was Lord of old,
In full-blown pride of place and valour bold,
  Hath fallen and is gone, even as an old tale told!
  And he that next held sway,
  By stronger grasp o'erthrown
  Hath pass'd away!
And whoso now shall bid the triumph-chant arise
  To Zeus, and Zeus alone,
He shall be found the truly wise.
'Tis Zeus alone who shows the perfect way
  Of knowledge: He hath ruled,
Men shall learn wisdom, by affliction schooled.
    In visions of the night, like dropping rain,
  Descend the many memories of pain
Before the spirit's sight: through tears and dole
  Comes wisdom o'er the unwilling soul—
  A boon, I wot, of all Divinity,
That holds its sacred throne in strength, above the sky!
    And then the elder chief, at whose command
  The fleet of Greece was manned,
  Cast on the seer no word of hate,
  But veered before the sudden breath of Fate—
    Ah, weary while! for, ere they put forth sail,
  Did every store, each minish'd vessel, fail,
    While all the Achaean host
    At Aulis anchored lay,
  Looking across to Chalics and the coast
  Where refluent waters welter, rock, and sway;
    And rife with ill delay
  From northern Strymon blew the thwarting blast—
    Mother of famine fell,
    That holds men wand'ring still
  Far from the haven where they fain would be!—
    And pitiless did waste
    Each ship and cable, rotting on the sea,
    And, doubling with delay each weary hour,
Withered with hope deferred th' Achaeans' warlike flower.
    But when, for bitter storm, a deadlier relief,
  And heavier with ill to either chief,

Pleading the ire of Artemis, the seer avowed,
  The two Atridae smote their sceptres on the plain,
  And, striving hard, could not their tears restrain!
  And then the elder monarch spake aloud—
    Ill lot were mine, to disobey!
    And ill, to smite my child, my household's love and pride!
  To stain with virgin Hood a father's hands, and slay
  My daughter, by the altar's side!
    'Twixt woe and woe I dwell—
  I dare not like a recreant fly,
And leave the league of ships, and fail each true ally;
  For rightfully they crave, with eager fiery mind,
  The virgin's blood, shed forth to lull the adverse wind—
    God send the deed be well!
        Thus on his neck he took
        Fate's hard compelling yoke;
Then, in the counter-gale of will abhorr'd, accursed,
    To recklessness his shifting spirit veered—
    Alas! that Frenzy, first of ills and worst,
With evil craft men's souls to sin hath ever stirred!
        And so he steeled his heart—ah, well-a-day—
        Aiding a war for one false woman's sake,
          His child to slay,
      And with her spilt blood make
An offering, to speed the ships upon their way!
        Lusting for war, the bloody arbiters
Closed heart and ears, and would nor hear nor heed
      The girl-voice plead,
  Pity me, Father! nor her prayers,
      Nor tender, virgin years.
        So, when the chant of sacrifice was done,
      Her father bade the youthful priestly train
Raise her, like some poor kid, above the altar-stone,
      From where amid her robes she lay
        Sunk all in swoon away—
Bade them, as with the bit that mutely tames the steed,
      Her fair lips' speech refrain,
Lest she should speak a curse on Atreus' home and seed,
        So, trailing on the earth her robe of saffron dye,

With one last piteous dart from her beseeching eye
   Those that should smite she smote—
Fair, silent, as a pictur'd form, but fain
  To plead, Is all forgot?
How oft those halls of old,
Wherein my sire high feast did hold,
 Rang to the virginal soft strain,
  When I, a stainless child,
 Sang from pure lips and undefiled,
  Sang of my sire, and all
His honoured life, and how on him should fall
  Heaven's highest gift and gain!
 And then—but I beheld not, nor can tell,
  What further fate befel:
 But this is sure, that Calchas' boding strain
  Can ne'er be void or vain.
 This wage from Justice' hand do sufferers earn,
  The future to discern:
 And yet—farewell, O secret of To-morrow!
  Fore-knowledge is fore-sorrow.
 Clear with the clear beams of the morrow's sun,
  The future presseth on.
 Now, let the house's tale, how dark soe'er,
  Find yet an issue fair!—
 So prays the loyal, solitary band
  That guards the Apian land.
  [They turn to Clytemnestra, who leaves the altars and comes forward.
  O queen, I come in reverence of thy sway—
For, while the ruler's kingly seat is void,
The loyal heart before his consort bends.
Now—be it sure and certain news of good,
Or the fair tidings of a flatt'ring hope,
That bids thee spread the light from shrine to shrine,
I, fain to hear, yet grudge not if thou hide.
CLYTEMNESTRA
  As saith the adage, From the womb of Night
Spring forth, with promise fair, the young child Light.
Ay—fairer even than all hope my news—
By Grecian hands is Priam's city ta'en!

CHORUS

    What say'st thou? doubtful heart makes treach'rous ear.

CLYTEMNESTRA

    Hear then again, and plainly—Troy is ours!

CHORUS

    Thrills thro' my heart such joy as wakens tears.

CLYTEMNESTRA

    Ay, thro' those tears thine eye looks loyalty.

CHORUS

    But hast thou proof, to make assurance sure?

CLYTEMNESTRA

    Go to; I have—unless the god has lied.

CHORUS

    Hath some night-vision won thee to belief?

CLYTEMNESTRA

    Out on all presage of a slumb'rous soul!

CHORUS

    But wert thou cheered by Rumour's wingless word?

CLYTEMNESTRA

    Peace—thou dost chide me as a credulous girl.

CHORUS

    Say then, how long ago the city fell?

CLYTEMNESTRA

    Even in this night that now brings forth the dawn.

CHORUS

    Yet who so swift could speed the message here?

CLYTEMNESTRA

    From Ida's top Hephaestus, lord of fire,
Sent forth his sign; and on, and ever on,
Beacon to beacon sped the courier-flame.
From Ida to the crag, that Hermes loves,
Of Lemnos; thence unto the steep sublime
Of Athos, throne of Zeus, the broad blaze flared.
Thence, raised aloft to shoot across the sea,
The moving light, rejoicing in its strength,
Sped from the pyre of pine, and urged its way,
In golden glory, like some strange new sun,
Onward, and reached Macistus' watching heights.
There, with no dull delay nor heedless sleep,

The watcher sped the tidings on in turn,
Until the guard upon Messapius' peak
Saw the far flame gleam on Euripus' tide,
And from the high-piled heap of withered furze
Lit the new sign and bade the message on.
Then the strong light, far flown and yet undimmed,
Shot thro' the sky above Asopus' plain,
Bright as the moon, and on Cithaeron's crag
Aroused another watch of flying fire.
And there the sentinels no whit disowned,
But sent redoubled on, the hest of flame—
Swift shot the light, above Gorgopis' bay,
To Aegiplanctus' mount, and bade the peak
Fail not the onward ordinance of fire.
And like a long beard streaming in the wind,
Full-fed with fuel, roared and rose the blaze,
And onward flaring, gleamed above the cape,
Beneath which shimmers the Saronic bay,
And thence leapt light unto Arachne's peak,
The mountain watch that looks upon our town.
Thence to th' Atrides' roof—in lineage fair,
A bright posterity of Ida's fire.
So sped from stage to stage, fulfilled in turn,
Flame after flame, along the course ordained,
And lo! the last to speed upon its way
Sights the end first, and glows unto the goal.
And Troy is ta'en, and by this sign my lord
Tells me the tale, and ye have learned my word.
CHORUS
    To heaven, O queen, will I upraise new song:
But, wouldst thou speak once more, I fain would hear
From first to last the marvel of the tale.
CLYTEMNESTRA
    Think you—this very morn—the Greeks in Troy,
And loud therein the voice of utter wail!
Within one cup pour vinegar and oil,
And look! unblent, unreconciled, they war.
So in the twofold issue of the strife
Mingle the victor's shout, the captives' moan.

For all the conquered whom the sword has spared
Cling weeping—some unto a brother slain,
Some childlike to a nursing father's form,
And wail the loved and lost, the while their neck
Bows down already 'neath the captive's chain.
And lo! the victors, now the fight is done,
Goaded by restless hunger, far and wide
Range all disordered thro' the town, to snatch
Such victual and such rest as chance may give
Within the captive halls that once were Troy—
Joyful to rid them of the frost and dew,
Wherein they couched upon the plain of old—
Joyful to sleep the gracious night all through,
Unsummoned of the watching sentinel.
Yet let them reverence well the city's gods,
The lords of Troy, tho' fallen, and her shrines;
So shall the spoilers not in turn be spoiled.
Yea, let no craving for forbidden gain
Bid conquerors yield before the darts of greed.
For we need yet, before the race be won,
Homewards, unharmed, to round the course once more.
For should the host wax wanton ere it come,
Then, tho' the sudden blow of fate be spared,
Yet in the sight of gods shall rise once more
    The great wrong of the slain, to claim revenge.
Now, hearing from this woman's mouth of mine,
The tale and eke its warning, pray with me,
Luck sway the scale, with no uncertain poise.
For my fair hopes are changed to fairer joys.
CHORUS
    A gracious word thy woman's lips have told,
Worthy a wise man's utterance, O my queen;
Now with clear trust in thy convincing tale
I set me to salute the gods with song,
Who bring us bliss to counterpoise our pain.
    [Exit Clytemnestra.
    Zeus, Lord of heaven! and welcome night
Of victory, that hast our might
  With all the glories crowned!

On towers of Ilion, free no more,
Hast flung the mighty mesh of war,
  And closely girt them round,
Till neither warrior may 'scape,
Nor stripling lightly overleap
The trammels as they close, and close,
Till with the grip of doom our foes
  In slavery's coil are bound!
   Zeus, Lord of hospitality,
In grateful awe I bend to thee—
  'Tis thou hast struck the blow!
  At Alexander, long ago,
  We marked thee bend thy vengeful bow,
But long and warily withhold
The eager shaft, which, uncontrolled
And loosed too soon or launched too high,
Had wandered bloodless through the sky.
   Zeus, the high God!—whate'er be dim in doubt,
  This can our thought track out—
The blow that fells the sinner is of God,
  And as he wills, the rod
   Of vengeance smiteth sore. One said of old,
  The gods list not to hold
A reckoning with him whose feet oppress
  The grace of holiness—
An impious word! for whensoe'er the sire
  Breathed forth rebellious fire—
What time his household overflowed the measure
  Of bliss and health and treasure—
His children's children read the reckoning plain,
  At last, in tears and pain.
On me let weal that brings no woe be sent,
  And therewithal, content!
Who spurns the shrine of Right, nor wealth nor power
  Shall be to him a tower,
To guard him from the gulf: there lies his lot,
  Where all things are forgot.
Lust drives him on—lust, desperate and wild,
  Fate's sin-contriving child—

And cure is none; beyond concealment clear,
  Kindles sin's baleful glare.
As an ill coin beneath the wearing touch
  Betrays by stain and smutch
Its metal false—such is the sinful wight.
  Before, on pinions light,
Fair Pleasure flits, and lures him childlike on,
  While home and kin make moan
Beneath the grinding burden of his crime;
  Till, in the end of time,
Cast down of heaven, he pours forth fruitless prayer
  To powers that will not hear.
    And such did Paris come
  Unto Atrides' home,
And thence, with sin and shame his welcome to repay,
  Ravished the wife away—
And she, unto her country and her kin
Leaving the clash of shields and spears and arming ships,
And bearing unto Troy destruction for a dower,
  And overbold in sin,
Went fleetly thro' the gates, at midnight hour.
  Oft from the prophets' lips
Moaned out the warning and the wail—Ah woe!
Woe for the home, the home! and for the chieftains, woe
  Woe for the bride-bed, warm
Yet from the lovely limbs, the impress of the form
  Of her who loved her lord, a while ago!
    And woe! for him who stands
Shamed, silent, unreproachful, stretching hands
  That find her not, and sees, yet will not see,
    That she is far away!
And his sad fancy, yearning o'er the sea,
  Shall summon and recall
Her wraith, once more to queen it in his hall.
    And sad with many memories,
The fair cold beauty of each sculptured face—
  And all to hatefulness is turned their grace,
Seen blankly by forlorn and hungering eyes!
  And when the night is deep,

Come visions, sweet and sad, and bearing pain
  Of hopings vain—
Void, void and vain, for scarce the sleeping sight
  Has seen its old delight,
When thro' the grasps of love that bid it stay
  It vanishes away
On silent wings that roam adown the ways of sleep.
    Such are the sights, the sorrows fell,
About our hearth—and worse, whereof I may not tell.
  But, all the wide town o'er,
Each home that sent its master far away
  From Hellas' shore,
Feels the keen thrill of heart, the pang of loss, to-day.
  For, truth to say,
The touch of bitter death is manifold!
Familiar was each face, and dear as life,
  That went unto the war,
But thither, whence a warrior went of old,
  Doth nought return—
Only a spear and sword, and ashes in an urn!
  For Ares, lord of strife,
Who doth the swaying scales of battle hold,
War's money-changer, giving dust for gold,
  Sends back, to hearts that held them dear,
Scant ash of warriors, wept with many a tear,
Light to the hand, but heavy to the soul;
  Yea, fills the light urn full
  With what survived the flame—
Death's dusty measure of a hero's frame!
    Alas! one cries, and yet alas again!
Our chief is gone, the hero of the spear,
  And hath not left his peer!
Ah woe! another moans—my spouse is slain,
  The death of honour, rolled in dust and blood,
Slain for a woman's sin, a false wife's shame!
  Such muttered words of bitter mood
Rise against those who went forth to reclaim;
  Yea, jealous wrath creeps on against th' Atrides' name.
    And others, far beneath the Ilian wall,

Sleep their last sleep—the goodly chiefs and tall,
  Couched in the foeman's land, whereon they gave
Their breath, and lords of Troy, each in his Trojan grave.
    Therefore for each and all the city's breast
  Is heavy with a wrath supprest,
As deep and deadly as a curse more loud
  Flung by the common crowd;
And, brooding deeply, doth my soul await
  Tidings of coming fate,
Buried as yet in darkness' womb.
For not forgetful is the high gods' doom
  Against the sons of carnage: all too long
Seems the unjust to prosper and be strong,
  Till the dark Furies come,
And smite with stern reversal all his home,
  Down into dim obstruction—he is gone,
And help and hope, among the lost, is none!
    O'er him who vaunteth an exceeding fame,
  Impends a woe condign;
The vengeful bolt upon his eyes doth flame,
  Sped from the hand divine.
This bliss be mine, ungrudged of God, to feel—
  To tread no city to the dust,
  Nor see my own life thrust
Down to a slave's estate beneath another's heel!
    Behold, throughout the city wide
Have the swift feet of Rumour hied,
  Roused by the joyful flame:
But is the news they scatter, sooth?
Or haply do they give for truth
  Some cheat which heaven doth frame?
A child were he and all unwise,
  Who let his heart with joy be stirred,
To see the beacon-fires arise,
  And then, beneath some thwarting word,
  Sicken anon with hope deferred.
  The edge of woman's insight still
  Good news from true divideth ill;
Light rumours leap within the bound

That fences female credence round,
But, lightly born, as lightly dies
The tale that springs of her surmise.
   Soon shall we know whereof the bale-fires tell,
The beacons, kindled with transmitted flame;
Whether, as well I deem, their tale is true.
Or whether like some dream delusive came
The welcome blaze but to befool our soul.
For lo! I see a herald from the shore
Draw hither, shadowed with the olive-wreath—
And thirsty dust, twin-brother of the clay,
Speaks plain of travel far and truthful news—
No dumb surmise, nor tongue of flame in smoke,
Fitfully kindled from the mountain pyre;
But plainlier shall his voice say, All is well,
Or—but away, forebodings adverse, now,
   And on fair promise fair fulfilment come!
And whoso for the state prays otherwise,
Himself reap harvest of his ill desire!
   Enter HERALD
   O land of Argos, fatherland of mine!
To thee at last, beneath the tenth year's sun,
My feet return; the bark of my emprise,
Tho' one by one hope's anchors broke away,
Held by the last, and now rides safely here.
Long, long my soul despaired to win, in death,
Its longed-for rest within our Argive land:
And now all hail, O earth, and hail to thee,
New-risen sun! and hail our country's God,
High-ruling Zeus, and thou, the Pythian lord,
Whose arrows smote us once—smite thou no more!
Was not thy wrath wreaked full upon our heads,
O king Apollo, by Scamander's side?
Turn thou, be turned, be saviour, healer, now!
And hail, all gods who rule the street and mart
And Hermes hail! my patron and my pride,
Herald of heaven, and lord of heralds here!
And Heroes, ye who sped us on our way—
To one and all I cry, Receive again

With grace such Argives as the spear has spared.
   Ah, home of royalty, beloved halls,
And solemn shrines, and gods that front the morn!
Benign as erst, with sun-flushed aspect greet
The king returning after many days.
For as from night flash out the beams of day,
So out of darkness dawns a light, a king,
On you, on Argos—Agamemnon comes.
Then hail and greet him well! such meed befits
Him whose right hand hewed down the towers of Troy
With the great axe of Zeus who righteth wrong—
And smote the plain, smote down to nothingness
Each altar, every shrine; and far and wide
Dies from the whole land's face its offspring fair.
   Such mighty yoke of fate he set on Troy—
Our lord and monarch, Atreus' elder son,
And comes at last with blissful honour home;
Highest of all who walk on earth to-day—
Not Paris nor the city's self that paid
Sin's price with him, can boast, Whate'er befal,
The guerdon we have won outweighs it all.
But at Fate's judgment-seat the robber stands
Condemned of rapine, and his prey is torn
Forth from his hands, and by his deed is reaped
A bloody harvest of his home and land
Gone down to death, and for his guilt and lust
His father's race pays double in the dust.
CHORUS
   Hail, herald of the Greeks, new-come from war.
HERALD
   All hail! not death itself can fright me now.
CHORUS
   Was thine heart wrung with longing for thy land?
HERALD
   So that this joy doth brim mine eyes with tears.
CHORUS
   On you too then this sweet distress did fall—
HERALD
   How say'st thou? make me master of thy word.

CHORUS
You longed for us who pined for you again.
HERALD
Craved the land us who craved it, love for love?
CHORUS
Yea till my brooding heart moaned out with pain.
HERALD
Whence thy despair, that mars the army's joy?
CHORUS
Sole cure of wrong is silence, saith the saw.
HERALD
Thy kings afar, couldst thou fear other men?
CHORUS
Death had been sweet, as thou didst say but now.
HERALD
'Tis true; Fate smiles at last. Throughout our toil,
These many years, some chances issued fair,
And some, I wot, were chequered with a curse.
But who, on earth, hath won the bliss of heaven,
Thro' time's whole tenor an unbroken weal?
I could a tale unfold of toiling oars,
Ill rest, scant landings on a shore rock-strewn,
All pains, all sorrows, for our daily doom.
And worse and hatefuller our woes on land;
For where we couched, close by the foeman's wall,
The river-plain was ever dank with dews,
Dropped from the sky, exuded from the earth,
A curse that clung unto our sodden garb,
And hair as horrent as a wild beast's fell.
Why tell the woes of winter, when the birds
Lay stark and stiff, so stern was Ida's snow?
Or summer's scorch, what time the stirless wave
Sank to its sleep beneath the noon-day sun?
Why mourn old woes? their pain has passed away;
And passed away, from those who fell, all care,
For evermore, to rise and live again.
Why sum the count of death, and render thanks
For life by moaning over fate malign?
Farewell, a long farewell to all our woes!

To us, the remnant of the host of Greece,
Comes weal beyond all counterpoise of woe;
Thus boast we rightfully to yonder sun,
Like him far-fleeted over sea and land.
The Argive host prevailed to conquer Troy,
And in the temples of the gods of Greece
Hung up these spoils, a shining sign to Time.
Let those who learn this legend bless aright
The city and its chieftains, and repay
The meed of gratitude to Zeus who willed
And wrought the deed. So stands the tale fulfilled.
CHORUS
   Thy words o'erbear my doubt: for news of good,
The ear of age hath ever youth enow:
But those within and Clytemnestra's self
Would fain hear all; glad thou their ears and mine.
   Re-enter CLYTEMNESTRA
   Last night, when first the fiery courier came,
In sign that Troy is ta'en and razed to earth,
So wild a cry of joy my lips gave out,
That I was chidden—Hath the beacon watch
Made sure unto thy soul the sack of Troy?
A very woman thou, whose heart leaps light
At wandering rumours!—and with words like these
They showed me how I strayed, misled of hope.
Yet on each shrine I set the sacrifice,
And, in the strain they held for feminine,
Went heralds thro' the city, to and fro,
With voice of loud proclaim, announcing joy;
And in each fane they lit and quenched with wine
The spicy perfumes fading in the flame.
All is fulfilled: I spare your longer tale—
The king himself anon shall tell me all.
   Remains to think what honour best may greet
My lord, the majesty of Argos, home.
What day beams fairer on a woman's eyes
Than this, whereon she flings the portal wide,
To hail her lord, heaven-shielded, home from war?
This to my husband, that he tarry not,

But turn the city's longing into joy!
Yea let him come, and coming may he find
A wife no other than he left her, true
And faithful as a watch-dog to his home,
His foemen's foe, in all her duties leal,
Trusty to keep for ten long years unmarred
The store whereon he set his master-seal.
Be steel deep-dyed, before ye look to see
Ill joy, ill fame, from other wight, in me!
HERALD
   'Tis fairly said: thus speaks a noble dame,
Nor speaks amiss, when truth informs the boast.
   [Exit Clytemnestra.
CHORUS
   So has she spoken—be it yours to learn
By clear interpreters her specious word.
Turn to me, herald—tell me if anon
The second well-loved lord of Argos comes?
Hath Menelaus safely sped with you?
HERALD
   Alas—brief boon unto my friends it were,
To flatter them, for truth, with falsehoods fair!
CHORUS
   Speak joy, if truth be joy, but truth, at worst— loo plainly, truth and joy are
here divorced.
HERALD
   The hero and his bark were rapt away
Far from the Grecian fleet? 'tis truth I say.
CHORUS
   Whether in all men's sight from Ilion borne,
Or from the fleet by stress of weather torn?
HERALD
   Full on the mark thy shaft of speech doth light,
And one short word hath told long woes aright.
CHORUS
   But say, what now of him each comrade saith?
What their forebodings, of his life or death?
HERALD
   Ask me no more: the truth is known to none,

Save the earth-fostering, all-surveying Sun,
CHORUS
   Say, by what doom the fleet of Greece was driven?
How rose, how sank the storm, the wrath of heaven?
HERALD
   Nay, ill it were to mar with sorrow's tale
The day of blissful news. The gods demand
Thanksgiving sundered from solicitude.
If one as herald came with rueful face
To say, The curse has fallen, and the host
Gone down to death; and one wide wound has reached
The city's heart, and out of many homes
Many are cast and consecrate to death,
Beneath the double scourge, that Ares loves,
The bloody pair, the fire and sword of doom—
If such sore burden weighed upon my tongue,
'Twere fit to speak such words as gladden fiends.
But—coming as he comes who bringeth news
Of safe return from toil, and issues fair,
To men rejoicing in a weal restored—
Dare I to dash good words with ill, and say
How the gods' anger smote the Greeks in storm?
For fire and sea, that erst held bitter feud,
Now swore conspiracy and pledged their faith,
Wasting the Argives worn with toil and war.
Night and great horror of the rising wave
Came o'er us, and the blasts that blow from Thrace
Clashed ship with ship, and some with plunging prow
Thro' scudding drifts of spray and raving storm
Vanished, as strays by some ill shepherd driven.
And when at length the sun rose bright, we saw
Th' Aegaean sea-field flecked with flowers of death,
Corpses of Grecian men and shattered hulls.
For us indeed, some god, as well I deem,
No human power, laid hand upon our helm,
Snatched us or prayed us from the powers of air,
And brought our bark thro' all, unharmed in hull:
And saving Fortune sat and steered us fair,
So that no surge should gulf us deep in brine,

Nor grind our keel upon a rocky shore.
   So 'scaped we death that lurks beneath the sea,
But, under day's white light, mistrustful all
Of fortune's smile, we sat and brooded deep,
Shepherds forlorn of thoughts that wandered wild,
O'er this new woe; for smitten was our host,
And lost as ashes scattered from the pyre.
Of whom if any draw his life-breath yet,
Be well assured, he deems of us as dead,
As we of him no other fate forebode.
But heaven save all! If Menelaus live,
He will not tarry, but will surely come:
Therefore if anywhere the high sun's ray
Descries him upon earth, preserved by Zeus,
Who wills not yet to wipe his race away,
Hope still there is that homeward he may wend.
Enough—thou hast the truth unto the end.
CHORUS
     Say, from whose lips the presage fell?
   Who read the future all too well,
     And named her, in her natal hour,
     Helen, the bride with war for dower?
   'Twas one of the Invisible,
     Guiding his tongue with prescient power.
   On fleet, and host, and citadel,
     War, sprung from her, and death did lour,
   When from the bride-bed's fine-spun veil
   She to the Zephyr spread her sail.
     Strong blew the breeze—the surge closed o'er
   The cloven track of keel and oar,
     But while she fled, there drove along,
     Fast in her wake, a mighty throng—
   Athirst for blood, athirst for war,
     Forward in fell pursuit they sprung,
   Then leapt on Simois' bank ashore,
     The leafy coppices among—
   No rangers, they, of wood and field,
   But huntsmen of the sword and shield.
     Heaven's jealousy, that works its will,

Sped thus on Troy its destined ill,
  Well named, at once, the Bride and Bane;
  And loud rang out the bridal strain;
But they to whom that song befel
  Did turn anon to tears again;
Zeus tarries, but avenges still
  The husband's wrong, the household's stain!
He, the hearth's lord, brooks not to see
Its outraged hospitality.
    Even now, and in far other tone,
Troy chants her dirge of mighty moan,
  Woe upon Paris, woe and hate!
  Who wooed his country's doom for mate—
This is the burthen of the groan,
  Wherewith she wails disconsolate
The blood, so many of her own
  Have poured in vain, to fend her fate;
Troy! thou hast fed and freed to roam
A lion-cub within thy home!

    A suckling creature, newly ta'en
From mother's teat, still fully fain
  Of nursing care; and oft caressed,
  Within the arms, upon the breast,
Even as an infant, has it lain;
  Or fawns and licks, by hunger pressed,
The hand that will assuage its pain;
  In life's young dawn, a well-loved guest,
A fondling for the children's play,
A joy unto the old and gray.
    But waxing time and growth betrays
The blood-thirst of the lion-race,
  And, for the house's fostering care,
  Unbidden all, it revels there,
And bloody recompense repays—
  Rent flesh of tine, its talons tare:
A mighty beast, that slays and slays,
  And mars with blood the household fair,
A God-sent pest invincible,
A minister of fate and hell.

Even so to Ilion's city came by stealth
 A spirit as of windless seas and skies,
 A gentle phantom-form of joy and wealth,
  With love's soft arrows speeding from its eyes—
Love's rose, whose thorn doth pierce the soul in subtle wise.
  Ah, well-a-day! the bitter bridal-bed,
 When the fair mischief lay by Paris' side!
What curse on palace and on people sped
  With her, the Fury sent on Priam's pride,
By angered Zeus! what tears of many a widowed bride!
  Long, long ago to mortals this was told,
  How sweet security and blissful state
 Have curses for their children—so men hold—
  And for the man of all-too prosperous fate
Springs from a bitter seed some woe insatiate.
  Alone, alone, I deem far otherwise;
  Not bliss nor wealth it is, but impious deed,
 From which that after-growth of ill doth rise!
  Woe springs from wrong, the plant is like the seed—
While Right, in honour's house, doth its own likeness breed.
  Some past impiety, some gray old crime,
  Breeds the young curse, that wantons in our ill,
 Early or late, when haps th' appointed time—
  And out of light brings power of darkness still,
A master-fiend, a foe, unseen, invincible;
  A pride accursed, that broods upon the race
  And home in which dark Atè holds her sway—
 Sin's child and Woe's, that wears its parents' face;
  While Right in smoky cribs shines clear as day,
And decks with weal his life, who walks the righteous way.
  From gilded halls, that hands polluted raise,
  Right turns away with proud averted eyes,
 And of the wealth, men stamp amiss with praise,
  Heedless, to poorer, holier temples hies,
And to Fate's goal guides all, in its appointed wise.
  Hail to thee, chief of Atreus' race,
  Returning proud from Troy subdued!
How shall I greet thy conquering face,
How nor a fulsome praise obtrude,

Nor stint the meed of gratitude?
For mortal men who fall to ill
Take little heed of open truth,
But seek unto its semblance still:
The show of weeping and of ruth
To the forlorn will all men pay,
But, of the grief their eyes display,
Nought to the heart doth pierce its way.
And, with the joyous, they beguile
Their lips unto a feigned smile,
And force a joy, unfelt the while;
But he who as a shepherd wise
  Doth know his flock, can ne'er misread
Truth in the falsehood of his eyes,
Who veils beneath a kindly guise
  A lukewarm love in deed.
And thou, our leader—when of yore
Thou badest Greece go forth to war
For Helen's sake—I dare avow
That then I held thee not as now;
That to my vision thou didst seem
Dyed in the hues of disesteem.
I held thee for a pilot ill,
And reckless, of thy proper will,
Endowing others doomed to die
With vain and forced audacity!
Now from my heart, ungrudgingly,
To those that wrought, this word be said—
Well fall the labour ye have sped—
Let time and search, O king, declare
What men within thy city's bound
Were loyal to the kingdom's care,
  And who were faithless found.

  [Enter Agamemnon in a chariot, accompanied by Cassandra. He speaks
without descending.

AGAMEMNON

  First, as is meet, a king's All-hail be said
To Argos, and the gods that guard the land—
Gods who with me availed to speed us home,

With me availed to wring from Priam's town
The due of justice. In the court of heaven
The gods in conclave sat and judged the cause,
Not from a pleader's tongue, and at the close,
Unanimous into the urn of doom
This sentence gave, On Ilion and her men,
Death: and where hope drew nigh to pardon's urn
No hand there was to cast a vote therein.
And still the smoke of fallen Ilion
Rises in sight of all men, and the flame
Of Atè's hecatomb is living yet,
And where the towers in dusty ashes sink,
Rise the rich fumes of pomp and wealth consumed.
For this must all men pay unto the gods
The meed of mindful hearts and gratitude:
For by our hands the meshes of revenge
Closed on the prey, and for one woman's sake
Troy trodden by the Argive monster lies—
The foal, the shielded band that leapt the wall,
What time with autumn sank the Pleiades.
Yea, o'er the fencing wall a lion sprang
Ravening, and lapped his fill of blood of kings.
   Such prelude spoken to the gods in full,
To you I turn, and to the hidden thing
Whereof ye spake but now: and in that thought
I am as you, and what ye say, say I.
For few are they who have such inborn grace,
As to look up with love, and envy not,
When stands another on the height of weal.
Deep in his heart, whom jealousy hath seized,
Her poison lurking doth enhance his load;
For now beneath his proper woes he chafes,
And sighs withal to see another's weal.
AGAMEMNON
   I speak not idly, but from knowledge sure—
There be who vaunt an utter loyalty,
That is but as the ghost of friendship dead,
A shadow in a glass, of faith gone by.
One only—he who went reluctant forth

Across the seas with me—Odysseus—he
Was loyal unto me with strength and will,
A trusty trace-horse bound unto my car.
Thus—be he yet beneath the light of day,
Or dead, as well I fear—I speak his praise.

  Lastly, whate'er be due to men or gods,
With joint debate, in public council held,
We will decide, and warily contrive
That all which now is well may so abide:
For that which haply needs the healer's art,
That will we medicine, discerning well
If cautery or knife befit the time.

  Now, to my palace and the shrines of home,
I will pass in, and greet you first and fair,
Ye gods, who bade me forth, and home again—
And long may Victory tarry in my train!

  [Enter Clytemnestra, followed by maidens bearing purple robes.
CLYTEMNESTRA

  Old men of Argos, lieges of our realm,
Shame shall not bid me shrink lest ye should see
The love I bear my lord. Such blushing fear
Dies at the last from hearts of human kind.
From mine own soul and from no alien lips,
I know and will reveal the life I bore,
Reluctant, through the lingering livelong years,
The while my lord beleaguered Ilion's wall.

  First, that a wife sat sundered from her lord,
In widowed solitude, was utter woe—
And woe, to hear how rumour's many tongues
  All boded evil—woe, when he who came
  And he who followed spake of ill on ill,
  Keening Lost, lost, all lost! thro' hail and bower.
  Had this my husband met so many wounds,
  As by a thousand channels rumour told,
  No network e'er was full of holes as he.
  Had he been slain, as oft as tidings came
  That he was dead, he well might boast him now
  A second Geryon of triple frame,
  With triple robe of earth above him laid—

For that below, no matter—triply dead,
Dead by one death for every form he bore.
And thus distraught by news of wrath and woe,
Oft for self-slaughter had I slung the noose,
But others wrenched it from my neck away.
Hence haps it that Orestes, thine and mine,
The pledge and symbol of our wedded troth,
Stands not beside us now, as he should stand.
Nor marvel thou at this: he dwells with one
Who guards him loyally; 'tis Phocis' king,
Strophius, who warned me erst, Bethink thee, queen,
What woes of doubtful issue well may fall!
Thy lord in daily jeopardy at Troy,
While here a populace uncurbed may cry
"Down with the council, down!" bethink thee too,
'Tis the world's way to set a harder heel
On fallen power.
            For thy child's absence then
Such mine excuse, no wily afterthought.
For me, long since the gushing fount of tears
Is wept away; no drop is left to shed.
Dim are the eyes that ever watched till dawn,
Weeping, the bale-fires, piled for thy return,
Night after night unkindled. If I slept,
Each sound—the tiny humming of a gnat,
Roused me again, again, from fitful dreams
Wherein I felt thee smitten, saw thee slain,
Thrice for each moment of mine hour of sleep.
  All this I bore, and now, released from woe,
I hail my lord as watch-dog of a fold,
As saving stay-rope of a storm-tossed ship,
As column stout that holds the roof aloft,
As only child unto a sire bereaved,
As land beheld, past hope, by crews forlorn,
As sunshine fair when tempest's wrath is past,
As gushing spring to thirsty wayfarer.
So sweet it is to 'scape the press of pain.
With such salute I bid my husband hail!
Nor heaven be wroth therewith! for long and hard

I bore that ire of old.
                    Sweet lord, step forth,
Step from thy car, I pray—nay, not on earth
Plant the proud foot, O king, that trod down Troy!
Women! why tarry ye, whose task it is
To spread your monarch's path with tapestry?
Swift, swift, with purple strew his passage fair,
That justice lead him to a home, at last,
He scarcely looked to see.
                    For what remains,
Zeal unsubdued by sleep shall nerve my hand
To work as right and as the gods command.

AGAMEMNON

    Daughter of Leda, watcher o'er my home,
Thy greeting well befits mine absence long,
For late and hardly has it reached its end.
Know, that the praise which honour bids us crave,
Must come from others' lips, not from our own:
See too that not in fashion feminine
Thou make a warrior's pathway delicate;
Not unto me, as to some Eastern lord,
Bowing thyself to earth, make homage loud.
Strew not this purple that shall make each step
An arrogance; such pomp beseems the gods,
Not me. A mortal man to set his foot
On these rich dyes? I hold such pride in fear,
And bid thee honour me as man, not god.

    Fear not—such footcloths and all gauds apart,
  Loud from the trump of Fame my name is blown;
  Best gift of heaven it is, in glory's hour,
  To think thereon with soberness: and thou?
  Bethink thee of the adage, Call none blest
  Till peaceful death have crowned a life of weal.
  'Tis said: I fain would fare unvexed by fear.

CLYTEMNESTRA

    Nay, but unsay it—thwart not thou my will!

AGAMEMNON

    Know, I have said, and will not mar my word.

CLYTEMNESTRA

Was it fear made this meekness to the gods?
CLYTEMNESTRA

AGAMEMNON

If cause be cause, 'tis mine for this resolve.
CLYTEMNESTRA

What, think'st thou, in thy place had Priam done?
AGAMEMNON

He surely would have walked on broidered robes.
CLYTEMNESTRA

Then fear not thou the voice of human blame.
AGAMEMNON

Yet mighty is the murmur of a crowd.
CLYTEMNESTRA

Shrink not from envy, appanage of bliss.
AGAMEMNON

War is not woman's part, nor war of words.
CLYTEMNESTRA

Yet happy victors well may yield therein.
AGAMEMNON

Dost crave for triumph in this petty strife?
CLYTEMNESTRA

Yield; of thy grace permit me to prevail!
AGAMEMNON

Then, if thou wilt, let some one stoop to loose
Swiftly these sandals, slaves beneath my foot:
And stepping thus upon the sea's rich dye,
I pray, Let none among the gods look down
With jealous eye on me—reluctant all,
To trample thus and mar a thing of price,
Wasting the wealth of garments silver-worth.
Enough hereof: and, for the stranger maid,
Lead her within, but gently: God on high
Looks graciously on him whom triumph's hour
Has made not pitiless. None willingly
Wear the slave's yoke—and she, the prize and flower
Of all we won, comes hither in my train,
Gift of the army to its chief and lord.
—Now, since in this my will bows down to thine,
I will pass in on purples to my home.
CLYTEMNESTRA

A Sea there is—and who shall stay its springs?
And deep within its breast, a mighty store,
Precious as silver, of the purple dye,
Whereby the dipped robe doth its tint renew.
Enough of such, O king, within thy halls
There lies, a store that cannot fail; but I—
I would have gladly vowed unto the gods
Cost of a thousand garments trodden thus,
(Had once the oracle such gift required)
Contriving ransom for thy life preserved.
  For while the stock is firm the foliage climbs,
  Spreading a shade what time the dog-star glows;
  And thou, returning to thine hearth and home,
  Art as a genial warmth in winter hours,
  Or as a coolness, when the lord of heaven
  Mellows the juice within the bitter grape.
  Such boons and more doth bring into a home
  The present footstep of its proper lord.
  Zeus, Zeus, Fulfilment's lord! my vows fulfil,
  And whatsoe'er it be, work forth thy will!
    [Exeunt all but Cassandra and the Chorus.
CHORUS
    Wherefore for ever on the wings of fear
    Hovers a vision drear
  Before my boding heart? a strain,
  Unbidden and unwelcome, thrills mine ear,
    Oracular of pain.
  Not as of old upon my bosom's throne
    Sits Confidence, to spurn
    Such fears, like dreams we know not to discern.
  Old, old and gray long since the time has grown,
    Which saw the linked cables moor
  The fleet, when erst it came to Ilion's sandy shore;
    And now mine eyes and not another's see
      Their safe return.
        Yet none the less in me
  The inner spirit sings a boding song,
    Self-prompted, sings the Furies' strain—
      And seeks, and seeks in vain,

To hope and to be strong!
  Ah! to some end of Fate, unseen, unguessed,
Are these wild throbbings of my heart and breast?
  Yea, of some doom they tell?
    Each pulse, a knell.
 Lief, lief I were, that all
To unfulfilment's hidden realm might fall.
    Too far, too far our mortal spirits strive,
  Grasping at utter weal, unsatisfied—
Till the fell curse, that dwelleth hard beside,
Thrust down the sundering wall. Too fair they blow,
  The gales that waft our bark on Fortune's tide!
  Swiftly we sail, the sooner all to drive
  Upon the hidden rock, the reef of woe.
    Then if the hand of caution warily
    Sling forth into the sea
Part of the freight, lest all should sink below,
From the deep death it saves the bark: even so,
  Doom-laden though it be, once more may rise
  His household, who is timely wise.
    How oft the famine-stricken field
Is saved by God's large gift, the new year's yield!
    But blood of man once spilled,
Once at his feet shed forth, and darkening the plain,—
  Nor chant nor charm can call it back again.
    So Zeus hath willed:
Else had he spared the leech Asclepius, skilled
  To bring man from the dead: the hand divine
Did smite himself with death—a warning and a sign.
    Ah me! if Fate, ordained of old,
Held not the will of gods constrained, controlled,
  Helpless to us ward, and apart—
  Swifter than speech my heart
Had poured its presage out!
Now, fretting, chafing in the dark of doubt,
  'Tis hopeless to unfold
Truth, from fear's tangled skein; and, yearning to proclaim
  Its thought, my soul is prophecy and flame.
  Re-enter CLYTEMNESTRA

Get thee within thou too, Cassandra, go!
For Zeus to thee in gracious mercy grants
To share the sprinklings of the lustral bowl,
Beside the altar of his guardianship,
Slave among many slaves. What, haughty still?
Step from the car; Alcmena's son, 'tis said,
Was sold perforce and bore the yoke of old.
Ay, hard it is, but, if such fate befall,
'Tis a fair chance to serve within a home
Of ancient wealth and power. An upstart lord,
To whom wealth's harvest came beyond his hope,
Is as a lion to his slaves, in all
Exceeding fierce, immoderate in sway.
Pass in: thou hearest what our ways will be.
CHORUS
    Clear unto thee, O maid, is her command,
But thou—within the toils of Fate thou art—
If such thy will, I urge thee to obey;
Yet I misdoubt thou dost nor hear nor heed.
CLYTEMNESTRA
    I wot—unless like swallows she doth use
Some strange barbarian tongue from oversea—
My words must speak persuasion to her soul.
CHORUS
    Obey: there is no gentler way than this.
Step from the car's high seat and follow her.
CLYTEMNESTRA
    Truce to this bootless waiting here without!
I will not stay: beside the central shrine
The victims stand, prepared for knife and fire—
Offerings from hearts beyond all hope made glad.
Thou—if thou reckest aught of my command,
'Twere well done soon: but if thy sense be shut
From these my words, let thy barbarian hand
Fulfil by gesture the default of speech.
CHORUS
    No native is she, thus to read thy words
Unaided: like some wild thing of the wood,
New-trapped, behold! she shrinks and glares on thee.

CLYTEMNESTRA
'Tis madness and the rule of mind distraught,
Since she beheld her city sink in fire,
And hither comes, nor brooks the bit, until
In foam and blood her wrath be champed away.
See ye to her; unqueenly 'tis for me,
Unheeded thus to cast away my words.
    [Exit Clytemnestra.
CHORUS
    But with me pity sits in anger's place.
Poor maiden, come thou from the car; no way
There is but this—take up thy servitude.
CASSANDRA
    Woe, woe, alas! Earth, Mother Earth! and thou
Apollo, Apollo!
CHORUS
    Peace! shriek not to the bright prophetic god,
Who will not brook the suppliance of woe.
CASSANDRA
    Woe, woe, alas! Earth, Mother Earth! and thou
Apollo, Apollo!
CHORUS
    Hark, with wild curse she calls anew on him,
Who stands far off and loathes the voice of wail.
CASSANDRA
    Apollo, Apollo!
God of all ways, but only Death's to me,
Once and again, O thou, Destroyer named,
Thou hast destroyed me, thou, my love of old!
CHORUS
    She grows presageful of her woes to come,
Slave tho' she be, instinct with prophecy.
CASSANDRA
    Apollo, Apollo!
God of all ways, but only Death's to me,
O thou Apollo, thou Destroyer named!
What way hast led me, to what evil home?
CHORUS
    Know'st thou it not? The home of Atreus' race:

Take these my words for sooth and ask no more.
CASSANDRA

  Home cursed of God! Bear witness unto me,
  Ye visioned woes within—
The blood-stained hands of them that smite their kin—
The strangling noose, and, spattered o'er
With human blood, the reeking floor!
CHORUS

  How like a sleuth-hound questing on the track,
Keen-scented unto blood and death she hies!
CASSANDRA

  Ah! can the ghostly guidance fail,
Whereby my prophet-soul is onwards led?
Look! for their flesh the spectre-children wail,
Their sodden limbs on which their father fed!
CHORUS

  Long since we knew of thy prophetic fame,—
But for those deeds we seek no prophet's tongue.
CASSANDRA

  God! 'tis another crime—
Worse than the storied woe of olden time,
Cureless abhorred, that one is plotting here—
A shaming death, for those that should be dear!
  Alas! and far away, in foreign land,
  He that should help doth stand!
CHORUS

  I knew th' old tales, the city rings withal—
But now thy speech is dark, beyond my ken.
CASSANDRA

  O wretch, O purpose fell!
Thou for thy wedded lord
The cleansing wave hast poured—
A treacherous welcome!
          How the sequel tell?
Too soon 'twill come, too soon, for now, even now,
She smites him, blow on blow!
CHORUS

  Riddles beyond my rede—I peer in vain
Thro' the dim films that screen the prophecy.

CASSANDRA

God! a new sight! a net, a snare of hell,
Set by her hand—herself a snare more fell!
  A wedded wife, she slays her lord,
Helped by another hand!
                    Ye powers, whose hate
  Of Atreus' home no blood can satiate,
Raise the wild cry above the sacrifice abhorred!

CHORUS

  Why biddest thou some fiend, I know not whom,
Shriek o'er the house? Thine is no cheering word.
  Back to my heart in frozen fear I feel
  My waning life-blood run—
  The blood that round the wounding steel
  Ebbs slow, as sinks life's parting sun—
Swift, swift and sure, some woe comes pressing on!

CASSANDRA

    Away, away—keep him away—
  The monarch of the herd, the pasture's pride,
  Far from his mate! In treach'rous wrath,
  Muffling his swarthy horns, with secret scathe
    She gores his fenceless side!
  Hark! in the brimming bath,
  The heavy plash—the dying cry—
Hark—in the laver—hark, he falls by treachery!

CHORUS

    I read amiss dark sayings such as thine,
  Yet something warns me that they tell of ill.
    O dark prophetic speech,
    Ill tidings dost thou teach
    Ever, to mortals here below!
    Ever some tale of awe and woe
    Thro' all thy windings manifold
    Do we unriddle and unfold!

CASSANDRA

    Ah well-a-day! the cup of agony,
  Whereof I chant, foams with a draught for me.
  Ah lord, ah leader, thou hast led me here—
  Was't but to die with thee whose doom is near?

CHORUS

    Distraught thou art, divinely stirred,
  And wailest for thyself a tuneless lay,
  As piteous as the ceaseless tale
  Wherewith the brown melodious bird
  Doth ever Itys! Itys! wail,
Deep-bowered in sorrow, all its little life-time's day!

CASSANDRA

    Ah for thy fate, O shrill-voiced nightingale!
  Some solace for thy woes did Heaven afford,
  Clothed thee with soft brown plumes, and life apart from wail?
  But for my death is edged the double-biting sword!

CHORUS

    What pangs are these, what fruitless pain,
   Sent on thee from on high?
  Thou chantest terror's frantic strain,
  Yet in shrill measured melody.
  How thus unerring canst thou sweep along
  The prophet's path of boding song?

CASSANDRA

    Woe, Paris, woe on thee! thy bridal joy
  Was death and fire upon thy race and Troy!
   And woe for thee, Scamander's flood!
   Beside thy banks, O river fair,
   I grew in tender nursing care
   From childhood unto maidenhood!
  Now not by thine, but by Cocytus' stream
  And Acheron's banks shall ring my boding scream.

CHORUS

    Too plain is all, too plain!
A child might read aright thy fateful strain.
  Deep in my heart their piercing fang
  Terror and sorrow set, the while I heard
  That piteous, low, tender word,
Yet to mine ear and heart a crushing pang.

   CASSANDRA

Woe for my city, woe for Ilion's fall!
  Father, how oft with sanguine stain
  Streamed on thine altar-stone the blood of cattle, slain

That heaven might guard our wall!
But all was shed in vain.
Low lie the shattered towers whereas they fell,
And I—ah burning heart!—shall soon lie low as well.
CHORUS
Of sorrow is thy song, of sorrow still!
Alas, what power of ill
Sits heavy on thy heart and bids thee tell
In tears of perfect moan thy deadly tale?
Some woe—I know not what—must close thy piteous wail.
CASSANDRA
List! for no more the presage of my soul,
Bride-like, shall peer from its secluding veil;
But as the morning wind blows clear the east,
More bright shall blow the wind of prophecy,
And as against the low bright line of dawn
Heaves high and higher yet the rolling wave,
So in the clearing skies of prescience
Dawns on my soul a further, deadlier woe,
And I will speak, but in dark speech no more.
Bear witness, ye, and follow at my side—
I scent the trail of blood, shed long ago.
Within this house a choir abidingly
Chants in harsh unison the chant of ill;
Yea, and they drink, for more enhardened joy,
Man's blood for wine, and revel in the halls,
Departing never, Furies of the home.
They sit within, they chant the primal curse,
Each spitting hatred on that crime of old,
The brother's couch, the love incestuous
That brought forth hatred to the ravisher.
Say, is my speech or wild and erring now,
Or doth its arrow cleave the mark indeed?
They called me once, The prophetess of lies,
The wandering hag, the pest of every door—
Attest ye now, She knows in very sooth
The house's curse, the storied infamy.
CHORUS
Yet how should oath—how loyally soe'er

I swear it—aught avail thee? In good sooth,
AGAMEMNON
   My wonder meets thy claim: I stand amazed
That thou, a maiden born beyond the seas,
Dost as a native know and tell aright
Tales of a city of an alien tongue.
CASSANDRA
   That is my power—a boon Apollo gave.
CHORUS
   God though he were, yearning for mortal maid?
CASSANDRA
   Ay! what seemed shame of old is shame no more.
CHORUS
   Such finer sense suits not with slavery.
CASSANDRA
   He strove to win me, panting for my love.
CHORUS
   Came ye by compact unto bridal joys?
CASSANDRA
   Nay—for I plighted troth, then foiled the god.
CHORUS
   Wert thou already dowered with prescience?
CASSANDRA
   Yea—prophetess to Troy of all her doom.
CHORUS
   How left thee then Apollo's wrath unscathed?
CASSANDRA
   I, false to him, seemed prophet false to all.
CHORUS
   Not so—to us at least thy words seem sooth.
CASSANDRA
   Woe for me, woe! Again the agony—
Dread pain that sees the future all too well
With ghastly preludes whirls and racks my soul.
Behold ye—yonder on the palace roof
The spectre-children sitting—look, such things
As dreams are made on, phantoms as of babes,
Horrible shadows, that a kinsman's hand
Hath marked with murder, and their arms are full—

A rueful burden—see, they hold them up,
The entrails upon which their father fed!
  For this, for this, I say there plots revenge
A coward lion, couching in the lair—
Guarding the gate against my master's foot—
My master—mine—I bear the slave's yoke now,
And he, the lord of ships, who trod down Troy,
Knows not the fawning treachery of tongue
Of this thing false and dog-like—how her speech
Glozes and sleeks her purpose, till she win
By ill fate's favour the desired chance,
Moving like Atè to a secret end.
O aweless soul! the woman slays her lord—
Woman? what loathsome monster of the earth
Were fit comparison? The double snake—
Or Scylla, where she dwells, the seaman's bane,
Girt round about with rocks? some hag of hell,
Raving a truceless curse upon her kin?
Hark—even now she cries exultingly
The vengeful cry that tells of battle turned—
How fain, forsooth, to greet her chief restored!
Nay then, believe me not: what skills belief
Or disbelief? Fate works its will—and thou
Wilt see and say in ruth, Her tale was true.
CHORUS
  Ah—'tis Thyestes' feast on kindred flesh—
I guess her meaning and with horror thrill,
Hearing no shadow'd hint of th' o'er-true tale,
But its full hatefulness: yet, for the rest,
Far from the track I roam, and know no more.
CASSANDRA
  'Tis Agamemnon's doom thou shalt behold.
CHORUS
  Peace, hapless woman, to thy boding words!
CASSANDRA
  Far from my speech stands he who sains and saves.
CHORUS
  Ay—were such doom at hand—which God forbid!
CASSANDRA

Thou prayest idly—these move swift to slay.
CHORUS
   What man prepares a deed of such despite?
CASSANDRA
   Fool! thus to read amiss mine oracles.
CHORUS
   Deviser and device are dark to me.
CASSANDRA
   Dark! all too well I speak the Grecian tongue.
CHORUS
   Ay—but in thine, as in Apollo's strains,
Familiar is the tongue, but dark the thought.
CASSANDRA
   Ah ah the fire! it waxes, nears me now—
Woe, woe for me, Apollo of the dawn!
   Lo, how the woman-thing, the lioness
Couched with the wolf—her noble mate afar—
Will slay me, slave forlorn! Yea, like some witch
She drugs the cup of wrath, that slays her lord
With double death—his recompense for me!
Ay, 'tis for me, the prey he bore from Troy,
That she hath sworn his death, and edged the steel!
Ye wands, ye wreaths that cling around my neck,
Ye showed me prophetess yet scorned of all—
I stamp you into death, or e'er I die—
Down, to destruction!
           Thus I stand revenged—
Go, crown some other with a prophet's woe.
Look! it is he, it is Apollo's self
Rending from me the prophet-robe he gave
God! while I wore it yet, thou saw'st me mocked
There at my home by each malicious mouth—
To all and each, an undivided scorn.
The name alike and fate of witch and cheat—
Woe, poverty, and famine—all I bore;
And at this last the god hath brought me here
Into death's toils, and what his love had made
His hate unmakes me now: and I shall stand
Not now before the altar of my home,

But me a slaughter-house and block of blood
Shall see hewn down, a reeking sacrifice.
Yet shall the gods have heed of me who die,
For by their will shall one requite my doom.
He, to avenge his father's blood outpoured,
Shall smite and slay with matricidal hand.
Ay, he shall come—tho' far away he roam,
A banished wanderer in a stranger's land—
To crown his kindred's edifice of ill,
Called home to vengeance by his father's fall:
Thus have the high gods sworn, and shall fulfil.

   And now why mourn I, tarrying on earth,
Since first mine Ilion has found its fate
And I beheld, and those who won the wall
Pass to such issue as the gods ordain?
I too will pass and like them dare to die!
   [Turns and looks upon the palace door.
   Portal of Hades, thus I bid thee hail!
Grant me one boon—a swift and mortal stroke,
That all unwrung by pain, with ebbing blood
Shed forth in quiet death, I close mine eyes.
CHORUS
   Maid of mysterious woes, mysterious lore,
Long was thy prophecy: but if aright
Thou readest all thy fate, how, thus unscared,
Dost thou approach the altar of thy doom,
As fronts the knife some victim, heaven-controlled?
CASSANDRA
   Friends, there is no avoidance in delay.
CHORUS
   Yet who delays the longest, his the gain.
CASSANDRA
   The day is come—flight were small gain to me!
CHORUS
   O brave endurance of a soul resolved!
CASSANDRA
   That were ill praise, for those of happier doom.
CHORUS
   All fame is happy, even famous death.

CASSANDRA

Ah sire, ah brethren, famous once were ye!

[She moves to enter the house, then starts back.

CHORUS

What fear is this that scares thee from the house?

CASSANDRA

Pah!

CHORUS

What is this cry? some dark despair of soul?

CASSANDRA

Pah! the house fumes with stench and spilth of blood.

CHORUS

How? 'tis the smell of household offerings.

CASSANDRA

'Tis rank as charnel-scent from open graves.

CHORUS

Thou canst not mean this scented Syrian nard?

CASSANDRA

Nay, let me pass within to cry aloud

The monarch's fate and mine—enough of life.

Ah friends!

Bear to me witness, since I fall in death,

That not as birds that shun the bush and scream

I moan in idle terror. This attest

When for my death's revenge another dies,

A woman for a woman, and a man

Falls, for a man ill-wedded to his curse.

Grant me this boon—the last before I die.

CHORUS

Brave to the last! I mourn thy doom foreseen.

CASSANDRA

Once more one utterance, but not of wail,

Though for my death—and then I speak no more.

I thou whose beam I shall not see again,

To thee I cry, Let those whom vengeance calls

To slay their kindred's slayers, quit withal

The death of me, the slave, the fenceless prey.

Ah state of mortal man! in time of weal,

A line, a shadow! and if ill fate fall,

One wet sponge-sweep wipes all our trace away—
And this I deem less piteous, of the twain.
　　[Exit into the palace.
CHORUS
　　Too true it is! our mortal state
With bliss is never satiate,
And none, before the palace high
And stately of prosperity,
Cries to us with a voice of fear,
Away! 'tis ill to enter here!
　　Lo! this our lord hath trodden down,
By grace of heaven, old Priam's town,
　　And praised as god he stands once more
　　On Argos' shore!
Yet now—if blood shed long ago
Cries out that other blood shall flow—
His life-blood, his, to pay again
The stern requital of the slain—
Peace to that braggart's vaunting vain,
Who, having heard the chieftain's tale,
Yet boasts of bliss untouched by bale!
　　[A loud cry from within.
VOICE OF AGAMEMNON
　　O I am sped—a deep, a mortal blow.
CHORUS
　　Listen, listen! who is screaming as in mortal agony?
VOICE OF AGAMEMNON
　　O! O! again, another, another blow!
CHORUS
　　The bloody act is over—I have heard the monarch cry—
Let us swiftly take some counsel, lest we too be doomed to die.
ONE OF THE CHORUS
　　'Tis best, I judge, aloud for aid to call,
"Ho! loyal Argives! to the palace, all!"
ANOTHER
　　Better, I deem, ourselves to bear the aid,
And drag the deed to light, while drips the blade.
ANOTHER
　　Such will is mine, and what thou say'st I say:

Swiftly to act! the time brooks no delay.
ANOTHER

   Ay, for 'tis plain, this prelude of their song
Foretells its close in tyranny and wrong.
ANOTHER

   Behold, we tarry—but thy name, Delay,
They spurn, and press with sleepless hand to slay.
ANOTHER

   I know not what 'twere well to counsel now—
Who wills to act, 'tis his to counsel how.
ANOTHER

   Thy doubt is mine: for when a man is slain,
I have no words to bring his life again.
ANOTHER

   What? e'en for life's sake, bow us to obey
These house-defilers and their tyrant sway?
ANOTHER

   Unmanly doom! 'twere better far to die—
Death is a gentler lord than tyranny.
ANOTHER

   Think well—must cry or sign of woe or pain
Fix our conclusion that the chief is slain?
ANOTHER

   Such talk befits us when the deed we see—
Conjecture dwells afar from certainty.
LEADER OF THE CHORUS

   I read one will from many a diverse word,
To know aright, how stands it with our lord!

   [The scene opens, disclosing Clytemnestra, who comes forward. The body
of Agamemnon lies, muffled in a long robe, within a silver-sided laver; the
corpse of Cassandra is laid beside him.
CLYTEMNESTRA

   Ho, ye who heard me speak so long and oft
The glozing word that led me to my will?
Hear how I shrink not to unsay it all!
How else should one who willeth to requite
Evil for evil to an enemy
Disguised as friend, weave the mesh straitly round him,
Not to be overleaped, a net of doom?

This is the sum and issue of old strife,
Of me deep-pondered and at length fulfilled.
All is avowed, and as I smote I stand
With foot set firm upon a finished thing!
I turn not to denial: thus I wrought
So that he could nor flee nor ward his doom,
Even as the trammel hems the scaly shoal,
I trapped him with inextricable toils,
The ill abundance of a baffling robe;
Then smote him, once, again—and at each wound
He cried aloud, then as in death relaxed
Each limb and sank to earth; and as he lay,
Once more I smote him, with the last third blow,
Sacred to Hades, saviour of the dead.
And thus he fell, and as he passed away,
Spirit with body chafed; each dying breath
Flung from his breast swift bubbling jets of gore,
And the dark sprinklings of the rain of blood
Fell upon me; and I was fain to feel
That dew—not sweeter is the rain of heaven
To cornland, when the green sheath teems with grain,
   Elders of Argos—since the thing stands so,
I bid you to rejoice, if such your will:
Rejoice or not, I vaunt and praise the deed,
And well I ween, if seemly it could be,
'Twere not ill done to pour libations here,
Justly—ay, more than justly—on his corpse
Who filled his home with curses as with wine,
And thus returned to drain the cup he filled.
CHORUS
   I marvel at thy tongue's audacity,
To vaunt thus loudly o'er a husband slain.
CLYTEMNESTRA
   Ye hold me as a woman, weak of will,
And strive to sway me: but my heart is stout,
Nor fears to speak its uttermost to you,
Albeit ye know its message. Praise or blame,
Even as ye list,—I reck not of your words.
Lo! at my feet lies Agamemnon slain,

My husband once—and him this hand of mine,
A right contriver, fashioned for his death.
Behold the deed!
CHORUS
    Woman, what deadly birth,
What venomed essence of the earth
Or dark distilment of the wave,
To thee such passion gave,
Nerving thine hand
To set upon thy brow this burning crown,
The curses of thy land?
Our king by thee cut off, hewn down!
Go forth—they cry—accursèd and forlorn,
To hate and scorn!

CLYTEMNESTRA
  O ye just men, who speak my sentence now,
The city's hate, the ban of all my realm!
Ye had no voice of old to launch such doom
On him, my husband, when he held as light
My daughter's life as that of sheep or goat,
One victim from the thronging fleecy fold!
Yea, slew in sacrifice his child and mine,
The well-loved issue of my travail-pangs,
To lull and lay the gales that blew from Thrace.
That deed of his, I say, that stain and shame,
Had rightly been atoned by banishment;
But ye, who then were dumb, are stern to judge
This deed of mine that doth affront your ears.
Storm out your threats, yet knowing this for sooth,
That I am ready, if your hand prevail
As mine now doth, to bow beneath your sway:
If God say nay, it shall be yours to learn
By chastisement a late humility.
CHORUS
  Bold is thy craft, and proud
Thy confidence, thy vaunting loud;
Thy soul, that chose a murd'ress' fate,
Is all with blood elate—

Maddened to know
The blood not yet avenged, the damnèd spot
Crimson upon thy brow.
But Fate prepares for thee thy lot—
Smitten as thou didst smite, without a friend,
To meet thine end!

CLYTEMNESTRA

    Hear then the sanction of the oath I swear?
By the great vengeance for my murdered child,
By Atè, by the Fury unto whom
This man lies sacrificed by hand of mine,
I do not look to tread the hall of Fear,
While in this hearth and home of mine there burns
The light of love—Aegisthus—as of old
Loyal, a stalwart shield of confidence—
As true to me as this slain man was false,
Wronging his wife with paramours at Troy,
Fresh from the kiss of each Chryseis there!
Behold him dead—behold his captive prize,
Seeress and harlot—comfort of his bed,
True prophetess, true paramour—I wot
The sea-bench was not closer to the flesh,
Full oft, of every rower, than was she.
See, ill they did, and ill requites them now.
His death ye know: she as a dying swan
Sang her last dirge, and lies, as erst she lay,
Close to his side, and to my couch has left
A sweet new taste of joys that know no fear.

CHORUS

    Ah woe and well-a-day! I would that Fate—
Not bearing agony too great,
Nor stretching me too long on couch of pain—
Would bid mine eyelids keep
The morningless and unawakening sleep!
For life is weary, now my lord is slain,
The gracious among kings!
Hard fate of old he bore and many grievous things,
And for a woman's sake, on Ilian land—
Now is his life hewn down, and by a woman's hand.

O Helen, O infatuate soul,
Who bad'st the tides of battle roll,
Overwhelming thousands, life on life,
'Neath Ilion's wall!
And now lies dead the lord of all.
The blossom of thy storied sin
Bears blood's inexpiable stain,
O thou that erst, these halls within,
Wert unto all a rock of strife,
A husband's bane!
CLYTEMNESTRA
Peace! pray not thou for death as though
Thine heart was whelmed beneath this woe,
Nor turn thy wrath aside to ban
The name of Helen, nor recall
How she, one bane of many a man,
Sent down to death the Danaan lords,
To sleep at Troy the sleep of swords,
And wrought the woe that shattered all.
CHORUS
Fiend of the race! that swoopest fell
Upon the double stock of Tantalus,
Lording it o'er me by a woman's will,
Stern, manful, and imperious?
A bitter sway to me!
Thy very form I see,
Like some grim raven, perched upon the slain,
Exulting o'er the crime, aloud, in tuneless strain!
CLYTEMNESTRA
Right was that word—thou namest well
The brooding race-fiend, triply fell!
From him it is that murder's thirst,
Blood-lapping, inwardly is nursed—
Ere time the ancient scar can sain,
New blood comes welling forth again.
CHORUS
Grim is his wrath and heavy on our home,
That fiend of whom thy voice has cried,
Alas, an omened cry of woe unsatisfied,

An all-devouring doom!
  Ah woe, ah Zeus! from Zeus all things befall—
Zeus the high cause and finisher of all!—
Lord of our mortal state, by him are willed
  All things, by him fulfilled!
    Yet ah my king, my king no more!
What words to say, what tears to pour
  Can tell my love for thee?
The spider-web of treachery
She wove and wound, thy life around,
  And lo! I see thee lie,
And thro' a coward, impious wound
  Pant forth thy life and die!
A death of shame—ah woe on woe!
A treach'rous hand, a cleaving blow!

CLYTEMNESTRA

  My guilt thou harpest, o'er and o'er!
I bid thee reckon me no more
  As Agamemnon's spouse.
The old Avenger, stern of mood
For Atreus and his feast of blood,
  Hath struck the lord of Atreus' house,
And in the semblance of his wife
  The king hath slain.—
Yea, for the murdered children's life,
  A chieftain's in requital ta'en.

CHORUS

  Thou guiltless of this murder, thou!
  Who dares such thought avow?
  Yet it may be, wroth for the parent's deed,
  The fiend hath holpen thee to slay the son.
    Dark Ares, god of death, is pressing on
    Thro' streams of blood by kindred shed,
    Exacting the accompt for children dead,
For clotted blood, for flesh on which their sire did feed.
      Yet ah my king, my king no more!
    What words to say, what tears to pour
      Can tell my love for thee?
    The spider-web of treachery

She wove and wound, thy life around,
  And lo! I see thee lie,
And thro' a coward, impious wound
  Pant forth thy life and die!
A death of shame—ah woe on woe!
A treach'rous hand, a cleaving blow!

CLYTEMNESTRA

  I deem not that the death he died
  Had overmuch of shame:
For this was he who did provide
  Foul wrong unto his house and name:
His daughter, blossom of my womb,
He gave unto a deadly doom,
Iphigenia, child of tears!
And as he wrought, even so he fares.
Nor be his vaunt too loud in hell;
For by the sword his sin he wrought,
And by the sword himself is brought
  Among the dead to dwell.

CHORUS

  Ah whither shall I fly?
For all in ruin sinks the kingly hall;
Nor swift device nor shift of thought have I,
  To 'scape its fall.
A little while the gentler rain-drops fail;
I stand distraught—a ghastly interval,
  Till on the roof-tree rings the bursting hail
  Of blood and doom. Even now fate whets the steel
On whetstones new and deadlier than of old,
  The steel that smites, in Justice' hold,
  Another death to deal.
O Earth! that I had lain at rest
And lapped for ever in thy breast,
Ere I had seen my chieftain fall
Within the laver's silver wall,
Low-lying on dishonoured bier!
And who shall give him sepulchre,
And who the wail of sorrow pour?
Woman, 'tis thine no more!

A graceless gift unto his shade
Such tribute, by his murd'ress paid!
Strive not thus wrongly to atone
The impious deed thy hand hath done.
Ah who above the god-like chief
Shall weep the tears of loyal grief?
Who speak above his lowly grave
The last sad praises of the brave?

CLYTEMNESTRA

    Peace! for such task is none of thine.
  By me he fell, by me he died,
  And now his burial rites be mine!
Yet from these halls no mourners' train
  Shall celebrate his obsequies;
Only by Acheron's rolling tide
His child shall spring unto his side,
  And in a daughter's loving wise
Shall clasp and kiss him once again!

CHORUS

  Lo! sin by sin and sorrow dogg'd by sorrow—
  And who the end can know?
The slayer of to-day shall die to-morrow—
  The wage of wrong is woe.
While Time shall be, while Zeus in heaven is lord,
  His law is fixed and stern;
On him that wrought shall vengeance be outpoured—
  The tides of doom return.
The children of the curse abide within
  These halls of high estate—
And none can wrench from off the home of sin
  The clinging grasp of fate.

CLYTEMNESTRA

    Now walks thy word aright, to tell
This ancient truth of oracle;
But I with vows of sooth will pray
To him, the power that holdeth sway
  O'er all the race of Pleisthenes—
Tho' dark the deed and deep the guilt,
With this last blood, my hands have spilt,

I pray thee let thine anger cease!
I pray thee pass from us away
  To some new race in other lands,
There, if than wilt, to wrong and slay
  The lives of men by kindred hands.
    For me 'tis all sufficient meed,
  Tho' little wealth or power were won,
So I can say, 'Tis past and done.
The bloody lust and murderous,
The inborn frenzy of our house,
  Is ended, by my deed!
  [Enter Aegisthus.
AEGISTHUS
  Dawn of the day of rightful vengeance, hail!
I dare at length aver that gods above
Have care of men and heed of earthly wrongs.
I, I who stand and thus exult to see
This man lie wound in robes the Furies wove,
Slain in requital of his father's craft.
Take ye the truth, that Atreus, this man's sire,
The lord and monarch of this land of old,
  Held with my sire Thyestes deep dispute,
  Brother with brother, for the prize of sway,
  And drave him from his home to banishment.
  Thereafter, the lorn exile homeward stole
  And clung a suppliant to the hearth divine,
  And for himself won this immunity?
  Not with his own blood to defile the land
  That gave him birth. But Atreus, godless sire
  Of him who here lies dead, this welcome planned—
  With zeal that was not love he feigned to hold
  In loyal joy a day of festal cheer,
  And bade my father to his board, and set
  Before him flesh that was his children once.
  First, sitting at the upper board alone,
  He hid the fingers and the feet, but gave
  The rest—and readily Thyestes took
  What to his ignorance no semblance wore
  Of human flesh, and ate: behold what curse

That eating brought upon our race and name!
For when he knew what all unhallowed thing
He thus had wrought, with horror's bitter cry
Back-starting, spewing forth the fragments foul,
On Pelops' house a deadly curse he spake?
As darkly as I spurn this damned food,
So perish all the race of Pleisthenes!
Thus by that curse fell he whom here ye see,
And I—who else?—this murder wove and planned;
For me, an infant yet in swaddling bands,
Of the three children youngest, Atreus sent
To banishment by my sad father's side:
But Justice brought me home once more, grown now
To manhood's years; and stranger tho' I was,
My right hand reached unto the chieftain's life,
Plotting and planning all that malice bade.
And death itself were honour now to me,
Beholding him in Justice' ambush ta'en.
   CHORUS
Aegisthus, for this insolence of thine
That vaunts itself in evil, take my scorn.
Of thine own will, thou sayest, thou hast slain
The chieftain, by thine own unaided plot
Devised the piteous death: I rede thee well,
Think not thy head shall 'scape, when right prevails,
The people's ban, the stones of death and doom.
AEGISTHUS
   This word from thee, this word from one who rows
Low at the oars beneath, what time we rule,
We of the upper tier? Thou'lt know anon,
'Tis bitter to be taught again in age,
By one so young, submission at the word.
But iron of the chain and hunger's throes
Can minister unto an o'erswoln pride
Marvellous well, ay, even in the old.
Hast eyes, and seest not this? Peace—kick not thus
Against the pricks, unto thy proper pain!
CHORUS
   Thou womanish man, waiting till war did cease,

Home-watcher and defiler of the couch,
And arch-deviser of the chieftain's doom!
AEGISTHUS
 Bold words again! but they shall end in tears.
The very converse, thine, of Orpheus' tongue:
He roused and led in ecstasy of joy
All things that heard his voice melodious;
But thou as with the futile cry of curs
Wilt draw men wrathfully upon thee. Peace!
Or strong subjection soon shall tame thy tongue.
CHORUS
 Ay, thou art one to hold an Argive down—
Thou, skilled to plan the murder of the king,
But not with thine own hand to smite the blow!

AEGISTHUS
 That fraudful force was woman's very part,
Not mine, whom deep suspicion from of old
Would have debarred. Now by his treasure's aid
My purpose holds to rule the citizens.
But whoso will not bear my guiding hand,
Him for his corn-fed mettle I will drive
Not as a trace-horse, light-caparisoned,
But to the shafts with heaviest harness bound.
Famine, the grim mate of the dungeon dark,
Shall look on him and shall behold him tame.
CHORUS
 Thou losel soul, was then thy strength too slight
To deal in murder, while a woman's hand,
Staining and shaming Argos and its gods,
Availed to slay him? Ho, if anywhere
The light of life smite on Orestes' eyes,
Let him, returning by some guardian fate,
Hew down with force her paramour and her!
AEGISTHUS
 How thy word and act shall issue, thou shalt shortly understand.
CHORUS
 Up to action, O my comrades! for the fight is hard at hand Swift, your right
hands to the sword hilt! bare the weapon as for strife—

AEGISTHUS

Lo! I too am standing ready, hand on hilt for death or life.

CHORUS

'Twas thy word and we accept it: onward to the chance of war!

CLYTEMNESTRA

Nay, enough, enough, my champion! we will smite and slay
no more.

Already have we reaped enough the harvest-field of guilt:

Enough of wrong and murder, let no other blood be spilt.

Peace, old men! and pass away unto the homes by Fate decreed,

Lest ill valour meet our vengeance—'twas a necessary deed.

But enough of toils and troubles—be the end, if ever, now,

Ere thy talon, O Avenger, deal another deadly blow.

'Tis a woman's word of warning, and let who will list thereto.

AEGISTHUS

But that these should loose and lavish reckless blossoms of the tongue,

And in hazard of their fortune cast upon me words of wrong,

And forget the law of subjects, and revile their ruler's word—

CHORUS

Ruler? but 'tis not for Argives, thus to own a dastard lord!

AEGISTHUS

I will follow to chastise thee in my coming days of sway.

CHORUS

Not if Fortune guide Orestes safely on his homeward way.

AEGISTHUS

Ah, well I know how exiles feed on hopes of their return.

CHORUS

Fare and batten on pollution of the right, while 'tis thy turn.

AEGISTHUS

Thou shalt pay, be well assured, heavy quittance for thy pride

CHORUS

Crow and strut, with her to watch thee, like a cock, his mate beside!

CLYTEMNESTRA

Heed not thou too highly of them—let the cur-pack growl and yell:

I and thou will rule the palace and will order all things well.

The Libation-Bearers

Dramatis Personae:
ORESTES
CHORUS OF CAPTIVE WOMEN
ELECTRA
A NURSE
CLYTEMNESTRA
AEGISTHUS
AN ATTENDANT
PYLADES

The Scene is the Tomb of Agamemnon at Mycenae; afterwards, the Palace of Atreus, hard by the Tomb.

Orestes

Lord of the shades and patron of the realm
That erst my father swayed, list now my prayer,
Hermes, and save me with thine aiding arm,
Me who from banishment returning stand
On this my country; lo, my foot is set
On this grave-mound, and herald-like, as thou,
Once and again, I bid my father hear.
And these twin locks, from mine head shorn, I bring,
And one to Inachus the river-god,
My young life's nurturer, I dedicate,
And one in sign of mourning unfulfilled
I lay, though late, on this my father's grave.
For O my father, not beside thy corse
Stood I to wail thy death, nor was my hand
Stretched out to bear thee forth to burial.

What sight is yonder? what this woman-throng
Hitherward coming, by their sable garb
Made manifest as mourners? What hath chanced?
Doth some new sorrow hap within the home?
Or rightly may I deem that they draw near
Bearing libations, such as soothe the ire

Of dead men angered, to my father's grave?
Nay, such they are indeed; for I descry
Electra mine own sister pacing hither,
In moody grief conspicuous. Grant, O Zeus,
Grant me my father's murder to avenge—
Be thou my willing champion!

        Pylades,
Pass we aside, till rightly I discern
Wherefore these women throng in suppliance.
  [Exeunt Pylades and Orestes; enter the Chorus bearing vessels for libation;
Electra follows them; they pace slowly towards the tomb of Agamemnon.
CHORUS
  Forth from the royal halls by high command
  I bear libations for the dead.
Rings on my smitten breast my smiting hand,
  And all my cheek is rent and red,
Fresh-furrowed by my nails, and all my soul
This many a day doth feed on cries of dole.
  And trailing tatters of my vest,
In looped and windowed raggedness forlorn,
  Hang rent around my breast,
Even as I, by blows of Fate most stern
  Saddened and torn.
    Oracular thro' visions, ghastly clear,
Bearing a blast of wrath from realms below,
And stiffening each rising hair with dread,
  Came out of dream-land Fear,
  And, loud and awful, bade
The shriek ring out at midnight's witching hour,
  And brooded, stern with woe,
Above the inner house, the woman's bower.
And seers inspired did read the dream on oaths,
  Chanting aloud In realms below
  The dead are wroth;
Against their slayers yet their ire doth glow.
  Therefore to bear this gift of graceless worth—
  O Earth, my nursing mother!—
The woman god-accurs'd doth send me forth.

Lest one crime bring another.
Ill is the very word to speak, for none
    Can ransom or atone
For blood once shed and darkening the plain.
  O hearth of woe and bane,
  O state that low doth lie!
Sunless, accursed of men, the shadows brood
  Above the home of murdered majesty.
   Rumour of might, unquestioned, unsubdued,
Pervading ears and soul of lesser men,
   Is silent now and dead.
   Yet rules a viler dread;
  For bliss and power, however won,
As gods, and more than gods, dazzle our mortal ken.
   Justice doth mark, with scales that swiftly sway,
  Some that are yet in light;
  Others in interspace of day and night,
   Till Fate arouse them, stay;
And some are lapped in night, where all things are undone.
   On the life-giving lap of Earth
  Blood hath flowed forth;
And now, the seed of vengeance, clots the plain—
  Unmelting, uneffaced the stain.
And Atè tarries long, but at the last
    The sinner's heart is cast
Into pervading, waxing pangs of pain.
   Lo, when man's force doth ope
The virgin doors, there is nor cure nor hope
  For what is lost,—even so, I deem,
Though in one channel ran Earth's every stream,
  Laving the hand defiled from murder's stain,
   It were vain.
   And upon me—ah me!—the gods have laid
  The woe that wrapped round Troy,
What time they led down from home and kin
    Unto a slave's employ—
   The doom to bow the head
   And watch our master's will
   Work deeds of good and ill—

To see the headlong sway of force and sin,
  And hold restrained the spirit's bitter hate,
  Wailing the monarch's fruitless fate,
Hiding my face within my robe, and fain
Of tears, and chilled with frost of hidden pain.
ELECTRA
  Hand maidens, orderers of the palace-halls,
Since at my side ye come, a suppliant train,
Companions of this offering, counsel me
As best befits the time: for I, who pour
Upon the grave these streams funereal,
With what fair word can I invoke my sire?
Shall I aver, Behold, I bear these gifts
From well-beloved wife unto her well-beloved lord,
When 'tis from her, my mother, that they come?
I dare not say it: of all words I fail
Wherewith to consecrate unto my sire
These sacrificial honours on his grave.
Or shall I speak this word, as mortals use—
Give back, to those who send these coronals
Full recompense—of ills for acts malign?
Or shall I pour this draught for Earth to drink,
Sans word or reverence, as my sire was slain,
And homeward pass with unreverted eyes,
Casting the bowl away, as one who flings
The household cleansings to the common road?
Be art and part, O friends, in this my doubt,
Even as ye are in that one common hate
Whereby we live attended: fear ye not
The wrath of any man, nor hide your word
Within your breast: the day of death and doom
Awaits alike the freeman and the slave.
Speak, then, if aught thou know'st to aid us more.
CHORUS
  Thou biddest; I will speak my soul's thought out,
Revering as a shrine thy father's grave.
ELECTRA
  Say then thy say, as thou his tomb reverest.
CHORUS

Speak solemn words to them that love, and pour.

ELECTRA

And of his kin whom dare I name as kind?

CHORUS

Thyself; and next, whoe'er Aegisthus scorns.

ELECTRA

Then 'tis myself and thou, my prayer must name.

CHORUS

Whoe'er they be, 'tis thine to know and name them.

ELECTRA

Is there no other we may claim as ours?

CHORUS

Think of Orestes, though far-off he be.

ELECTRA

Right well in this too hast thou schooled my thought.

CHORUS

Mindfully, next, on those who shed the blood—

ELECTRA

Pray on them what? expound, instruct my doubt.

CHORUS

This; Upon them some god or mortal come——

ELECTRA

As judge or as avenger? speak thy thought.

CHORUS

Pray in set terms, Who shall the slayer slay.

ELECTRA

Beseemeth it to ask such boon of heaven?

CHORUS

How not, to wreak a wrong upon a foe?

ELECTRA

O mighty Hermes, warder of the shades,
Herald of upper and of under world,
Proclaim and usher down my prayer's appeal
Unto the gods below, that they with eyes
Watchful behold these halls, my sire's of old—
And unto Earth, the mother of all things,
And foster-nurse, and womb that takes their seed.

Lo, I that pour these draughts for men now dead,

Call on my father, who yet holds in ruth
Me and mine own Orestes, Father, speak—
How shall thy children rule thine halls again?
Homeless we are and sold; and she who sold
Is she who bore us; and the price she took
Is he who joined with her to work thy death,
Aegisthus, her new lord. Behold me here
Brought down to slave's estate, and far away
Wanders Orestes, banished from the wealth
That once was thine, the profit of thy care,
Whereon these revel in a shameful joy.
Father, my prayer is said; 'tis thine to hear—
Grant that some fair fate bring Orestes home,
And unto me grant these—a purer soul
Than is my mother's, a more stainless hand.

These be my prayers for us; for thee, O sire,
I cry that one may come to smite thy foes,
And that the slayers may in turn be slain.
Cursed is their prayer, and thus I bar its path,
Praying mine own, a counter-curse on them.
And thou, send up to us the righteous boon
For which we pray: thine aids be heaven and earth,
And justice guide the right to victory,
    [To the Chorus
    Thus have I prayed, and thus I shed these streams,
And follow ye the wont, and as with flowers
Crown ye with many a tear and cry the dirge,
Your lips ring out above the dead man's grave.
    [She pours the libations.
CHORUS
        Woe, woe, woe!
Let the teardrop fall, plashing on the ground
    Where our lord lies low:
Fall and cleanse away the cursed libation's stain,
    Shed on this grave-mound,
Fenced wherein together, gifts of good or bane
    From the dead are found.
        Lord of Argos, hearken!
Though around thee darken

Mist of death and hell, arise and hear!
Hearken and awaken to our cry of woe!
    Who with might of spear
     Shall our home deliver?
    Who like Ares bend until it quiver,
    Bend the northern bow?
Who with hand upon the hilt himself will thrust with glaive,
    Thrust and slay and save?

ELECTRA
     Lo! the earth drinks them, to my sire they pass—
  Learn ye with me of this thing new and strange.

CHORUS
  Speak thou; my breast doth palpitate with fear.

ELECTRA
  I see upon the tomb a curl new shorn.

CHORUS
  Shorn from what man or what deep-girded maid?

ELECTRA
  That may he guess who will; the sign is plain.

CHORUS
  Let me learn this of thee; let youth prompt age.

ELECTRA
  None is there here but I, to clip such gift.

CHORUS
  For they who thus should mourn him hate him sore.

ELECTRA
  And lo! in truth the hair exceeding like—

CHORUS
  Like to what locks and whose? instruct me that.

ELECTRA
  Like unto those my father's children wear.

CHORUS
  Then is this lock Orestes' secret gift?

ELECTRA
  Most like it is unto the curls he wore,

CHORUS
  Yet how dared he to come unto his home?

ELECTRA
  He hath but sent it, clipt to mourn his sire.

CHORUS

   It is a sorrow grievous as his death,
That he should live yet never dare return.

ELECTRA

   Yea, and my heart o'erflows with gall of grief,
And I am pierced as with a cleaving dart;
Like to the first drops after drought, my tears
Fall down at will, a bitter bursting tide,
As on this lock I gaze; I cannot deem
That any Argive save Orestes' self
Was ever lord thereof; nor, well I wot,
Hath she, the murd'ress, shorn and laid this lock
To mourn him whom she slew—my mother she,
Bearing no mother's heart, but to her race
A loathing spirit, loathed itself of heaven!
Yet to affirm, as utterly made sure,
That this adornment cometh of the hand
Of mine Orestes, brother of my soul,
I may not venture, yet hope flatters fair!
Ah well-a-day, that this dumb hair had voice
To glad mine ears, as might a messenger,
Bidding me sway no more 'twixt fear and hope,
Clearly commanding, Cast me hence away,
Clipped was I from some head thou lovest not;
Or, I am kin to thee, and here, as thou,
I come to weep and deck our father's grave.
Aid me, ye gods! for well indeed ye know
How in the gale and counter-gale of doubt,
Like to the seaman's bark, we whirl and stray.
But, if God will our life, how strong shall spring,
From seed how small, the new tree of our home!—
Lo ye, a second sign—these footsteps, look,—
Like to my own, a corresponsive print;
And look, another footmark,—this his own,
And that the foot of one who walked with him.
Mark, how the heel and tendons' print combine,
Measured exact, with mine coincident!
Alas! for doubt and anguish rack my mind.

   ORESTES (approaching suddenly)

Pray thou, in gratitude for prayers fulfilled, Fair fall the rest of what I ask
of heaven.
ELECTRA
Wherefore? what win I from the gods by prayer?
ORESTES
This, that thine eyes behold thy heart's desire.

ELECTRA
On whom of mortals know'st thou that I call?
ORESTES
I know thy yearning for Orestes deep.
ELECTRA
Say then, wherein event hath crowned my prayer?
ORESTES
I, I am he; seek not one more akin.
ELECTRA
Some fraud, O stranger, weavest thou for me?
ORESTES
Against myself I weave it, if I weave.
ELECTRA
Ah thou hast mind to mock me in my woe!
ORESTES
'Tis at mine own I mock then, mocking thine.
ELECTRA
Speak I with thee then as Orestes' self?
ORESTES
My very face thou see'st and know'st me not,
And yet but now, when thou didst see the lock
Shorn for my father's grave, and when thy quest
Was eager on the footprints I had made,
Even I, thy brother, shaped and sized as thou,
Fluttered thy spirit, as at sight of me!
Lay now this ringlet whence 'twas shorn, and judge,
And look upon this robe, thine own hands' work,
The shuttle-prints, the creature wrought thereon—
Refrain thyself, nor prudence lose in joy,
For well I wot, our kin are less than kind.
ELECTRA
O thou that art unto our father's home

Love, grief and hope, for thee the tears ran down,
For thee, the son, the saviour that should be;
Trust thou thine arm and win thy father's halls!
O aspect sweet of fourfold love to me,
Whom upon thee the heart's constraint bids call
As on my father, and the claim of love
From me unto my mother turns to thee,
For she is very hate; to thee too turns
What of my heart went out to her who died
A ruthless death upon the altar-stone;
And for myself I love thee—thee that wast
A brother leal, sole stay of love to me.
Now by thy side be strength and right, and Zeus
Saviour almighty, stand to aid the twain!

ORESTES

Zeus, Zeus! look down on our estate and us,
The orphaned brood of him, our eagle-sire,
Whom to his death a fearful serpent brought
Enwinding him in coils; and we, bereft
And foodless, sink with famine, all too weak
To bear unto the eyrie, as he bore,
Such quarry as he slew. Lo! I and she,
Electra, stand before thee, fatherless,
And each alike cast out and homeless made.

ELECTRA

And if thou leave to death the brood of him
Whose altar blazed for thee, whose reverence
Was thine, all thine,—whence, in the after years,
Shall any hand like his adorn thy shrine
With sacrifice of flesh? the eaglets slain,
Thou wouldst not have a messenger to bear
Thine omens, once so clear, to mortal men;
So, if this kingly stock be withered all,
None on high festivals will fend thy shrine
Stoop thou to raise us! strong the race shall show,
Though puny now it seem, and fallen low.

CHORUS

O children, saviours of your father's home,
Beware ye of your words, lest one should hear

And bear them, for the tongue hath lust to tell,
Unto our masters—whom God grant to me
In pitchy reek of fun'ral flame to see!
ORESTES
   Nay, mighty is Apollo's oracle
And shall not fail me, whom it bade to pass
Thro' all this peril; clear the voice rang out
With many warnings, sternly threatening
To my hot heart the wintry chill of pain,
Unless upon the slayers of my sire
I pressed for vengeance: this the god's command—
That I, in ire for home and wealth despoiled,
Should with a craft like theirs the slayers slay:
Else with my very life I should atone
This deed undone, in many a ghastly wise
For he proclaimed unto the ears of men
That offerings, poured to angry power of death,
Exude again, unless their will be done,
As grim disease on those that poured them forth—
As leprous ulcers mounting on the flesh
And with fell fangs corroding what of old
Wore natural form; and on the brow arise
White poisoned hairs, the crown of this disease.
He spake moreover of assailing fiends
Empowered to quit on me my father's blood,
Wreaking their wrath on me, what time in night
Beneath shut lids the spirit's eye sees clear.
The dart that flies in darkness, sped from hell
By spirits of the murdered dead who call
Unto their kin for vengeance, formless fear,
The night-tide's visitant, and madness' curse
Should drive and rack me; and my tortured frame
Should be chased forth from man's community
As with the brazen scorpions of the scourge.
For me and such as me no lustral bowl
Should stand, no spilth of wine be poured to God
For me, and wrath unseen of my dead sire
Should drive me from the shrine; no man should dare
To take me to his hearth, nor dwell with me:

Slow, friendless, cursed of all should be mine end,
And pitiless horror wind me for the grave,
This spake the god—this dare I disobey?
Yea, though I dared, the deed must yet be done;
For to that end diverse desires combine,—
The god's behest, deep grief for him who died,
And last, the grievous blank of wealth despoiled—
All these weigh on me, urge that Argive men,
Minions of valour, who with soul of fire
Did make of fenced Troy a ruinous heap,
Be not left slaves to two and each a woman!
For he, the man, wears woman's heart; if not
Soon shall he know, confronted by a man.

[Orestes, Electra, and the Chorus gather round the tomb of Agamemnon
for the invocation which follows.

CHORUS
　　Mighty Fates, on you we call!
　Bid the will of Zeus ordain
　Power to those, to whom again
　Justice turns with hand and aid!
　Grievous was the prayer one made—
　Grievous let the answer fall!
　Where the mighty doom is set,
　Justice claims aloud her debt
　Who in blood hath dipped the steel,
　Deep in blood her meed shall feel!
　List an immemorial word—
　　Whosoe'er shall take the sword
　　Shall perish by the sword.

ORESTES
　Father, unblest in death, O father mine!
　　What breath of word or deed
Can I waft on thee from this far confine
　　Unto thy lowly bed,—
Waft upon thee, in midst of darkness lying,
　　Hope's counter-gleam of fire?
Yet the loud dirge of praise brings grace undying
　　Unto each parted sire.

CHORUS

O child, the spirit of the dead,
Altho' upon his flesh have fed
  The grim teeth of the flame,
Is quelled not; after many days
The sting of wrath his soul shall raise,
  A vengeance to reclaim!
To the dead rings loud our cry—
Plain the living's treachery—
Swelling, shrilling, urged on high,
  The vengeful dirge, for parents
  Shall strive and shall attain.
ELECTRA
    Hear me too, even me, O father, hear!
Not by one child alone these groans, these tears are shed
    Upon thy sepulchre.
  Each, each, where thou art lowly laid,
  Stands, a suppliant, homeless made:
    Ah, and all is full of ill,
  Comfort is there none to say!
  Strive and wrestle as we may,
    Still stands doom invincible.
CHORUS
    Nay, if so he will, the god
  Still our tears to joy can turn
  He can bid a triumph-ode
  Drown the dirge beside this urn;
  He to kingly halls can greet
The child restored, the homeward-guided feet.
ORESTES
  Ah my father! hadst thou lain
  Under Ilion's wall,
By some Lycian spearman slain,
  Thou hadst left in this thine hall
Honour; thou hadst wrought for us
Fame and life most glorious.
  Over-seas if thou had'st died,
Heavily had stood thy tomb,
  Heaped on high; but, quenched in pride,
Grief were light unto thy home.

CHORUS
 Loved and honoured hadst thou lain
 By the dead that nobly fell,
In the under-world again,
 Where are throned the kings of hell,
 Full of sway adorable
Thou hadst stood at their right hand—
Thou that wert, in mortal land,
 By Fate's ordinance and law,
King of kings who bear the crown
 And the staff, to which in awe
Mortal men bow down.

ELECTRA
 Nay O father, I were fain
Other fate had fallen on thee.
 Ill it were if thou hadst lain
 One among the common slain,
 Fallen by Scamander's side—
Those who slew thee there should be!
Then, untouched by slavery,
 We had heard as from afar
Deaths of those who should have died
 'Mid the chance of war.

CHORUS
 O child, forbear! things all too high thou sayest.
 Easy, but vain, thy cry!
A boon above all gold is that thou prayest,
 An unreached destiny,
As of the blessèd land that far aloof
 Beyond the north wind lies;
Yet doth your double prayer ring loud reproof;
 A double scourge of sighs
Awakes the dead; th' avengers rise, though late;
 Blood stains the guilty pride
Of the accursed who rule on earth, and Fate
 Stands on the children's side.

ELECTRA
 That hath sped thro' mine ear, like a shaft from a bow!
Zeus, Zeus! it is thou who dost send from below

A doom on the desperate doer—ere long
On a mother a father shall visit his wrong.
CHORUS
   Be it mine to upraise thro' the reek of the pyre
The chant of delight, while the funeral fire
  Devoureth the corpse of a man that is slain
    And a woman laid low!
For who bids me conceal it! out-rending control,
Blows ever stern blast of hate thro' my soul,
  And before me a vision of wrath and of bane
   Flits and waves to and fro.
ORESTES
   Zeus, thou alone to us art parent now.
   Smite with a rending blow
  Upon their heads, and bid the land be well:
Set right where wrong hath stood; and thou give ear,
   O Earth, unto my prayer—
Yea, hear O mother Earth, and monarchy of hell!
CHORUS
   Nay, the law is sternly set—
  Blood-drops shed upon the ground
Plead for other bloodshed yet;
  Loud the call of death doth sound,
Calling guilt of olden time,
A Fury, crowning crime with crime.
ELECTRA
   Where, where are ye, avenging powers,
   Puissant Furies of the slain?
  Behold the relics of the race
  Of Atreus, thrust from pride of place!
 O Zeus, what home henceforth is ours,
   What refuge to attain?
CHORUS
  Lo, at your wail my heart throbs, wildly stirred;
   Now am I lorn with sadness,
Darkened in all my soul, to hear your sorrow's word
  Anon to hope, the seat of strength, I rise,—
  She, thrusting grief away, lifts up mine eyes
   To the new dawn of gladness.

ORESTES
    Skills it to tell of aught save wrong on wrong,
   Wrought by our mother's deed?
  Though now she fawn for pardon, sternly strong
   Standeth our wrath, and will nor hear nor heed;
 Her children's soul is wolfish, born from hers,
   And softens not by prayers.
CHORUS
     I dealt upon my breast the blow
     That Asian mourning women know;
     Wails from my breast the fun'ral cry,
     The Cissian weeping melody;
   Stretched rendingly forth, to tatter and tear,
   My clenched hands wander, here and there,
    From head to breast; distraught with blows
      Throb dizzily my brows.
ELECTRA
    Aweless in hate, O mother, sternly brave!
    As in a foeman's grave
  Thou laid'st in earth a king, but to the bier
    No citizen drew near,—
 Thy husband, thine, yet for his obsequies,
   Thou bad'st no wail arise!
ORESTES
    Alas the shameful burial thou dost speak!
 Yet I the vengeance of his shame will wreak—
    That do the gods command!
    That shall achieve mine hand!
 Grant me to thrust her life away, and I
     Will dare to die!
CHORUS
  List thou the deed! Hewn down and foully torn,
   He to the tomb was borne;
 Yea, by her hand, the deed who wrought,
 With like dishonour to the grave was brought,
 And by her hand she strove, with strong desire,
 Thy life to crush, O child, by murder of thy sire:
  Bethink thee, hearing, of the shame, the pain
    Wherewith that sire was slain!

ELECTRA

    Yea, such was the doom of my sire; well-a-day,
    I was thrust from his side,—
As a dog from the chamber they thrust me away,
And in place of my laughter rose sobbing and tears
      As in darkness I lay.
O father, if this word can pass to thine ears,
    To thy soul let it reach and abide!

CHORUS

    Let it pass, let it pierce, through the sense of thine ear,
   To thy soul, where in silence it waiteth the hour!
The past is accomplished; but rouse thee to hear
What the future prepareth; awake and appear,
    Our champion, in wrath and in power!

ORESTES

    O father, to thy loved ones come in aid.

ELECTRA

    With tears I call on thee.

CHORUS

      Listen and rise to light!
Be thou with us, be thou against the foe!
Swiftly this cry arises—even so
   Pray we, the loyal band, as we have prayed!

ORESTES

    Let their might meet with mine, and their right with my right.

ELECTRA

    O ye Gods, it is yours to decree.

CHORUS

    Ye call unto the dead; I quake to hear.
Fate is ordained of old, and shall fulfil your prayer.

ELECTRA

    Alas, the inborn curse that haunts our home,
   Of Atè's bloodstained scourge the tuneless sound!
Alas, the deep insufferable doom,
   The stanchless wound!

ORESTES

    It shall be stanched, the task is ours,—
   Not by a stranger's, but by kindred hand,
Shall be chased forth the blood-fiend of our land.

Be this our spoken spell, to call Earth's nether powers!

CHORUS

    Lords of a dark eternity,
  To you has come the children's cry,
  Send up from hell, fulfil your aid
    To them who prayed.

ORESTES

  O father, murdered in unkingly wise,
Fulfil my prayer, grant me thine halls to sway.

ELECTRA

  To me too, grant this boon—dark death to deal
Unto Aegisthus, and to 'scape my doom.

ORESTES

  So shall the rightful feasts that mortals pay
Be set for thee; else, not for thee shall rise
The scented reek of altars fed with flesh,
But thou shall lie dishonoured: hear thou me!

ELECTRA

  I too, from my full heritage restored,
Will pour the lustral streams, what time I pass
Forth as a bride from these paternal halls,
And honour first, beyond all graves, thy tomb.

ORESTES

  Earth, send my sire to fend me in the fight!

ELECTRA

  Give fair-faced fortune, O Persephone!

ORESTES

  Bethink thee, father, in the laver slain—

ELECTRA

  Bethink thee of the net they handselled for thee!

ORESTES

  Bonds not of brass ensnared thee, father mine.

ELECTRA

  Yea, the ill craft of an enfolding robe.

ORESTES

  By this our bitter speech arise, O sire!

ELECTRA

  Raise thou thine head at love's last, dearest call!

ORESTES
   Yea, speed forth Right to aid thy kinsmen's cause;
Grip for grip, let them grasp the foe, if thou
Willest in triumph to forget thy fall.
ELECTRA
   Hear me, O father, once again hear me.
Lo! at thy tomb, two fledglings of thy brood—
A man-child and a maid; hold them in ruth,
Nor wipe them out, the last of Pelops' line.
For while they live, thou livest from the dead;
Children are memory's voices, and preserve
The dead from wholly dying: as a net
Is ever by the buoyant corks upheld,
Which save the flex-mesh, in the depth submerged.
Listen, this wail of ours doth rise for thee,
And as thou heedest it thyself art saved.
CHORUS
   In sooth, a blameless prayer ye spake at length—
The tomb's requital for its dirge denied:
Now, for the rest, as thou art fixed to do,
Take fortune by the hand and work thy will.
ORESTES
   The doom is set; and yet I fain would ask—
Not swerving from the course of my resolve,—
Wherefore she sent these offerings, and why
She softens all too late her cureless deed?
An idle boon it was, to send them here
Unto the dead who recks not of such gifts.
I cannot guess her thought, but well I ween
Such gifts are skilless to atone such crime.
Be blood once spilled, an idle strife he strives
Who seeks with other wealth or wine outpoured
To atone the deed. So stands the word, nor fails.
Yet would I know her thought; speak, if thou knowest.
CHORUS
   I know it, son; for at her side I stood.
'Twas the night-wandering terror of a dream
That flung her shivering from her couch, and bade her—
Her, the accursed of God—these offerings send.

ORESTES
  Heard ye the dream, to tell it forth aright?
  CHORUS
Yea, from herself; her womb a serpent bare.
ORESTES
  What then the sum and issue of the tale?
CHORUS
  Even as a swaddled child, she lull'd the thing.
ORESTES
  What suckling craved the creature, born full-fanged?
CHORUS
  Yet in her dreams she proffered it the breast.
ORESTES
  How? did the hateful thing not bite her teat?
CHORUS
  Yea, and sucked forth a blood-gout in the milk.
ORESTES
  Not vain this dream—it bodes a man's revenge.
CHORUS
  Then out of sleep she started with a cry,
And thro' the palace for their mistress' aid
Full many lamps, that erst lay blind with night
Flared into light; then, even as mourners use,
She sends these offerings, in hope to win
A cure to cleave and sunder sin from doom.
ORESTES
  Earth and my father's grave, to you I call—
Give this her dream fulfilment, and thro' me.
I read it in each part coincident,
With what shall be; for mark, that serpent sprang
From the same womb as I, in swaddling bands
By the same hands was swathed, lipped the same breast.
And sucking forth the same sweet mother's-milk
Infused a clot of blood; and in alarm
She cried upon her wound the cry of pain.
The rede is clear: the thing of dread she nursed,
The death of blood she dies; and I, 'tis I,
In semblance of a serpent, that must slay her.
Thou art my seer, and thus I read the dream.

CHORUS
   So do; yet ere thou doest, speak to us,
Siding some act, some, by not acting, aid.
ORESTES
   Brief my command: I bid my sister pass
In silence to the house, and all I bid
This my design with wariness conceal,
That they who did by craft a chieftain slay
May by like craft and in like noose be ta'en
Dying the death which Loxias foretold—
Apollo, king and prophet undisproved.
I with this warrior Pylades will come
In likeness of a stranger, full equipt
As travellers come, and at the palace gates
Will stand, as stranger yet in friendship's bond
Unto this house allied; and each of us
Will speak the tongue that round Parnassus sounds,
Feigning such speech as Phocian voices use.
And what if none of those that tend the gates
Shall welcome us with gladness, since the house
With ills divine is haunted? if this hap,
We at the gate will bide, till, passing by,
Some townsman make conjecture and proclaim,
How? is Aegisthus here, and knowingly
Keeps suppliants aloof, by bolt and bar?
Then shall I win my way; and if I cross
The threshold of the gate, the palace' guard,
And find him throned where once my father sat—
Or if he come anon, and face to face
Confronting, drop his eyes from mine—I swear
He shall not utter, Who art thou and whence?
Ere my steel leap, and compassed round with death
Low he shall lie: and thus, full-fed with doom,
The Fury of the house shall drain once more
A deep third draught of rich unmingled blood.
But thou, O sister, look that all within
Be well prepared to give these things event.
And ye—I say 'twere well to bear a tongue
Full of fair silence and of fitting speech

As each beseems the time; and last, do thou,
Hermes the warder-god, keep watch and ward,
And guide to victory my striving sword.
   [Exit with Pylades.
CHORUS
   Many and marvellous the things of fear
   Earth's breast doth bear;
 And the sea's lap with many monsters teems,
 And windy levin-bolts and meteor gleams
   Breed many deadly things—
Unknown and flying forms, with fear upon their wings,
   And in their tread is death;
 And rushing whirlwinds, of whose blasting breath
   Man's tongue can tell.
   But who can tell aright the fiercer thing,
   The aweless soul, within man's breast inhabiting?
   Who tell, how, passion-fraught and love-distraught
   The woman's eager, craving thought
   Doth wed mankind to woe and ruin fell?
   Yea, how the loveless love that doth possess
   The woman, even as the lioness,
   Doth rend and wrest apart, with eager strife,
     The link of wedded life?
   Let him be the witness, whose thought is not borne on light wings
   thro' the air,
But abideth with knowledge, what thing was wrought by Althea's
   despair;
For she marr'd the life-grace of her son, with ill counsel rekindled
   the flame
That was quenched as it glowed on the brand, what time from his mother
   he came,
With the cry of a new-born child; and the brand from the burning she
   won,
For the Fates had foretold it coeval, in life and in death, with her
   son.
   Yea, and man's hate tells of another, even Scylla of murderous guile,
Who slew for an enemy's sake her father, won o'er by the wile
And the gifts of Cretan Minos, the gauds of the high-wrought gold;
For she clipped from her father's head the lock that should never

wax old,
As he breathed in the silence of sleep, and knew not her craft and
    her crime—
But Hermes, the guard of the dead, doth grasp her, in fulness of
    time.
    And since of the crimes of the cruel I tell, let my singing record
The bitter wedlock and loveless, the curse on these halls outpoured,
The crafty device of a woman, whereby did a chieftain fall,
A warrior stern in his wrath; the fear of his enemies all,—
A song of dishonour, untimely! and cold is the hearth that was warm
And ruled by the cowardly spear, the woman's unwomanly arm.
    But the summit and crown of all crimes is that which in Lemnos befell;
A woe and a mourning it is, a shame and a spitting to tell;
And he that in after time doth speak of his deadliest thought,
Doth say, It is like to the deed that of old time in Lemnos was
    wrought;
And loathed of men were the doers, and perished, they and their seed,
For the gods brought hate upon them; none loveth the impious deed.
    It is well of these tales to tell; for the sword in the grasp of Right
With a cleaving, a piercing blow to the innermost heart doth smite,
And the deed unlawfully done is not trodden down nor forgot,
When the sinner out-steppeth the law and heedeth the high God not;
But Justice hath planted the anvil, and Destiny forgeth the sword
That shall smite in her chosen time; by her is the child restored;
And, darkly devising, the Fiend of the house, world-cursed, will repay
The price of the blood of the slain that was shed in the bygone day.
    [Enter Orestes and Pylades, in guise of travellers.
    ORESTES (knocking at the palace gate)
What ho! slave, ho! I smite the palace gate
In vain, it seems; what ho, attend within,—
Once more, attend; come forth and ope the halls
If yet Aegisthus holds them hospitable.
    SLAVE (from within)
    Anon, anon! [Opens the door. Speak, from what land art thou, and sent
from whom?
ORESTES
    Go, tell to them who rule the palace-halls,
Since 'tis to them I come with tidings new—
(Delay not—Night's dark car is speeding on,

And time is now for wayfarers to cast
Anchor in haven, wheresoe'er a house
Doth welcome strangers)—that there now come forth
Some one who holds authority within—
The queen, or, if some man, more seemly were it;
For when man standeth face to face with man,
No stammering modesty confounds their speech,
But each to each doth tell his meaning clear.
   [Enter Clytemnestra,
CLYTEMNESTRA
   Speak on, O strangers; have ye need of aught?
Here is whate'er beseems a house like this—
Warm bath and bed, tired Nature's soft restorer,
And courteous eyes to greet you; and if aught
Of graver import needeth act as well,
That, as man's charge, I to a man will tell.
ORESTES
   A Daulian man am I, from Phocis bound,
And as with mine own travel-scrip self-laden
I went toward Argos, parting hitherward
With travelling foot, there did encounter me
One whom I knew not and who knew not me,
But asked my purposed way nor hid his own,
And, as we talked together, told his name—
Strophius of Phocis; then he said, "Good sir,
Since in all case thou art to Argos bound,
Forget not this my message, heed it well,
Tell to his own, Orestes is no more.
And—whatsoe'er his kinsfolk shall resolve,
Whether to bear his dust unto his home,
Or lay him here, in death as erst in life
Exiled for aye, a child of banishment—
Bring me their hest, upon thy backward road;
For now in brazen compass of an urn
His ashes lie, their dues of weeping paid."
So much I heard, and so much tell to thee,
Not knowing if I speak unto his kin
Who rule his home; but well, I deem, it were,
Such news should earliest reach a parent's ear.

CLYTEMNESTRA

Ah woe is me! thy word our ruin tells;
From roof-tree unto base are we despoiled.—
O thou whom nevermore we wrestle down,
Thou Fury of this home, how oft and oft
Thou dost descry what far aloof is laid,
Yea, from afar dost bend th' unerring bow
And rendest from my wretchedness its friends;
As now Orestes—who, a brief while since,
Safe from the mire of death stood warily,—
Was the home's hope to cure th' exulting wrong;
Now thou ordainest, Let the ill abide.

ORESTES

To host and hostess thus with fortune blest,
Lief had I come with better news to bear
Unto your greeting and acquaintanceship;
For what goodwill lies deeper than the bond
Of guest and host? and wrong abhorred it were,
As well I deem, if I, who pledged my faith
To one, and greetings from the other had,
Bore not aright the tidings 'twixt the twain.

CLYTEMNESTRA

Whate'er thy news, thou shalt not welcome lack,
Meet and deserved, nor scant our grace shall be.
Hadst them thyself not come, such tale to tell
Another, sure, had borne it to our ears.
But lo! the hour is here when travelling guests
Fresh from the daylong labour of the road,
Should win their rightful due. Take him within
[To the slave.
To the man-chamber's hospitable rest—
Him and these fellow-farers at his side
Give them such guest-right as beseems our halls;
I bid thee do as thou shalt answer for it
And I unto the prince who rules our home
Will tell the tale, and, since we lack not friends,
With them will counsel how this hap to bear
    [Exit Clytemnestra.

CHORUS

So be it done—
Sister-servants, when draws nigh
Time for us aloud to cry
Orestes and his victory?
    O holy earth and holy tomb
Over the grave-pit heaped on high,
Where low doth Agamemnon lie,
    The king of ships, the army's lord!
Now is the hour—give ear and come,
    For now doth Craft her aid afford,
And Hermes, guard of shades in hell,
Stands o'er their strife, to sentinel
    The dooming of the sword.
I wot the stranger worketh woe within—
For lo! I see come forth, suffused with tears,
Orestes' nurse. What ho, Kilissa—thou
Beyond the doors? Where goest thou? Methinks
Some grief unbidden walketh at thy side.
    [Enter Kilissa, a nurse.

KILISSA

    My mistress bids me, with what speed I may,
Call in Aegisthus to the stranger guests,
    That he may come, and standing face to face,
    A man with men, may thus more clearly learn
    This rumour new. Thus speaking, to her slaves
    She hid beneath the glance of fictive grief
    Laughter for what is wrought—to her desire
    Too well; but ill, ill, ill besets the house,
    Brought by the tale these guests have told so clear.
    And he, God wot, will gladden all his heart
    Hearing this rumour. Woe and well-a-day!
    The bitter mingled cup of ancient woes,
    Hard to be borne, that here in Atreus' house
    Befel, was grievous to mine inmost heart,
    But never yet did I endure such pain.
    All else I bore with set soul patiently;
    But now—alack, alack!—Orestes dear,
    The day and night-long travail of my soul!
    Whom from his mother's womb, a new-born child,

I clasped and cherished! Many a time and oft
Toilsome and profitless my service was,
When his shrill outcry called me from my couch!
For the young child, before the sense is born,
Hath but a dumb thing's life, must needs be nursed
As its own nature bids. The swaddled thing
Hath nought of speech, whate'er discomfort come—
Hunger or thirst or lower weakling need,—
For the babe's stomach works its own relief.
Which knowing well before, yet oft surprised,
'Twas mine to cleanse the swaddling clothes—poor I
Was nurse to tend and fuller to make white;
Two works in one, two handicrafts I took,
When in mine arms the father laid the boy.
And now he's dead—alack and well-a-day!
Yet must I go to him whose wrongful power
Pollutes this house—fair tidings these to him!
CHORUS
    Say then, with what array she bids him come?
KILISSA
    What say'st thou! Speak more clearly for mine ear.
CHORUS
    Bids she bring henchmen, or to come alone?
    KILISSA
    She bids him bring a spear-armed body-guard.
CHORUS
      Nay, tell not that unto our loathèd lord,
    But speed to him, put on the mien of joy,
    Say, Come along, fear nought, the news is good:
    A bearer can tell straight a twisted tale.
KILISSA
    Does then thy mind in this new tale find joy?
CHORUS
    What if Zeus bid our ill wind veer to fair?
KILISSA
    And how? the home's hope with Orestes dies.
CHORUS
    Not yet-a seer, though feeble, this might see.
KILISSA

What say'st thou? Know'st thou aught, this tale belying?
CHORUS
Go, tell the news to him, perform thine hest,—
What the gods will, themselves can well provide.
KILISSA
Well, I will go, herein obeying thee;
And luck fall fair, with favour sent from heaven.
[Exit.
CHORUS
Zeus, sire of them who on Olympus dwell,
Hear thou, O hear my prayer!
Grant to my rightful lords to prosper well
Even as their zeal is fair!
For right, for right goes up aloud my cry—
Zeus, aid him, stand anigh!
Into his father's hall he goes
To smite his father's foes.
Bid him prevail! by thee on throne of triumph set,
Twice, yea and thrice with joy shall he acquit the debt.
Bethink thee, the young steed, the orphan foal
Of sire beloved by thee, unto the car
Of doom is harnessed fast.
Guide him aright, plant firm a lasting goal,
Speed thou his pace,—O that no chance may mar
The homeward course, the last!
And ye who dwell within the inner chamber
Where shines the storèd joy of gold—
Gods of one heart, O hear ye, and remember;
Up and avenge the blood shed forth of old,
With sudden rightful blow;
Then let the old curse die, nor be renewed
With progeny of blood,—
Once more, and not again, be latter guilt laid low!
O thou who dwell'st in Delphi's mighty cave,
Grant us to see this home once more restored
Unto its rightful lord!
Let it look forth, from veils of death, with joyous eye
Unto the dawning light of liberty;
And Hermes, Maia's child, lend hand to save,

Willing the right, and guide
Our state with Fortune's breeze adown the favouring
      tide.
Whate'er in darkness hidden lies,
   He utters at his will;
He at his will throws darkness on our eye
  By night and eke by day inscrutable.
   Then, then shall wealth atone
 The ills that here were done.
   Then, then will we unbind,
   Fling free on wafting wind
Of joy, the woman's voice that waileth now
In piercing accents for a chief laid low;
   And this our song shall be—
  Hail to the commonwealth restored!
   Hail to the freedom won to me!
All hail! for doom hath passed from him, my well—
      loved lord!
   And thou, O child, when Time and Chance agree,
Up to the deed that for thy sire is done!
And if she wail unto thee, Spare, O son—
Cry, Aid, O father—and achieve the deed,
The horror of man's tongue, the gods' great need!
Hold in thy breast such heart as Perseus had,
The bitter woe work forth,
Appease the summons of the dead,
The wrath of friends on earth;
Yea, set within a sign of blood and doom,
And do to utter death him that pollutes thy home.
   [Enter Aegisthus.
AEGISTHUS
   Hither and not unsummoned have I come;
For a new rumour, borne by stranger men
Arriving hither, hath attained mine ears,
Of hap unwished-for, even Orestes' death.
This were new sorrow, a blood-bolter'd load
Laid on the house that doth already bow
Beneath a former wound that festers deep.
Dare I opine these words have truth and life?

Or are they tales, of woman's terror born,
That fly in the void air, and die disproved?
Canst thou tell aught, and prove it to my soul?
CHORUS
    What we have heard, we heard; go thou within
  Thyself to ask the strangers of their tale.
  Strengthless are tidings, thro' another heard;
  Question is his, to whom the tale is brought.
AEGISTHUS
    I too will meet and test the messenger,
  Whether himself stood witness of the death,
  Or tells it merely from dim rumour learnt:
  None shall cheat me, whose soul hath watchful eyes.
    [Exit.
CHORUS
    Zeus, Zeus! what word to me is given?
  What cry or prayer, invoking heaven,
  Shall first by me be uttered?
  What speech of craft? nor all revealing,
  Nor all too warily concealing?
  Ending my speech, shall aid the deed?
  For lo! in readiness is laid
  The dark emprise, the rending blade;
  Blood-dropping daggers shall achieve
  The dateless doom of Atreus' name,
  Or? kindling torch and joyful flame
  In sign of new-won liberty?
  Once more Orestes shall retrieve
  His father's wealth, and, throned on high,
  Shall hold the city's fealty.
  So mighty is the grasp whereby,
  Heaven-holpen, he shall trip and throw,
  Unseconded, a double foe
  Ho for the victory!
    [A loud cry within.
VOICE OF AEGISTHUS
  Help, help, alas!
CHORUS
  Ho there, ho! how is't within?

Is't done? is't over? Stand we here aloof
While it is wrought, that guiltless we may seem
Of this dark deed; with death is strife fulfilled.
    [Enter a slave
SLAVE
    O woe, O woe, my lord is done to death!
Woe, woe, and woe again, AEgisthus gone!
Hasten, fling wide the doors, unloose the bolts
Of the queen's chamber. O for some young strength
To match the need! but aid availeth nought
To him laid low for ever. Help, help, help!
Sure to deaf ears I shout, and call in vain
To slumber ineffectual. What ho!
The queen! how fareth Clytemnestra's self?
Her neck too, hers, is close upon the steel,
And soon shall sink, hewn thro' as justice wills.
    [Enter Clytemnestra.
CLYTEMNESTRA
    What ails thee, raising this ado for us?
SLAVE
    I say the dead are come to slay the living.
CLYTEMNESTRA
    Alack, I read thy riddles all too clear?
We slew by craft and by like craft shall die.
Swift, bring the axe that slew my lord of old;
I'll know anon or death or victory?
So stands the curse, so I confront it here.
    [Enter Orestes, his sword dropping with blood,
ORESTES
    Thee too I seek: for him what's done will serve.
CLYTEMNESTRA
    Woe, woe! Aegisthus, spouse and champion, slain!
ORESTES
    What lov'st the man? then in his grave lie down,
Be his in death, desert him nevermore!
CLYTEMNESTSA
    Stay, child, and fear to strike. O son, this breast
Pillowed thine head full oft, while, drowsed with sleep,
Thy toothless mouth drew mother's milk from me.

ORESTES

Can I my mother spare? speak, Pylades,

PYLADES

Where then would fall the hest Apollo gave
At Delphi, where the solemn compact sworn?
Choose thou the hate of all men, not of gods.

ORESTES

Thou dost prevail; I hold thy counsel good.
[To Clytemnestra.
Follow; I will slay thee at his side.
With him whom in his life thou lovedst more
Than Agamemnon, sleep in death, the meed
For hate where love, and love where hate was due!

CLYTEMNESTRA

I nursed thee young; must I forego mine eld?

ORESTES

Thou slew'st my father; shalt thou dwell with me?

CLYTEMNESTRA

Fate bore a share in these things, O my child!

ORESTES

Fate also doth provide this doom for thee.

CLYTEMNESTRA

Beware, O my child, a parent's dying curse.

ORESTES

A parent who did cast me out to ill!

CLYTEMNESTRA

Not cast thee out, but to a friendly home.

ORESTES

Born free, I was by twofold bargain sold.

CLYTEMNESTRA

Where then the price that I received for thee?

ORESTES

The price of shame; I taunt thee not more plainly.

CLYTEMNESTRA

Nay, but recount thy father's lewdness too.

ORESTES

Home-keeping, chide not him who toils without.

CLYTEMNESTRA

'Tis hard for wives to live as widows, child.
ORESTES
   The absent husband toils for them at home.
CLYTEMNESTRA
   Thou growest fain to slay thy mother, child
ORESTES
   Nay, 'tis thyself wilt slay thyself, not I.
CLYTEMNESTRA
   Beware thy mother's vengeful hounds from hell.
ORESTES
   How shall I 'scape my father's, sparing thee?
CLYTEMNESTRA
   Living, I cry as to a tomb, unheard.
ORESTES
   My father's fate ordains this doom for thee.
CLYTEMNESTRA
   Ah, me! this snake it was I bore and nursed.
ORESTES
   Ay, right prophetic was thy visioned fear.
Shameful thy deed was—die the death of shame!
   [Exit, driving Clytemnestra before him.
CHORUS
   Lo, even for these I mourn, a double death:
Yet since Orestes, driven on by doom,
Thus crowns the height of murders manifold,
I say, 'tis well—that not in night and death
Should sink the eye and light of this our home.

   There came on Priam's race and name
  A vengeance; though it tarried long,
   With heavy doom it came.
Came, too, on Agamemnon's hall
  A lion-pair, twin swordsmen strong.
And last, the heritage doth fall
  To him, to whom from Pythian cave
  The god his deepest counsel gave.
Cry out, rejoice! our kingly hall
  Hath 'scaped from ruin—ne'er again
Its ancient wealth be wasted all
   By two usurpers, sin-defiled—

An evil path of woe and bane!
On him who dealt the dastard blow
   Comes Craft, Revenge's scheming child.
And hand in hand with him doth go,
     Eager for fight,
The child of Zeus, whom men below
 Call Justice, naming her aright.
    And on her foes her breath
    Is as the blast of death;
For her the god who dwells in deep recess
    Beneath Parnassus' brow,
   Summons with loud acclaim
   To rise, though late and lame,
And come with craft that worketh righteousness.
   For even o'er Powers divine this law is strong—
   Thou shalt not serve the wrong.
To that which ruleth heaven beseems it that we bow.
   Lo, freedom's light hath come!
   Lo, now is rent away
The grim and curbing bit that held us dumb.
 Up to the light, ye halls! this many a day
   Too low on earth ye lay.
 And Time, the great Accomplisher,
 Shall cross the threshold, whensoe'er
 He choose with purging hand to cleanse
 The palace, driving all pollution thence.
 And fair the cast of Fortune's die
 Before our state's new lords shall lie,
 Not as of old, but bringing fairer doom
   Lo, freedom's light hath come!

[The scene opens, disclosing Orestes standing over the corpses of Aegisthus and Clytemnestra; in one hand he holds his sword, in the other the robe in which Agamemnon was entangled and slain.

ORESTES
   There lies our country's twofold tyranny,
My father's slayers, spoilers of my home.
Erst were they royal, sitting on the throne,
And loving are they yet,—their common fate
Tells the tale truly, shows their trothplight firm.

They swore to work mine ill-starred father's death,
They swore to die together; 'tis fulfilled.
O ye who stand, this great doom's witnesses,
Behold this too, the dark device which bound
My sire unhappy to his death,—behold
The mesh which trapped his hands, enwound his feet!
Stand round, unfold it—'tis the trammel-net
That wrapped a chieftain; holds it that he see,
The father—not my sire, but he whose eye
Is judge of all things, the all-seeing Sun!
Let him behold my mother's damnèd deed,
Then let him stand, when need shall be to me,
Witness that justly I have sought and slain
My mother; blameless was Aegisthus' doom—
He died the death law bids adulterers die.
But she who plotted this accursèd thing
To slay her lord, by whom she bare beneath
Her girdle once the burden of her babes,
Beloved erewhile, now turned to hateful foes—
What deem ye of her? or what venomed thing,
Sea-snake or adder, had more power than she
To poison with a touch the flesh unscarred?
So great her daring, such her impious will.
How name her, if I may not speak a curse?
A lion-springe! a laver's swathing cloth,
Wrapping a dead man, twining round his feet—
A net, a trammel, an entangling robe?
Such were the weapon of some strangling thief,
The terror of the road, a cut-purse hound—
With such device full many might he kill,
Full oft exult in heat of villainy.
Ne'er have my house so cursed an indweller—
Heaven send me, rather, childless to be slain!
CHORUS
   Woe for each desperate deed!
Woe for the queen, with shame of life bereft!
And ah, for him who still is left,
Madness, dark blossom of a bloody seed!
ORESTES

Did she the deed or not? this robe gives proof,
Imbrued with blood that bathed Aegisthus' sword;
Look, how the spurted stain combines with time
To blur the many dyes that once adorned
Its pattern manifold! I now stand here,
Made glad, made sad with blood, exulting, wailing—
Hear, O thou woven web that slew my sire!
I grieve for deed and death and all my home—
Victor, pollution's damnèd stain for prize.
CHORUS
Alas, that none of mortal men
Can pass his life untouched by pain!
Behold, one woe is here—
Another loometh near.
ORESTES
Hark ye and learn—for what the end shall be
For me I know not: breaking from the curb
My spirit whirls me off, a conquered prey,
Borne as a charioteer by steeds distraught
Far from the course, and madness in my breast
Burneth to chant its song, and leap, and rave—
Hark ye and learn, friends, ere my reason goes!
I say that rightfully I slew my mother,
A thing God-scorned, that foully slew my sire
And chiefest wizard of the spell that bound me
Unto this deed I name the Pythian seer
Apollo, who foretold that if I slew,
The guilt of murder done should pass from me;
But if I spared, the fate that should be mine
I dare not blazon forth—the bow of speech
Can reach not to the mark, that doom to tell.
And now behold me, how with branch and crown
I pass, a suppliant made meet to go
Unto Earth's midmost shrine, the holy ground
Of Loxias, and that renownèd light
Of ever-burning fire, to 'scape the doom
Of kindred murder: to no other shrine
(So Loxias bade) may I for refuge turn.
Bear witness, Argives, in the after time,

How came on me this dread fatality.
Living, I pass a banished wanderer hence,
To leave in death the memory of this cry.
CHORUS
  Nay, but the deed is well; link not thy lips
To speech ill-starred, nor vent ill-boding words—
Who hast to Argos her full freedom given,
Lopping two serpents' heads with timely blow.
ORESTES
  Look, look, alas!
Handmaidens, see—what Gorgon shapes throng up;
Dusky their robes and all their hair enwound—
Snakes coiled with snakes—off, off, I must away!
CHORUS
  Most loyal of all sons unto thy sire,
What visions thus distract thee? Hold, abide;
Great was thy victory, and shalt thou fear?
ORESTES
  These are no dreams, void shapes of haunting ill,
But clear to sight my mother's hell-hounds come!
CHORUS
  Nay, the fresh bloodshed still imbrues thine hands,
And thence distraction sinks into thy soul.
ORESTES
  O king Apollo—see, they swarm and throng—
Black blood of hatred dripping from their eyes!
CHORUS
  One remedy thou hast; go, touch the shrine
Of Loxias, and rid thee of these woes.
ORESTES
  Ye can behold them not, but I behold them.
Up and away! I dare abide no more.
  [Exit
CHORUS
  Farewell then as thou mayst,—the god thy friend
Guard thee and aid with chances favouring.
  Behold, the storm of woe divine
That the raves and beats on Atreus' line
  Its great third blast hath blown.
First was Thyestes' loathly woe—

The rueful feast of long ago,
  On children's flesh, unknown.
And next the kingly chief's despite,
When he who led the Greeks to fight
  Was in the bath hewn down.
And now the offspring of the race
Stands in the third, the saviour's place,
  To save—or to consume?
O whither, ere it be fulfilled,
Ere its fierce blast be hushed and stilled,
  Shall blow the wind of doom?
    [Exeunt.

The Furies

Dramatis Personae:
THE PYTHIAN
PRIESTESS
APOLLO
ORESTES
THE GHOST OF CLYTEMNESTRA
CHORUS OF FURIES
ATHENA
ATTENDANTS OF ATHENA
TWELVE ATHENIAN CITIZENS

The Scene of the Drama is the Temple of Apollo, at Delphi: afterwards the Temple of Athena, on the Acropolis of Athens, and the adjoining Areopagus.

The Temple at Delphi

The Pythian Priestess

First, in this prayer, of all the gods I name
The prophet mother Earth; and Themis next,
Second who sat—for so with truth is said—
On this her mother's shrine oracular.
Then by her grace, who unconstrained allowed,
There sat thereon another child of Earth—
Titanian Phoebe. She, in after time,
Gave o'er the throne, as birthgift to a god,
Phoebus, who in his own bears Phoebe's name.
He from the lake and ridge of Delos' isle
Steered to the port of Pallas' Attic shores,
The home of ships; and thence he passed and came
Unto this land and to Parnassus' shrine.
And at his side, with awe revering him,
There went the children of Hephaestus' seed,
The hewers of the sacred way, who tame
The stubborn tract that erst was wilderness.
And all this folk, and Delphos, chieftain-king
Of this their land, with honour gave him home;
And in his breast Zeus set a prophet's soul,
And gave to him this throne, whereon he sits,

Fourth prophet of the shrine, and, Loxias hight,
Gives voice to that which Zeus his sire decrees.
    Such gods I name in my preluding prayer,
And after them, I call with honour due
On Pallas, wardress of the fane, and Nymphs
Who dwell around the rock Corycian,
Where in the hollow cave, the wild birds' haunt,
Wander the feet of lesser gods; and there,
Right well I know it, Bromian Bacchus dwells,
Since he in godship led his Maenad host,
Devising death for Pentheus, whom they rent
Piecemeal, as hare among the hounds. And last,
I call on Pleistus' springs, Poseidon's might,
And Zeus most high, the great Accomplisher.
Then as a seeress to the sacred chair
I pass and sit; and may the powers divine
Make this mine entrance fruitful in response
Beyond each former advent, triply blest.
And if there stand without, from Hellas bound,
Men seeking oracles, let each pass in
In order of the lot, as use allows;
For the god guides whate'er my tongue proclaims.
    [She goes into the interior of the temple; after a short interval, she returns
in great fear.
    Things fell to speak of, fell for eyes to see,
Have sped me forth again from Loxias' shrine,
With strength unstrung, moving erect no more,
But aiding with my hands my failing feet,
Unnerved by fear. A beldame's force is naught—
Is as a child's, when age and fear combine.
For as I pace towards the inmost fane
Bay-filleted by many a suppliant's hand,
Lo, at the central altar I descry
One crouching as for refuge—yea, a man
Abhorredd of heaven; and from his hands, wherein
A sword new-drawn he holds, blood reeked and fell:
A wand he bears, the olive's topmost bough,
Twined as of purpose with a deep close tuft
Of whitest wool. This, that I plainly saw,
Plainly I tell. But lo, in front of him,
Crouched on the altar-steps, a grisly band

Of women slumbers—not like women they,
But Gorgons rather; nay, that word is weak,
Nor may I match the Gorgons' shape with theirs!
Such have I seen in painted semblance erst—
Winged Harpies, snatching food from Phineus' board,—
But these are wingless, black, and all their shape
The eye's abomination to behold.
Fell is the breath—let none draw nigh to it—
Wherewith they snort in slumber; from their eyes
Exude the damned drops of poisonous ire:
And such their garb as none should dare to bring
To statues of the gods or homes of men.
I wot not of the tribe wherefrom can come
So fell a legion, nor in what land Earth
Could rear, unharmed, such creatures, nor avow
That she had travailed and brought forth death.
But, for the rest, be all these things a care
Unto the mighty Loxias, the lord
Of this our shrine: healer and prophet he,
Discerner he of portents, and the cleanser
Of other homes—behold, his own to cleanse!
　　[Exit.
　　[The scene opens, disclosing the interior of the temple: Orestes clings to
the central altar; the Furies lie slumbering at a little distance; Apollo and
Hermes appear from the innermost shrine.
APOLLO
　　Lo, I desert thee never: to the end,
Hard at thy side as now, or sundered far,
I am thy guard, and to thine enemies
Implacably oppose me: look on them,
These greedy fiends, beneath my craft subdued!
See, they are fallen on sleep, these beldames oid,
Unto whose grim and wizened maidenhood
Nor god nor man nor beast can e'er draw near.
Yea, evil were they born, for evil's doom,
Evil the dark abyss of Tartarus
Wherein they dwell, and they themselves the hate
Of men on earth, and of Olympian gods.
But thou, flee far and with unfaltering speed;
For they shall hunt thee through the mainland wide
Where'er throughout the tract of travelled earth

Thy foot may roam, and o'er and o'er the seas
And island homes of men. Faint not nor fail,
Too soon and timidly within thy breast
Shepherding thoughts forlorn of this thy toil;
But unto Pallas' city go, and there
Crouch at her shrine, and in thine arms enfold
Her ancient image: there we well shall find
Meet judges for this cause and suasive pleas,
Skilled to contrive for thee deliverance
From all this woe. Be such my pledge to thee,
For by my hest thou didst thy mother slay.
ORESTES
    O king Apollo, since right well thou know'st
What justice bids, have heed, fulfil the same,—
Thy strength is all-sufficient to achieve.
APOLLO
    Have thou too heed, nor let thy fear prevail
Above thy will. And do thou guard him, Hermes,
Whose blood is brother unto mine, whose sire
The same high God. Men call thee guide and guard,
Guide therefore thou and guard my suppliant;
For Zeus himself reveres the outlaw's right,
Boon of fair escort, upon man conferred.
    [Exeunt Apollo, Hermes, and Orestes The Ghost of Clytemnestra near
GHOST OF CLYTEMNESTRA
    Sleep on! awake! what skills your sleep to me—
Me, among all the dead by you dishonoured—
Me from whom never, in the world of death,
Dieth this curse, 'Tis she who smote and slew,
And shamed and scorned I roam? Awake, and hear
My plaint of dead men's hate intolerable.
Me, sternly slain by them that should have loved,
Me doth no god arouse him to avenge,
Hewn down in blood by matricidal hands.
Mark ye these wounds from which the heart's blood ran,
And by whose hand, bethink ye! for the sense
When shut in sleep hath then the spirit-sight,
But in the day the inward eye is blind.
List, ye who drank so oft with lapping tongue
The wineless draught by me outpoured to soothe
Your vengeful ire! how oft on kindled shrine

I laid the feast of darkness, at the hour
Abhorred of every god but you alone!
Lo, all my service trampled down and scorned!
And he hath baulked your chase, as stag the hounds;
Yea, lightly bounding from the circling toils,
Hath wried his face in scorn, and flieth far.
Awake and hear—for mine own soul I cry—
Awake, ye powers of hell! the wandering ghost
That once was Clytemnestra calls—Arise!

[The Furies mutter grimly, as in a dream. Mutter and murmur! He hath
flown afar— My kin have gods to guard them, I have none!

[The Furies mutter as before. O drowsed in sleep too deep to heed my
pain! Orestes flies, who me, his mother, slew.

[The Furies give a confused cry. Yelping, and drowsed again? Up and be
doing That which alone is yours, the deed of hell!

[The Furies give another cry. Lo, sleep and toil, the sworn confederates,
Have quelled your dragon-anger, once so fell!

THE FURIES (muttering more fiercely and loudly)

Seize, seize, seize, seize—mark, yonder!

GHOST

In dreams ye chase a prey, and like some hound,
That even in sleep doth ply his woodland toil,
Ye bell and bay. What do ye, sleeping here?
Be not o'ercome with toil, nor sleep-subdued,
Be heedless of my wrong. Up! thrill your heart
With the just chidings of my tongue,—such words
Are as a spur to purpose firmly held.
Blow forth on him the breath of wrath and blood,
Scorch him with reek of fire that burns in you,
Waste him with new pursuit—swift, hound him down!

[Ghost sinks.

FIRST FURY (awaking)

Up! rouse another as I rouse thee; up!
Sleep'st thou? Rise up, and spurning sleep away,
See we if false to us this prelude rang.

CHORUS OF FURIES

Alack, alack, O sisters, we have toiled,
O much and vainly have we toiled and borne!
Vainly! and all we wrought the gods have foiled,
        And turnèd us to scorn!
He hath slipped from the net, whom we chased: he

hath 'scaped us who should be our prey—
O'ermastered by slumber we sank, and our quarry hath stolen away!
Thou, child of the high God Zeus, Apollo, hast robbed us and wronged;
Thou, a youth, hast down-trodden the right that is godship more
    ancient belonged;
Thou hast cherished thy suppliant man; the slayer the God-forsaken,
The bane of a parent, by craft from out of our grasp thou hast taken:
A god, thou hast stolen from us the avengers a matricide son—
And who shall consider thy deed and say, It is rightfully done?
      The sound of chiding scorn
      Came from the land of dream;
  Deep to mine inmost heart I felt it thrill and burn,
    Thrust as a strong-grasped goad, to urge
      Onward the chariot's team.
    Thrilled, chilled with bitter inward pain
  I stand as one beneath the doomsman's scourge.
  Shame on the younger gods who tread down right,
    Sitting on thrones of might!
  Woe on the altar of earth's central fane!
    Clotted on step and shrine,
Behold, the guilt of blood, the ghastly stain!
  Woe upon thee, Apollo! uncontrolled,
    Unbidden, hast thou, prophet-god, imbrued
    The pure prophetic shrine with wrongful blood!
  For thou too heinous a respect didst hold
Of man, too little heed of powers divine!
    And us the Fates, the ancients of the earth,
    Didst deem as nothing worth.
Scornful to me thou art, yet shalt not fend
  My wrath from him; though unto hell he flee,
      There too are we!
And he the blood defiled, should feel and rue,
Though I were not, fiend-wrath that shall not end,
Descending on his head who foully slew.
    [Re-enter Apollo from the inner shrine.
APOLLO
  Out! I command you. Out from this my home—
Haste, tarry not! Out from the mystic shrine,
Lest thy lot be to take into thy breast
The winged bright dart that from my golden string
Speeds hissing as a snake,—lest, pierced and thrilled

With agony, thou shouldst spew forth again
Black frothy heart's-blood, drawn from mortal men,
Belching the gory clots sucked forth from wounds.
These be no halls where such as you can prowl—
Go where men lay on men the doom of blood,
Heads lopped from necks, eyes from their Sphere plucked out,
Hacked flesh, the flower of youthful seed crushed or
Feet hewn away, and hands, and death beneath
The smiting stone, low moans and piteous
Of men impaled—Hark, hear ye for what feast
Ye hanker ever, and the loathing gods
Do spit upon your craving? Lo, your shape
Is all too fitted to your greed; the cave
Where lurks some lion, lapping gore, were home
More meet for you. Avaunt from sacred shrines,
Nor bring pollution by your touch on all
That nears you. Hence! and roam unshepherded—
No god there is to tend such herd as you.

CHORUS

    O king Apollo, in our turn hear us'
Thou hast'not only part in these ill things,
But art chief cause and doer of the same.

APOLLO

    How? stretch thy speech to tell this, and have done.

CHORUS

    Thine oracle bade this man slay his mother.

APOLLO

    I bade him quit his sire's death,—wherefore not?

CHORUS

    Then didst thou aid and guard red-handed crime.

APOLLO

    Yea, and I bade him to this temple flee.

CHORUS

    And yet forsooth dost chide us following him!

APOLLO

    Ay—not for you it is, to near this fane.

CHORUS

    Yet is such office ours, imposed by fate.

APOLLO

    What office? vaunt the thing ye deem so fair.

CHORUS
From home to home we chase the matricide.
APOLLO
What? to avenge a wife who slays her lord?
CHORUS
That is not blood outpoured by kindred hands.
APOLLO
How darkly ye dishonour and annul
The troth to which the high accomplishers,
Hera and Zeus, do honour. Yea, and thus
Is Aphrodite to dishonour cast,
The queen of rapture unto mortal men.
Know, that above the marriage-bed ordained
For man and woman standeth Right as guard,
Enhancing sanctity of troth-plight sworn;
Therefore, if thou art placable to those
Who have their consort slain, nor will'st to turn
On them the eye of wrath, unjust art thou
In hounding to his doom the man who slew
His mother. Lo, I know thee full of wrath
Against one deed, but all too placable
Unto the other, minishing the crime.
But in this cause shall Pallas guard the right.
CHORUS
Deem not my quest shall ever quit that man.
APOLLO
Follow then, make thee double toil in vain!
CHORUS
Think not by speech mine office to curtail.
APOLLO
None hast thou, that I would accept of thee!
CHORUS
Yea, high thine honour by the throne of Zeus:
But I, drawn on by scent of mother's blood,
Seek vengeance on this man and hound him down.
APOLLO
But I will stand beside him; 'tis for me
To guard my suppliant: gods and men alike
Do dread the curse of such an one betrayed,
And in me Fear and Will say Leave him not.
    [Exeunt omnes

The scene changes to Athens. In the foreground, the Temple of Athena on the Acropolis; her statue stands in the centre; Orestes is seen dinging to it.

ORESTES

Look on me, queen Athena; lo, I come
By Loxias' behest; thou of thy grace
Receive me, driven of avenging powers—
Not now a red-hand slayer unannealed,
But with guilt fading, half-effaced, outworn
On many homes and paths of mortal men.
For to the limit of each land, each sea,
I roamed, obedient to Apollo's hest,
And come at last, O Goddess, to thy fane,
And clinging to thine image, bide my doom.
 [Enter the Chorus of Furies, questing like hounds

CHORUS

Ho! clear is here the trace of him we seek:
Follow the track of blood, the silent sign!
Like to some hound that hunts a wounded fawn,
We snuff along the scent of dripping gore,
And inwardly we pant, for many a day
Toiling in chase that shall fordo the man;
For o'er and o'er the wide land have I ranged,
And o'er the wide sea, flying without wings,
Swift as a sail I pressed upon his track,
Who now hard by is crouching, well I wot,
For scent of mortal blood allures me here.

Follow, seek him—round and round
Scent and snuff and scan the ground,
Lest unharmed he slip away,
 He who did his mother slay!
Hist—he is there! See him his arms entwine
Around the image of the maid divine—
 Thus aided, for the deed he wrought
Unto the judgment wills he to be brought.
 It may not be! a mother's blood, poured forth
 Upon the stainèd earth,
None gathers up: it lies—bear witness, Hell!—
 For aye indelible!
And thou who sheddest it shalt give thine own
 That shedding to atone!

Yea, from thy living limbs I suck it out,
　　Red, clotted, gout by gout,—
A draught abhorred of men and gods; but I
　　Will drain it, suck thee dry;
Yea, I will waste thee living, nerve and vein;
　　Yea, for thy mother slain,
Will drag thee downward, there where thou shalt dree
　　The weird of agony!
And thou and whatsoe'er of men hath sinned—
　　Hath wronged or God, or friend,
Or parent,—learn ye how to all and each
　　The arm of doom can reach!
Sternly requiteth, in the world beneath,
　　The judgment-seat of Death;
Yea, Death, beholding every man's endeavour
　　Recordeth it for ever.

ORESTES
　　I, schooled in many miseries, have learnt
How many refuges of cleansing shrines
There be; I know when law alloweth speech
And when imposeth silence. Lo, I stand
Fixed now to speak, for he whose word is wise
Commands the same. Look, how the stain of blood
Is dull upon mine hand and wastes away,
And laved and lost therewith is the deep curse
Of matricide; for while the guilt was new,
'Twas banished from me at Apollo's hearth,
Atoned and purified by death of swine.
Long were my word if I should sum the tale,
How oft since then among my fellow-men
I stood and brought no curse. Time cleanses all—
Time, the coeval of all things that are.
Now from pure lips, in words of omen fair,
I call Athena, lady of this land,
To come, my champion: so, in aftertime,
She shall not fail of love and service deal,
Not won by war, from me and from my land
And all the folk of Argos, vowed to her.
　　Now, be she far away in Libyan land
Where flows from Triton's lake her natal wave,—
Stand she with planted feet, or in some hour

Of rest conceal them, champion of her friends
Where'er she be,—or whether o'er the plain
Phlegraean she look forth, as warrior bold—
I cry to her to come, where'er she be,
(And she, as goddess, from afar can hear,)
And aid and free me, set among my foes.
CHORUS
   Thee not Apollo nor Athena's strength
Can save from perishing, a castaway
Amid the Lost, where no delight shall meet
Thy soul—a bloodless prey of nether powers,
A shadow among shadows. Answerest thou
Nothing? dost cast away my words with scorn,
Thou, prey prepared and dedicate to me?
Not as a victim slain upon the shrine,
But living shalt thou see thy flesh my food.
Hear now the binding chant that makes thee mine.
    Weave the weird dance,—behold the hour
  To utter forth the chant of hell,
  Our sway among mankind to tell,
The guidance of our power.
Of Justice are we ministers,
  And whosoe'er of men may stand
  Lifting a pure unsullied hand,
That man no doom of ours incurs,
  And walks thro' all his mortal path
  Untouched by woe, unharmed by wrath.
  But if, as yonder man, he hath
Blood on the hands he strives to hide,
  We stand avengers at his side,
Decreeing, Thou hast wronged the dead:
  We are doom's witnesses to thee.
The price of blood, his hands have shed,
We wring from him; in life, in death,
  Hard at his side are we!
   Night, Mother Night, who brought me forth, a torment
     To living men and dead,
Hear me, O hear! by Leto's stripling son
     I am dishonourèd:
He hath ta'en from me him who cowers in refuge,
     To me made consecrate,—

A rightful victim, him who slew his mother.
    Given o'er to me and fate.
      Hear the hymn of hell,
    O'er the victim sounding,—
    Chant of frenzy, chant of ill,
     Sense and will confounding!
    Round the soul entwining
     Without lute or lyre—
    Soul in madness pining,
     Wasting as with fire!
 Fate, all-pervading Fate, this service spun, commanding
    That I should bide therein:
Whosoe'er of mortals, made perverse and lawless,
    Is stained with blood of kin,
By his side are we, and hunt him ever onward,
    Till to the Silent Land,
The realm of death, he cometh; neither yonder
    In freedom shall he stand.
      Hear the hymn of hell,
    O'er the victim sounding,—
    Chant of frenzy, chant of ill,
     Sense and will confounding!
    Round the soul entwining
     Without lute or lyre—
    Soul in madness pining,
     Wasting as with fire!
 When from womb of Night we sprang, on us this labour
    Was laid and shall abide.
Gods immortal are ye, yet beware ye touch not
    That which is our pride!
None may come beside us gathered round the blood feast—
    For us no garments white
Gleam on a festal day; for us a darker fate is,
    Another darker rite.
That is mine hour when falls an ancient line—
    When in the household's heart
The god of blood doth slay by kindred hands,—
    Then do we bear our part:
On him who slays we sweep with chasing cry:
Though he be triply strong,
We wear and waste him; blood atones for blood,

New pain for ancient wrong.
　I hold this task—'tis mine, and not another's.
The very gods on high,
Though they can silence and annul the prayers
Of those who on us cry,
They may not strive with us who stand apart,
A race by Zeus abhorred,
Blood-boltered, held unworthy of the council
And converse of Heaven's lord.
Therefore the more I leap upon my prey;
Upon their head I bound;
My foot is hard; as one that trips a runner
I cast them to the ground;
Yea, to the depth of doom intolerable;
And they who erst were great,
And upon earth held high their pride and glory,
Are brought to low estate.
In underworld they waste and are diminished,
The while around them fleet
Dark wavings of my robes, and, subtly woven,
The paces of my feet.
　Who falls infatuate, he sees not, neither knows he
That we are at his side;
So closely round about him, darkly flitting,
The cloud of guilt doth glide.
Heavily 'tis uttered, how around his hearthstone
The mirk of hell doth rise.
Stern and fixed the law is; we have hands t'achieve it,
Cunning to devise.
Queens are we and mindful of our solemn vengeance.
Not by tear or prayer
Shall a man avert it. In unhonoured darkness,
Far from gods, we fare,
Lit unto our task with torch of sunless regions,
And o'er a deadly way—
Deadly to the living as to those who see not
　Life and light of day—
Hunt we and press onward. Who of mortals hearing
　Doth not quake for awe,
Hearing all that Fate thro' hand of God hath given us
　For ordinance and law?

Yea, this right to us, in dark abysm and backward
    Of ages it befel:
None shall wrong mine office, tho' in nether regions
    And sunless dark I dwell.
[Enter Athena from above

ATHENA
    Far off I heard the clamour of your cry,
As by Scamander's side I set my foot
Asserting right upon the land given o'er
To me by those who o'er Achaia's host
Held sway and leadership: no scanty part
Of all they won by spear and sword, to me
They gave it, land and all that grew theron,
As chosen heirloom for my Theseus' clan.
Thence summoned, sped I with a tireless foot,—
Hummed on the wind, instead of wings, the fold
Of this mine aegis, by my feet propelled,
As, linked to mettled horses, speeds a car.
And now, beholding here Earth's nether brood,
I fear it nought, yet are mine eyes amazed
With wonder. Who are ye? of all I ask,
And of this stranger to my statue clinging.
But ye—your shape is like no human form,
Like to no goddess whom the gods behold,
Like to no shape which mortal women wear.
Yet to stand by and chide a monstrous form
Is all unjust—from such words Right revolts.

CHORUS
    O child of Zeus, one word shall tell thee all.
We are the children of eternal Night,
And Furies in the underworld are called.

ATHENA
    I know your lineage now and eke your name.

CHORUS
    Yea, and eftsoons indeed my rights shalt know.

ATHENA
    Fain would I learn them; speak them clearly forth.

CHORUS
    We chase from home the murderers of men.

ATHENA
    And where at last can he that slew make pause?

CHORUS

Where this is law—All joy abandon here.

ATHENA

Say, do ye bay this man to such a flight?

CHORUS

Yea, for of choice he did his mother slay.

ATHENA

Urged by no fear of other wrath and doom?

CHORUS

What spur can rightly goad to matricide?

ATHENA

Two stand to plead—one only have I heard.

CHORUS

He will not swear nor challenge us to oath.

ATHENA

The form of justice, not its deed, thou willest.

CHORUS

Prove thou that word; thou art not scant of skill.

ATHENA

I say that oaths shall not enforce the wrong.

CHORUS

Then test the cause, judge and award the right.

ATHENA

Will ye to me then this decision trust?

CHORUS

Yea, reverencing true child of worthy sire.

ATHENA (to Orestes)

O man unknown, make thou thy plea in turn
Speak forth thy land, thy lineage, and thy woes;
Then, if thou canst, avert this bitter blame—
If, as I deem, in confidence of right
Thou sittest hard beside my holy place,
Clasping this statue, as Ixion sat,
A sacred suppliant for Zeus to cleanse,—
To all this answer me in words made plain.

ORESTES

O queen Athena, first from thy last words
Will I a great solicitude remove.
Not one blood-guilty am I; no foul stain
Clings to thine image from my clinging hand;
Whereof one potent proof I have to tell.

Lo, the law stands—The slayer shall not plead,
Till by the hand of him who cleanses blood
A suckling creature's blood besprinkle him.
Long since have I this expiation done—
In many a home, slain beasts and running streams
Have cleansed me. Thus I speak away that fear.
Next, of my lineage quickly thou shalt learn:
An Argive am I, and right well thou know'st
My sire, that Agamemnon who arrayed
The fleet and them that went therein to war—
That chief with whom thy hand combined to crush
To an uncitied heap what once was Troy;
That Agamemnon, when he homeward came,
Was brought unto no honourable death,
Slain by the dark-souled wife who brought me forth
To him,—enwound and slain in wily nets,
Blazoned with blood that in the laver ran.
And I, returning from an exiled youth,
Slew her, my mother—lo, it stands avowed!
With blood for blood avenging my loved sire;
And in this deed doth Loxias bear part,
Decreeing agonies, to goad my will,
Unless by me the guilty found their doom.
Do thou decide if right or wrong were done—
Thy dooming, whatsoe'er it be, contents me.
ATHENA
    Too mighty is this matter, whatsoe'er
Of mortals claims to judge hereof aright.
Yea, me, even me, eternal Right forbids
To judge the issues of blood-guilt, and wrath
That follows swift behind. This too gives pause,
That thou as one with all due rites performed
Dost come, unsinning, pure, unto my shrine.
Whate'er thou art, in this my city's name,
As uncondemned, I take thee to my side,—
Yet have these foes of thine such dues by fate,
I may not banish them: and if they fail,
O'erthrown in judgment of the cause, forthwith
Their anger's poison shall infect the land—
A dropping plague-spot of eternal ill.
Thus stand we with a woe on either hand:

Stay they, or go at my commandment forth,
Perplexity or pain must needs befall.
Yet, as on me Fate hath imposed the cause,
I choose unto me judges that shall be
An ordinance for ever, set to rule
The dues of blood-guilt, upon oath declared.
But ye, call forth your witness and your proof,
Words strong for justice, fortified by oath;
And I, whoe'er are truest in my town,
Them will I chose and bring, and straitly charge,
Look on this cause, discriminating well,
And pledge your oath to utter nought of wrong.
  [Exit Athena.
CHORUS
  Now are they all undone, the ancient laws,
    If here the slayer's cause
Prevail; new wrong for ancient right shall be
    If matricide go free.
Henceforth a deed like his by all shall stand,
    Too ready to the hand:
Too oft shall parents in the aftertime
    Rue and lament this crime,—
Taught, not in false imagining, to feel
    Their children's thrusting steel:
No more the wrath, that erst on murder fell
      From us, the queens of Hell.
Shall fall, no more our watching gaze impend—
    Death shall smite unrestrained.
    Henceforth shall one unto another cry Lo, they are stricken, lo, they fall
and die Around me! and that other answers him, O thou that lookest that
thy woes should cease, Behold, with dark increase They throng and press
upon thee; yea, and dim Is all the cure, and every comfort vain!
    Let none henceforth cry out, when falls the blow
    Of sudden-smiting woe,
    Cry out in sad reiterated strain
  O Justice, aid! aid, O ye thrones of Hell!
    So though a father or a mother wail
    New-smitten by a son, it shall no more avail,
Since, overthrown by wrong, the fane of Justice fell!
    Know, that a throne there is that may not pass away,
    And one that sitteth on it—even Fear,

Searching with steadfast eyes man's inner soul:
Wisdom is child of pain, and born with many a tear;
    But who henceforth,
What man of mortal men, what nation upon earth,
  That holdeth nought in awe nor in the light
  Of inner reverence, shall worship Right
    As in the older day?
    Praise not, O man, the life beyond control,
  Nor that which bows unto a tyrant's sway.
    Know that the middle way
Is dearest unto God, and they thereon who wend,
    They shall achieve the end;
  But they who wander or to left or right
    Are sinners in his sight.
  Take to thy heart this one, this soothfast word—
  Of wantonness impiety is sire;
  Only from calm control and sanity unstirred
  Cometh true weal, the goal of every man's desire.
    Yea, whatsoe'er befall, hold thou this word of mine:
    Bow down at Justice' shrine,
    Turn thou thine eyes away from earthly lure,
  Nor with a godless foot that altar spurn.
  For as thou dost shall Fate do in return,
    And the great doom is sure.
    Therefore let each adore a parent's trust,
    And each with loyalty revere the guest
    That in his halls doth rest.
For whoso uncompelled doth follow what is just,
    He ne'er shall be unblest;
    Yea, never to the gulf of doom
    That man shall come.
But he whose will is set against the gods,
  Who treads beyond the law with foot impure,
  Till o'er the wreck of Right confusion broods—
Know that for him, though now he sail secure,
The day of storm shall be; then shall he strive and fail,
  Down from the shivered yard to furl the sail,
And call on Powers, that heed him nought, to save
  And vainly wrestle with the whirling wave,
    Hot was his heart with pride—
    I shall not fall, he cried.

But him with watching scorn
The god beholds, forlorn,
Tangled in toils of Fate beyond escape,
Hopeless of haven safe beyond the cape—
Till all his wealth and bliss of bygone day
Upon the reef of Rightful Doom is hurled,
And he is rapt away
Unwept, for ever, to the dead forgotten world.
[Re-enter Athena, with twelve Athenian citizens.
ATHENA
O herald, make proclaim, bid all men come.
Then let the shrill blast of the Tyrrhene trump,
Fulfilled with mortal breath, thro' the wide air
Peal a loud summons, bidding all men heed.
For, till my judges fill this judgment-seat,
Silence behoves,—that this whole city learn,
What for all time mine ordinance commands,
And these men, that the cause be judged aright.
[Apollo approaches.
CHORUS
O king Apollo, rule what is thine own,
But in this thing what share pertains to thee?
APOLLO
First, as a witness come I, for this man
Is suppliant of mine by sacred right,
Guest of my holy hearth and cleansed by me
Of blood-guilt: then, to set me at his side
And in his cause bear part, as part I bore
Erst in his deed, whereby his mother fell.
Let whoso knoweth now announce the cause.
ATHENA (to the Chorus)
'Tis I announce the cause—first speech be yours;
For rightfully shall they whose plaint is tried
Tell the tale first and set the matter clear.
CHORUS
Though we be many, brief shall be our tale.
(To Orestes) Answer thou, setting word to match with
word;
And first avow—hast thou thy mother slain?
ORESTES
I slew her. I deny no word hereof.

CHORUS
Three falls decide the wrestle—this is one.
ORESTES
Thou vauntest thee—but o'er no final fall.
CHORUS
Yet must thou tell the manner of thy deed.
ORESTES
Drawn sword in hand, I gashed her neck. Tis told.
CHORUS
But by whose word, whose craft, wert thou impelled?
ORESTES
By oracles of him who here attests me.

CHORUS
The prophet-god bade thee thy mother slay?
ORESTES
Yea, and thro' him less ill I fared, till now.
CHORUS
If the vote grip thee, thou shalt change that word.
ORESTES
Strong is my hope; my buried sire shall aid.
CHORUS
Go to now, trust the dead, a matricide!
ORESTES
Yea, for in her combined two stains of sin.
CHORUS
How? speak this clearly to the judges' mind.
ORESTES
Slaying her husband, she did slay my sire.
CHORUS
Therefore thou livest; death assoils her deed.
ORESTES
Then while she lived why didst thou hunt her not?
CHORUS
She was not kin by blood to him she slew.
ORESTES
And I, am I by blood my mother's kin?
CHORUS
O cursed with murder's guilt, how else wert thou
The burden of her womb? Dost thou forswear
Thy mother's kinship, closest bond of love?

ORESTES

It is thine hour, Apollo—speak the law,
Averring if this deed were justly done;
For done it is, and clear and undenied.
But if to thee this murder's cause seem right
Or wrongful, speak—that I to these may tell.

APOLLO

To you, Athena's mighty council-court,
Justly for justice will I plead, even I,
The prophet-god, nor cheat you by one word.
For never spake I from my prophet-seat
One word, of man, of woman, or of state,
Save what the Father of Olympian gods
Commanded unto me. I rede you then,
Bethink you of my plea, how strong it stands,
And follow the decree of Zeus our sire,—
For oaths prevail not over Zeus' command.

CHORUS

Go to; thou sayest that from Zeus befel
The oracle that this Orestes bade
With vengeance quit the slaying of his sire,
And hold as nought his mother's right of kin!

APOLLO

Yea, for it stands not with a common death,
That he should die, a chieftain and a king
Decked with the sceptre which high heaven confers—
Die, and by female hands, not smitten down
By a far-shooting bow, held stalwartly
By some strong Amazon. Another doom
Was his: O Pallas, hear, and ye who sit
In judgment, to discern this thing aright!—
She with a specious voice of welcome true
Hailed him, returning from the mighty mart
Where war for life gives fame, triumphant home;
Then o'er the laver, as he bathed himself,
She spread from head to foot a covering net,
And in the endless mesh of cunning robes
Enwound and trapped her lord, and smote him down.
Lo, ye have heard what doom this chieftain met,
The majesty of Greece, the fleet's high lord:
Such as I tell it, let it gall your ears,

Who stand as judges to decide this cause.
CHORUS
   Zeus, as thou sayest, holds a father's death
As first of crimes,—yet he of his own act
Cast into chains his father, Cronos old:
How suits that deed with that which now ye tell?
O ye who judge, I bid ye mark my words!
APOLLO
   O monsters loathed of all, O scorn of gods,
He that hath bound may loose: a cure there is,
Yea, many a plan that can unbind the chain.
But when the thirsty dust sucks up man's blood
Once shed in death, he shall arise no more.
No chant nor charm for this my Sire hath wrought.
All else there is, he moulds and shifts at will,
Not scant of strength nor breath, whate'er he do.
CHORUS
   Think yet, for what acquittal thou dost plead:
He who hath shed a mother's kindred blood,
Shall he in Argos dwell, where dwelt his sire?
How shall he stand before the city's shrines,
How share the clansmen's holy lustral bowl?
APOLLO
   This too I answer; mark a soothfast word,
Not the true parent is the woman's womb
That bears the child; she doth but nurse the seed
New-sown: the male is parent; she for him,
As stranger for a stranger, hoards the germ
Of life; unless the god its promise blight.
And proof hereof before you will I set.
Birth may from fathers, without mothers, be:
See at your side a witness of the same,
Athena, daughter of Olympian Zeus,
Never within the darkness of the womb
Fostered nor fashioned, but a bud more bright
Than any goddess in her breast might bear.
And I, O Pallas, howsoe'er I may,
Henceforth will glorify thy town, thy clan,
And for this end have sent my suppliant here
Unto thy shrine; that he from this time forth
Be loyal unto thee for evermore,

O goddess-queen, and thou unto thy side
Mayst win and hold him faithful, and his line,
And that for aye this pledge and troth remain
To children's children of Athenian seed.
ΛTHENΛ
    Enough is said; I bid the judges now
With pure intent deliver just award.
CHORUS
    We too have shot our every shaft of speech,
And now abide to hear the doom of law.
    ATHENA (to Apollo and Orestes)
    Say, how ordaining shall I 'scape your blame?
APOLLO
    I spake, ye heard; enough. O stranger men,
Heed well your oath as ye decide the cause.
ATHENA
    O men of Athens, ye who first do judge
The law of bloodshed, hear me now ordain.
Here to all time for Aegeus' Attic host
Shall stand this council-court of judges sworn,
Here the tribunal, set on Ares' Hill
Where camped of old the tented Amazons,
What time in hate of Theseus they assailed
Athens, and set against her citadel
A counterwork of new sky-pointing towers,
And there to Ares held their sacrifice,
Where now the rock hath name, even Ares' Hill.
And hence shall Reverence and her kinsman Fear
Pass to each free man's heart, by day and night
Enjoining, Thou shalt do no unjust thing,
So long as law stands as it stood of old
Unmarred by civic change. Look you, the spring
Is pure; but foul it once with influx vile
    And muddy clay, and none can drink thereof.
Therefore, O citizens, I bid ye bow
In awe to this command, Let no man live
Uncurbed by law nor curbed by tyranny;
Nor banish ye the monarchy of Awe
Beyond the walls; untouched by fear divine,
No man doth justice in the world of men.
Therefore in purity and holy dread

Stand and revere; so shall ye have and hold
A saving bulwark of the state and land,
Such as no man hath ever elsewhere known,
Nor in far Scythia, nor in Pelops' realm.
Thus I ordain it now, a council-court
Pure and unsullied by the lust of gain,
Sacred and swift to vengeance, wakeful ever
To champion men who sleep, the country's guard.
Thus have I spoken, thus to mine own clan
Commended it for ever. Ye who judge,
Arise, take each his vote, mete out the right,
Your oath revering. Lo, my word is said.

[The twelve judges come forward, one by one, to the urns of decision; the first votes; as each of the others follows, the Chorus and Apollo speak alternately.

CHORUS

I rede ye well, beware! nor put to shame,
In aught, this grievous company of hell.

APOLLO

I too would warn you, fear mine oracles—
From Zeus they are,—nor make them void of fruit.

CHORUS

Presumptuous is thy claim, blood-guilt to judge,
And false henceforth thine oracles shall be.

APOLLO

Failed then the counsels of my sire, when turned
Ixion, first of slayers, to his side?

CHORUS

These are but words; but I, if justice fail me,
Will haunt this land in grim and deadly deed.

APOLLO

Scorn of the younger and the elder gods
Art thou: 'tis I that shall prevail anon.

CHORUS

Thus didst thou too of old in Pheres' halls,
O'erreaching Fate to make a mortal deathless.

APOLLO

Was it not well, my worshipper to aid,
Then most of all when hardest was the need?

CHORUS

I say thou didst annul the lots of life,

Cheating with wine the deities of eld.
APOLLO
I say thou shalt anon, thy pleadings foiled,
Spit venom vainly on thine enemies.
CHORUS
Since this young god o'errides mine ancient right
I tarry but to claim your law, not knowing
If wrath of mine shall blast your state or spare
ATHENA
Mine is the right to add the final vote,
And I award it to Orestes' cause.
For me no mother bore within her womb,
And, save for wedlock evermore eschewed,
I vouch myself the champion of the man,
Not of the woman, yea, with all my soul,—
In heart, as birth, a father's child alone.
Thus will I not too heinously regard
A woman's death who did her husband slay,
The guardian of her home; and if the votes
Equal do fall, Orestes shall prevail.
Ye of the judges who are named thereto,
Swiftly shake forth the lots from either urn.
[Two judges come forward, one to each urn.
ORESTES
O bright Apollo, what shall be the end?
CHORUS
O Night, dark mother mine, dost mark these things?
OSESTES
Now shall my doom be life, or strangling cords.
CHORUS
And mine, lost honour or a wider sway.
APOLLO
O stranger judges, sum aright the count
Of votes cast forth, and, parting them, take heed
Ye err not in decision. The default
Of one vote only bringeth ruin deep,
One, cast aright, doth stablish house and home.
ATHENA
Behold, this man is free from guilt of blood,
For half the votes condemn him, half set free!
ORESTES

O Pallas, light and safety of my home,
Thou, thou hast given me back to dwell once more
In that my fatherland, amerced of which
I wandered; now shall Grecian lips say this,
The man is Argive once again, and dwells
Again within his father's wealthy hall,
By Pallas saved, by Loxias, and by Him,
The great third saviour, Zeus omnipotent—
Who thus in pity for my father's fate
Doth pluck me from my doom, beholding these,
Confederates of my mother. Lo, I pass
To mine own home, but proffering this vow
Unto thy land and people: Nevermore,
Thro' all the manifold years of Time to be,
Shall any chieftain of mine Argive land
Bear hitherward his spears for fight arrayed.
For we, though lapped in earth we then shall lie,
By thwart adversities will work our will
On them who shall transgress this oath of mine,
Paths of despair and journeyings ill-starred
For them ordaining, till their task they rue.
But if this oath be rightly kept, to them
Will we the dead be full of grace, the while
With loyal league they honour Pallas' town.
And now farewell, thou and thy city's folk—
Firm be thine arm's grasp, closing with thy foes
And, strong to save, bring victory to thy spear.
  [Exit Orestes, with Apollo.
CHORUS
  Woe on you, younger gods! the ancient right
Ye have o'erridden, rent it from my hands.
  I am dishonoured of you, thrust to scorn!
  But heavily my wrath
Shall on this land fling forth the drops that blast and burn
 Venom of vengeance, that shall work such scathe
 As I have suffered; where that dew shall fall,
   Shall leafless blight arise,
 Wasting Earth's offspring,—Justice, hear my call!—
 And thorough all the land in deadly wise
 Shall scatter venom, to exude again
   In pestilence on men.

What cry avails me now, what deed of blood,
Unto this land what dark despite?
 Alack, alack, forlorn
Are we, a bitter injury have borne!
Alack, O sisters, O dishonoured brood
 Of mother Night!

ATHENA

 Nay, bow ye to my words, chafe not nor moan:
Ye are not worsted nor disgraced; behold,
With balanced vote the cause had issue fair,
Nor in the end did aught dishonour thee.
But thus the will of Zeus shone clearly forth,
And his own prophet-god avouched the same,
Orestes slew: his slaying is atoned.
Therefore I pray you, not upon this land
Shoot forth the dart of vengeance; be appeased,
Nor blast the land with blight, nor loose thereon
Drops of eternal venom, direful darts
Wasting and marring nature's seed of growth.
 For I, the queen of Athens' sacred right,
Do pledge to you a holy sanctuary
Deep in the heart of this my land, made just
By your indwelling presence, while ye sit
Hard by your sacred shrines that gleam with oil
Of sacrifice, and by this folk adored.

CHORUS

 Woe on you, younger gods! the ancient right
Ye have o'erridden, rent it from my hands.
 I am dishonoured of you, thrust to scorn!
 But heavily my wrath
Shall on his land fling forth the drops that blast and burn.
 Venom of vengeance, that shall work such scathe
 As I have suffered; where that dew shall fall,
  Shall leafless blight arise,
Wasting Earth's offspring,—Justice, hear my call!—
And thorough all the land in deadly wise
Shall scatter venom, to exude again
 In pestilence of men.
What cry avails me now, what deed of blood,
Unto this land what dark despite?
 Alack, alack, forlorn

Are we, a bitter injury have borne!
Alack, O sisters, O dishonoured brood
  Of mother Night!
ATHENA
  Dishonoured are ye not; turn not, I pray.
As goddesses your swelling wrath on men,
Nor make the friendly earth despiteful to them.
I too have Zeus for champion—'tis enough—
I only of all goddesses do know.
To ope the chamber where his thunderbolts
Lie stored and sealed; but here is no such need.
Nay, be appeased, nor cast upon the ground
The malice of thy tongue, to blast the world;
Calm thou thy bitter wrath's black inward surge,
For high shall be thine honour, set beside me
For ever in this land, whose fertile lap
Shall pour its teeming firstfruits unto you,
Gifts for fair childbirth and for wedlock's crown:
Thus honoured, praise my spoken pledge for aye.
CHORUS
  I, I dishonoured in this earth to dwell,—
Ancient of days and wisdom! I breathe forth
Poison and breath of frenzied ire. O Earth,
  Woe, woe, for thee, for me!
From side to side what pains be these that thrill?
Hearken, O mother Night, my wrath, mine agony!
Whom from mine ancient rights the gods have thrust
  And brought me to the dust—
Woe, woe is me!—with craft invincible.
ATHENA
  Older art thou than I, and I will bear
With this thy fury. Know, although thou be
More wise in ancient wisdom, yet have I
From Zeus no scanted measure of the same,
Wherefore take heed unto this prophecy—
If to another land of alien men
Ye go, too late shall ye feel longing deep
For mine. The rolling tides of time bring round
A day of brighter glory for this town;
And thou, enshrined in honour by the halls
Where dwelt Erechtheus, shalt a worship win

From men and from the train of womankind,
Greater than any tribe elsewhere shall pay.
Cast thou not therefore on this soil of mine
Whetstones that sharpen souls to bloodshedding.
The burning goads of youthful hearts, made hot
With frenzy of the spirit, not of wine.
Nor pluck as 'twere the heart from cocks that strive,
To set it in the breasts of citizens
Of mine, a war-god's spirit, keen for fight,
Made stern against their country and their kin.
The man who grievously doth lust for fame,
War, full, immitigable, let him wage
Against the stranger; but of kindred birds
I hold the challenge hateful. Such the boon
I proffer thee—within this land of lands,
Most loved of gods, with me to show and share
Fair mercy, gratitude and grace as fair.
CHORUS
   I, I dishonoured in this earth to dwell,—
Ancient of days and wisdom! I breathe forth
Poison and breath of frenzied ire. O Earth,
     Woe, woe for thee, for me!
From side to side what pains be these that thrill?
Hearken, O mother Night, my wrath, mine agony!
Whom from mine ancient rights the gods have thrust,
     And brought me to the dust—
Woe, woe is me!—with craft invincible.
ATHENA
   I will not weary of soft words to thee,
That never mayst thou say, Behold me spurned,
An elder by a younger deity,
And from this land rejected and forlorn,
Unhonoured by the men who dwell therein.
But, if Persuasion's grace be sacred to thee,
Soft in the soothing accents of my tongue,
Tarry, I pray thee; yet, if go thou wilt,
Not rightfully wilt thou on this my town
Sway down the scale that beareth wrath and teen
Or wasting plague upon this folk. 'Tis thine,
If so thou wilt, inheritress to be
Of this my land, its utmost grace to win.

CHORUS

O queen, what refuge dost thou promise me?

ATHENA

Refuge untouched by bale: take thou my boon.

CHORUS

What, if I take it, shall mine honour be?

ATHENA

No house shall prosper without grace of thine.

CHORUS

Canst thou achieve and grant such power to me?

ATHENA

Yea, for my hand shall bless thy worshippers.

CHORUS

And wilt thou pledge me this for time eterne?

ATHENA

Yea: none can bid me pledge beyond my power.

CHORUS

Lo, I desist from wrath, appeased by thee.

ATHENA

Then in the land's heart shalt thou win thee friends.

CHORUS

What chant dost bid me raise, to greet the land?

ATHENA

Such as aspires towards a victory
Unrued by any: chants from breast of earth,
From wave, from sky; and let the wild winds' breath
Pass with soft sunlight o'er the lap of land,—
Strong wax the fruits of earth, fair teem the kine,
Unfailing, for my town's prosperity,
And constant be the growth of mortal seed.
But more and more root out the impious,
For as a gardener fosters what he sows,
So foster I this race, whom righteousness
Doth fend from sorrow. Such the proffered boon.
But I, if wars must be, and their loud clash
And carnage, for my town, will ne'er endure
That aught but victory shall crown her fame.

CHORUS

Lo, I accept it; at her very side
Doth Pallas bid me dwell:
I will not wrong the city of her pride,

Which even Almighty Zeus and Ares hold
   Heaven's earthly citadel,
Loved home of Grecian gods, the young, the old,
   The sanctuary divine,
   The shield of every shrine!
For Athens I say forth a gracious prophecy,—
  The glory of the sunlight and the skies
  Shall bid from earth arise
Warm wavelets of new life and glad prosperity.
ATHENA
    Behold, with gracious heart well pleased
   I for my citizens do grant
   Fulfilment of this covenant:
  And here, their wrath at length appeased,
   These mighty deities shall stay,
  For theirs it is by right to sway
The lot that rules our mortal day,
   And he who hath not inly felt
   Their stern decree, ere long on him,
   Not knowing why and whence, the grim
   Life-crushing blow is dealt.
   The father's sin upon the child
   Descends, and sin is silent death,
   And leads him on the downward path,
   By stealth beguiled,
   Unto the Furies: though his state
   On earth were high, and loud his boast,
   Victim of silent ire and hate
   He dwells among the Lost.

CHORUS
  To my blessing now give ear.—
Scorching blight nor singèd air
Never blast thine olives fair!
Drouth, that wasteth bud and plant,
Keep to thine own place. Avaunt,
Famine fell, and come not hither
Stealthily to waste and wither!
Let the land, in season due,
Twice her waxing fruits renew;
Teem the kine in double measure;

Rich in new god-given treasure;
Here let men the powers adore
For sudden gifts unhoped before!
ATHENA
   O hearken, warders of the wall
  That guards mine Athens, what a dower
  Is unto her ordained and given!
For mighty is the Furies' power,
  And deep-revered in courts of heaven
And realms of hell; and clear to all
  They weave thy doom, mortality!
And some in joy and peace shall sing;
But unto other some they bring
  Sad life and tear-dimmed eye.
CHORUS
   And far away I ban thee and remove,
  Untimely death of youths too soon brought low!
And to each maid, O gods, when time is come for love,
  Grant ye a warrior's heart, a wedded life to know.
Ye too, O Fates, children of mother Night,
  Whose children too are we, O goddesses
Of just award, of all by sacred right
  Queens who in time and in eternity
Do rule, a present power for righteousness,
  Honoured beyond all Gods, hear ye and grant my cry!
ATHENA
   And I too, I with joy am fain,
Hearing your voice this gift ordain
Unto my land. High thanks be thine,
Persuasion, who with eyes divine
Into my tongue didst look thy strength,
  To bend and to appease at length
Those who would not be comforted.
  Zeus, king of parley, doth prevail,
And ye and I will strive nor fail,
  That good may stand in evil's stead,
And lasting bliss for bale.
CHORUS
   And nevermore these walls within
Shall echo fierce sedition's din
  Unslaked with blood and crime;

The thirsty dust shall nevermore
Suck up the darkly streaming gore
Of civic broils, shed out in wrath
And vengeance, crying death for death!
But man with man and state with state
Shall vow The pledge of common hate
And common friendship, that for man
Hath oft made blessing out of ban,
Be ours unto all time.
ATHENA
   Skill they, or not, the path to find
Of favouring speech and presage kind?
Yea, even from these, who, grim and stern,
   Glared anger upon you of old,
O citizens, ye now shall earn
   A recompense right manifold.
Deck them aright, extol them high,
Be loyal to their loyalty,
   And ye shall make your town and land
   Sure, propped on Justice' saving hand,
And Fame's eternity.
CHORUS
     Hail ye, all hail! and yet again, all hail
    O Athens, happy in a weal secured!
   O ye who sit by Zeus' right hand, nor fail
    Of wisdom set among you and assured,
   Loved of the well-loved Goddess-Maid! the King
Of gods doth reverence you, beneath her guarding wing.
ATHENA
   All hail unto each honoured guest!
Whom to the chambers of your rest
'Tis mine to lead, and to provide
The hallowed torch, the guard and guide.
Pass down, the while these altars glow
With sacred fire, to earth below
   And your appointed shrine.
There dwelling, from the land restrain
The force of fate, the breath of bane,
But waft on us the gift and gain
   Of Victory divine!
And ye, the men of Cranaos' seed,

I bid you now with reverence lead
These alien Powers that thus are made
Athenian evermore. To you
Fair be their will henceforth, to do
  Whate'er may bless and aid!
  CHORUS
Hail to you all! hail yet again,
All who love Athens, Gods and men,
  Adoring her as Pallas' home!
And while ye reverence what ye grant—
My sacred shrine and hidden haunt—
  Blameless and blissful be your doom!
  ATHENA
Once more I praise the promise of your vows,
And now I bid the golden torches' glow
Pass down before you to the hidden depth
Of earth, by mine own sacred servants borne,
My loyal guards of statue and of shrine.
Come forth, O flower of Theseus' Attic land,
O glorious band of children and of wives,
And ye, O train of matrons crowned with eld!
Deck you with festal robes of scarlet dye
In honour of this day: O gleaming torch,
Lead onward, that these gracious powers of earth
Henceforth be seen to bless the life of men.

[Athena leads the procession downwards into the Cave of the Furies, under Areopagus: as they go, the escort of women and children chant aloud.
CHANT
  With loyalty we lead you; proudly go,
Night's childless children, to your home below!
  (O citizens, awhile from words forbear!)
  To darkness' deep primeval lair,
  Far in Earth's bosom, downward fare,
  Adored with prayer and sacrifice.
  (O citizens, forbear your cries!)
  Pass hitherward, ye powers of Dread,
  With all your former wrath allayed,
  Into the heart of this loved land;
  With joy unto your temple wend,
  The while upon your steps attend
  The flames that fed upon the brand—

(Now, now ring out your chant, your joy's acclaim!)
   Behind them, as they downward fare,
   Let holy hands libations bear,
     And torches' sacred flame.
   All-seeing Zeus and Fate come down
   To battle fair for Pallas' town!
Ring out your chant, ring out your joy's acclaim!
   [Exeunt omnes.

Prometheus Bound

Dramatis Personae:
STRENGTH AND FORCE.
HEPHAESTUS.
PROMETHEUS.
CHORUS OF SEA-NYMPHS,
DAUGHTERS OF OCEANUS.
OCEANUS.
IO.
HERMES.

ARGUMENT
  In the beginning, Ouranos and Gaia held sway over Heaven and Earth.
And manifold children were born unto them, of whom were Cronos, and
Okeanos, and the Titans, and the Giants. But Cronos cast down his father
Ouranos, and ruled in his stead, until Zeus his son cast him down in his
turn, and became King of Gods and men. Then were the Titans divided,
for some had good will unto Cronos, and others unto Zeus; until Prometheus, son of the Titan Iapetos, by wise counsel, gave the victory to Zeus.
But Zeus held the race of mortal men in scorn, and was fain to destroy
them from the face of the earth; yet Prometheus loved them, and gave
secretly to them the gift of fire, and arts whereby they could prosper upon
the earth. Then was Zeus sorely angered with Prometheus, and bound him
upon a mountain, and afterward overwhelmed him in an earthquake, and
devised other torments against him for many ages; yet could he not slay
Prometheus, for he was a God.
  Scene—A rocky ravine in the mountains of Scythia.
STRENGTH
    Lo, the earth's bound and limitary land,
  The Scythian steppe, the waste untrod of men!
  Look to it now, Hephaestus—thine it is,
  Thy Sire obeying, this arch-thief to clench
  Against the steep-down precipice of rock,
  With stubborn links of adamantine chain.
  Look thou: thy flower, the gleaming plastic fire,

He stole and lent to mortal man—a sin
That gods immortal make him rue to-day,
Lessoned hereby to own th' omnipotence
Of Zeus, and to repent his love to man!
HEPHAESTUS
   O Strength and Force, for you the best of Zeus
Stands all achieved, and nothing bars your will:
But I—I dare not bind to storm-vext cleft
One of our race, immortal as are we.
Yet, none the less, necessity constrains,
For Zeus, defied, is heavy in revenge!
                 (To PROMETHEUS)
   O deep-devising child of Themis sage,
Small will have I to do, or thou to bear,
What yet we must. Beyond the haunt of man
Unto this rock, with fetters grimly forged,
I must transfix and shackle up thy limbs,
Where thou shalt mark no voice nor human form,
But, parching in the glow and glare of sun,
Thy body's flower shall suffer a sky-change;
And gladly wilt thou hail the hour when Night
Shall in her starry robe invest the day,
Or when the Sun shall melt the morning rime.
But, day or night, for ever shall the load
Of wasting agony, that may not pass,
Wear thee away; for know, the womb of Time
Hath not conceived a power to set thee free.
Such meed thou hast, for love toward mankind
For thou, a god defying wrath of gods,
Beyond the ordinance didst champion men,
And for reward shalt keep a sleepless watch,
Stiff-kneed, erect, nailed to this dismal rock,
With manifold laments and useless cries
Against the will inexorable of Zeus.
Hard is the heart of fresh-usurpèd power!
STRENGTH
   Enough of useless ruth! why tarriest thou?
Why pitiest one whom all gods wholly hate,
One who to man gave o'er thy privilege?
HEPHAESTUS
   Kinship and friendship wring my heart for him.

STRENGTH

Ay—but how disregard our Sire's command?
Is not thy pity weaker than thy fear?

HEPHAESTUS

Ruthless as ever, brutal to the full!

STRENGTH

Tears can avail him nothing: strive not thou,
Nor waste thine efforts thus unaidingly.

HEPHAESTUS

Out on my cursed mastery of steel!

STRENGTH

Why curse it thus? In sooth that craft of thine
Standeth assoiled of all that here is wrought.

HEPHAESTUS

Would that some other were endowed therewith!

STRENGTH

All hath its burden, save the rule of Heaven,
And freedom is for Zeus, and Zeus alone.

HEPHAESTUS

I know it; I gainsay no word hereof.

STRENGTH

Up, then, and hasten to do on his bonds,
Lest Zeus behold thee indolent of will!

HEPHAESTUS

Ah well—behold the armlets ready now!

STRENGTH

Then cast them round his arms and with sheer strength
Swing down the hammer, clinch him to the crags.

HEPHAESTUS

Lo, 'tis toward—no weakness in the work!

STRENGTH

Smite harder, wedge it home—no faltering here!
He hath a craft can pass th' impassable!

HEPHAESTUS

This arm is fast, inextricably bound.

STRENGTH

Then shackle safe the other, that he know
His utmost craft is weaker far than Zeus.

HEPHAESTUS

He, but none other, can accuse mine art!

STRENGTH

Now, strong and sheer, drive thro' from breast to back
The adamantine wedge's stubborn fang.

HEPHAESTUS

Alas, Prometheus! I lament thy pain.

STRENGTH

Thou, faltering and weeping sore for those
Whom Zeus abhors! 'ware, lest thou rue thy tears!

HEPHAESTUS

Thou gazest on a scene that poisons sight.

STRENGTH

I gaze on one who suffers his desert.
Now between rib and shoulder shackle him—

HEPHAESTUS

Do it I must—hush thy superfluous charge!

STRENGTH

Urge thee I will—ay, hound thee to the prey.
Step downward now, enring his legs amain!

HEPHAESTUS

Lo, it is done—'twas but a moment's toil.

STRENGTH

Now, strongly strike, drive in the piercing gyves—
Stern is the power that oversees thy task!

HEPHAESTUS

Brutish thy form, thy speech brutality!

STRENGTH

Be gentle, an thou wilt, but blame not me
For this my stubbornness and anger fell!

HEPHAESTUS

Let us go hence; his legs are firmly chained.

STRENGTH (To PROMETHEUS)

Aha! there play the insolent, and steal,
For creatures of a day, the rights of gods!
O deep delusion of the powers that named thee
Prometheus, the Fore-thinker! thou hast need
Of others' forethought and device, whereby
Thou may'st elude this handicraft of ours!

> [Exeunt HEPHAESTUS, STRENGTH,
> and FORCE.—A pause.

PROMETHEUS

O Sky divine, O Winds of pinions swift,

O fountain-heads of Rivers, and O thou,
Illimitable laughter of the Sea!
O Earth, the Mighty Mother, and thou Sun,
Whose orbed light surveyeth all—attest,
What ills I suffer from the gods, a god!
Behold me, who must here sustain
The marring agonies of pain,
Wrestling with torture, doomed to bear
Eternal ages, year on year!
Such and so shameful is the chain
Which Heaven's new tyrant doth ordain
To bind me helpless here.
Woe! for the ruthless present doom!
Woe! for the Future's teeming womb!
On what far dawn, in what dim skies,
Shall star of my deliverance rise?

   Truce to this utterance! to its dimmest verge
I do foreknow the future, hour by hour,
Nor can whatever pang may smite me now
Smite with surprise. The destiny ordained
I must endure to the best, for well I wot
That none may challenge with Necessity.
Yet is it past my patience, to reveal,
Or to conceal, these issues of my doom.
Since I to mortals brought prerogatives,
Unto this durance dismal am I bound:
Yea, I am he who in a fennel-stalk,
By stealthy sleight, purveyed the fount of fire,
The teacher, proven thus, and arch-resource
Of every art that aideth mortal men.
Such was my sin: I earn its recompense,
Rock-riveted, and chained in height and cold.
                   [A pause.
Listen! what breath of sound,
what fragrance soft hath risen
Upward to me? is it some godlike essence,
Or being half-divine, or mortal presence?
Who to the world's end comes, unto my craggy prison?
Craves he the sight of pain, or what would he behold?
Gaze on a god in tortures manifold,
Heinous to Zeus, and scorned by all

Whose footsteps tread the heavenly hall,
Because too deeply, from on high,
I pitied man's mortality!
Hark, and again! that fluttering sound
Of wings that whirr and circle round,
And their light rustle thrills the air—
How all things that unseen draw near
Are to me Fear!

                [Enter the CHORUS OF OCEANIDES,
                    in winged cars]

CHORUS
    Ah, fear us not! as friends, with rivalry
Of swiftly-vying wings, we came together
Unto this rock and thee!
With our sea-sire we pleaded hard, until
We won him to our will,
And swift the wafting breezes bore us hither.
The heavy hammer's steely blow
Thrilled to our ocean-cavern from afar,
Banished soft shyness from our maiden brow,
And with unsandalled feet we come, in winged car!

PROMETHEUS
    Ah well-a-day! ye come, ye come
From the Sea-Mother's teeming home—
Children of Tethys and the sire
Who around Earth rolls, gyre on gyre,
His sleepless ocean-tide!
Look on me—shackled with what chain,
Upon this chasm's beetling side
I must my dismal watch sustain!

CHORUS
    Yea, I behold, Prometheus! and my fears
Draw swiftly o'er mine eyes a mist fulfilled of tears,
When I behold thy frame
Bound, wasting on the rock, and put to shame
By adamantine chains!
The rudder and the rule of Heaven
Are to strange pilots given:
Zeus with new laws and strong caprice holds sway,
Unkings the ancient Powers, their might constrains,
And thrusts their pride away!

PROMETHEUS

   Had he but hurled me, far beneath
The vast and ghostly halls of Death,
Down to the limitless profound Of Tartarus,
in fetters bound, Fixed by his unrelenting hand!
So had no man, nor God on high,
Exulted o'er mine agony—
But now, a sport to wind and sky,
Mocked by my foes, I stand!

CHORUS

   What God can wear such ruthless heart
As to delight in ill?
Who in thy sorrow bears not part?
Zeus, Zeus alone! for he, with wrathful will,
Clenched and inflexible,
Bears down Heaven's race—nor end shall be, till hate
His soul shall satiate,
Or till, by some device, some other hand
Shall wrest from him his sternly-clasped command!

PROMETHEUS

   Yet,—though in shackles close and strong
I lie in wasting torments long,—
Yet the new tyrant, 'neath whose nod
Cowers down each blest subservient god,
One day, far hence, my help shall need,
The destined stratagem to read,
Whereby, in some yet distant day,
Zeus shall be reaved of pride and sway:
And no persuasion's honied spell
Shall lure me on, the tale to tell;
And no stern threat shall make me cower
And yield the secret to his power,
Until his purpose be foregone,
And shackles yield, and he atone
The deep despite that he hath done!

CHORUS

   O strong in hardihood, thou striv'st amain
Against the stress of pain!
But yet too free, too resolute thy tongue
In challenging thy wrong!
Ah, shuddering dread doth make my spirit quiver,

And o'er thy fate sits Fear!
I see not to what shore of safety ever
Thy bark can steer—
In depths unreached the will of Zeus doth dwell,
Hidden, implacable!
PROMETHEUS
    Ay, stern is Zeus, and Justice stands,
Wrenched to his purpose, in his hands—
Yet shall he learn, perforce, to know
A milder mood, when falls the blow—
His ruthless wrath he shall lay still,
And he and I with mutual will
In concord's bond shall go.
CHORUS
    Unveil, say forth to us the tale entire,
Under what imputation Zeus laid hands
On thee, to rack thee thus with shameful pangs?
Tell us—unless the telling pain thee—all!
PROMETHEUS
    Grievous alike are these things for my tongue,
Grievous for silence—rueful everyway.
Know that, when first the gods began their strife,
And heaven was all astir with mutual feud—
Some willing to fling Cronos from his throne,
And set, forsooth, their Zeus on high as king,
And other some in contrariety
Striving to bar him from heaven's throne for aye—
Thereon I sought to counsel for the best
The Titan brood of Ouranos and Earth;
Yet I prevailed not, for they held in scorn
My glozing wiles, and, in their hardy pride,
Deemed that sans effort they could grasp the sway.
But, for my sake, my mother Themis oft,
And Earth, one symbol of names manifold,
Had held me warned, how in futurity
It stood ordained that not by force or power,
But by some wile, the victors must prevail.
In such wise I interpreted; but they
Deigned not to cast their heed thereon at all.
Then, of things possible, I deemed it best,
Joining my mother's wisdom to mine own,

To range myself with Zeus, two wills in one.
Thus, by device of mine, the murky depth
Of Tartarus enfoldeth Cronos old
And those who strove beside him. Such the aid
I gave the lord of heaven—my meed for which
He paid me thus, a penal recompense!
For 'tis the inward vice of tyranny,
To deem of friends as being secret foes.
Now, to your question—hear me clearly show
On what imputed fault he tortures me.
Scarce was he seated on his father's throne,
When he began his doles of privilege
Among the lesser gods, allotting power
In trim division; while of mortal men
Nothing he recked, nor of their misery
Nay, even willed to blast their race entire
To nothingness, and breed another brood;
And none but I was found to cross his will.
I dared it, I alone; I rescued men
From crushing ruin and th' abyss of hell—
Therefore am I constrained in chastisement
Grievous to bear and piteous to behold,—
Yea, firm to feel compassion for mankind,
Myself was held unworthy of the same—
Ay, beyond pity am I ranged and ruled
To sufferance—a sight that shames his sway!

CHORUS
   A heart of steel, a mould of stone were he,
Who could complacently behold thy pains
I came not here as craving for this sight,
 And, seeing it, I stand heart-wrung with pain.

PROMETHEUS
  Yea truly, kindly eyes must pity me!

CHORUS
  Say, didst thou push transgression further still?

PROMETHEUS
  Ay, man thro' me ceased to foreknow his death.

CHORUS
  What cure couldst thou discover for this curse?

PROMETHEUS
  Blind hopes I sent to nestle in man's heart.

CHORUS
   This was a goodly gift thou gavest them.
PROMETHEUS
   Yet more I gave them, even the boon of fire.
CHORUS
   What? radiant fire, to things ephemeral?
PROMETHEUS
   Yea—many an art too shall they learn thereby!
CHORUS
   Then, upon imputation of such guilt,
   Doth Zeus without surcease torment thee thus?
   Is there no limit to thy course of pain?
PROMETHEUS
   None, till his own will shall decree an end.
CHORUS
   And how shall he decree it? say, what hope?
   Seëst thou not thy sin? yet of that sin
   It irks me sore to speak, as thee to hear.
   Nay, no more words hereof; bethink thee now,
   From this ordeal how to find release.
PROMETHEUS
   Easy it is, for one whose foot is set
   Outside the slough of pain, to lesson well
   With admonitions him who lies therein.
   With perfect knowledge did I all I did,
   I willed to sin, and sinned, I own it all—
   I championed men, unto my proper pain.
   Yet scarce I deemed that, in such cruel doom,
   Withering upon this skyey precipice,
   I should inherit lonely mountain crags,
   Here, in a vast tin-neighboured solitude.
   Yet list not to lament my present pains,
   But, stepping from your cars unto the ground,
   Listen, the while I tell the future fates
   Now drawing near, until ye know the whole.
   Grant ye, O grant my prayer, be pitiful
   To one now racked with woe! the doom of pain
   Wanders, but settles, soon or late, on all.
CHORUS
   To willing hearts, and schooled to feel,
   Prometheus, came thy tongue's appeal;

Therefore we leave, with lightsome tread,
The flying cars in which we sped—
We leave the stainless virgin air
Where winged creatures float and fare,
And by thy side, on rocky land,
Thus gently we alight and stand,
Willing, from end to end, to know
Thine history of woe.

> [The CHORUS alight from their winged cars.
> Enter OCEANUS, mounted on a griffin.

OCEANUS

Thus, over leagues and leagues of space
I come, Prometheus, to thy place—
By will alone, not rein, I guide
The winged thing on which I ride;
And much, be sure, I mourn thy case—
Kinship is Pity's bond, I trow;
And, wert thou not akin, I vow
None other should have more than thou
Of my compassion's grace!
'Tis said, and shall be proved; no skill
Have I to gloze and feign goodwill!
Name but some mode of helpfulness,
And thou wilt in a trice confess
That I, Oceanus, am best
Of all thy friends, and trustiest.

PROMETHEUS

Ho, what a sight of marvel! what, thou too
Comest to contemplate my pains, and darest—
(Yet how, I wot not!) leaving far behind
The circling tide, thy namefellow, and those
Rock-arched, self-hollowed caverns—thus to come
Unto this land, whose womb bears iron ore?
Art come to see my lot, resent with me
The ills I bear? Well, gaze thy fill! behold
Me, friend of Zeus, part-author of his power—
Mark, in what ruthlessness he bows me down!

OCEANUS

Yea, I behold, Prometheus! and would warn
Thee, spite of all thy wisdom, for thy weal!
Learn now thyself to know, and to renew

A rightful spirit within thee, for, made new
With pride of place, sits Zeus among the gods!
Now, if thou choosest to fling forth on him
Words rough with anger thus and edged with scorn,
Zeus, though he sit aloof, afar, on high,
May hear thine utterance, and make thee deem
His present wrath a mere pretence of pain.
Banish, poor wretch! the passion of thy soul,
And seek, instead, acquittance from thy pangs!
Belike my words seem ancientry to thee—
Such, natheless, O Prometheus, is the meed
That doth await the overweening tongue!
Meek wert thou never, wilt not crouch to pain,
But, set amid misfortunes, cravest more!
Now—if thou let thyself be schooled by me—
Thou must not kick against the goad. Thou knowest,
A despot rules, harsh, resolute, supreme,
Whose law is will. Yet shall I go to him,
With all endeavour to relieve thy plight—
So thou wilt curb the tempest of thy tongue!
Surely thou knowest, in thy wisdom deep,
The saw—Who vaunts amiss, quick pain is his.

PROMETHEUS

    O enviable thou, and unaccused—
Thou who wast art and part in all I dared!
And now, let be! make this no care of thine,
For Zeus is past persuasion—urge him not!
Look to thyself, lest thine emprise thou rue

OCEANUS

    Thou hast more skill to school thy neighbour's fault
Than to amend thine own: 'tis proved and plain,
By fact, not hearsay, that I read this well.
Yet am I fixed to go—withhold me not—
Assured I am, assured, that Zeus will grant
The boon I crave, the loosening of thy bonds.

PROMETHEUS

    In part I praise thee, to the end will praise;
Goodwill thou lackest not, but yet forbear
Thy further trouble! If thy heart be fain,
Bethink thee that thy toil avails me not.

Nay, rest thee well, aloof from danger's brink!
I will not ease my woe by base relief
In knowing others too involved therein.
Away the thought! for deeply do I rue
My brother Atlas' doom. Far off he stands
In sunset land, and on his shoulder bears
The pillar'd mountain-mass whose base is earth,
Whose top is heaven, and its ponderous load
Too great for any grasp. With pity too
I saw Earth's child, the monstrous thing of war,
That in Cilicia's hollow places dwelt—
Typho; I saw his hundred-headed form
Crushed and constrained; yet once his stride was fierce,
His jaws gaped horror and their hiss was death,
And all heaven's host he challenged to the fray,
While, as one vowed to storm the power of Zeus,
Forth from his eyes he shot a demon glare.
It skilled not: the unsleeping bolt of Zeus,
The downward levin with its rush of flame,
Smote on him, and made dumb for evermore
The clamour of his vaunting: to the heart
Stricken he lay, and all that mould of strength
Sank thunder-shattered to a smouldering ash;
And helpless now and laid in ruin huge
He lieth by the narrow strait of sea,
Crushed at the root of Etna's mountain-pile.
High on the pinnacles whereof there sits
Hephaestus, sweltering at the forge; and thence
On some hereafter day shall burst and stream
The lava-floods, that shall with ravening fangs
Gnaw thy smooth lowlands, fertile Sicily!
Such ire shall Typho from his living grave
Send seething up, such jets of fiery surge,
Hot and unslaked, altho' himself be laid
In quaking ashes by Zeus' thunderbolt.
But thou dost know hereof, nor needest me
To school thy sense: thou knowest safety's road—
Walk then thereon! I to the dregs will drain,
Till Zeus relent from wrath, my present woe.
OCEANUS

Nay, but, Prometheus, know'st thou not the saw— Words can appease
the angry soul's disease?
PROMETHEUS
    Ay—if in season one apply their salve,
  Not scorching wrath's proud flesh with caustic tongue.
OCEANUS
    But in wise thought and venturous essay
  Perceivest thou a danger? prithee tell!
PROMETHEUS
  I see a fool's good nature, useless toil.
OCEANUS
    Let me be sick of that disease; I know,
  Loyalty, masked as folly, wins the way.
PROMETHEUS
  But of thy blunder I shall bear the blame.
OCEANUS
    Clearly, thy word would send me home again.
PROMETHEUS
  Lest thy lament for me should bring thee hate.
OCEANUS
  Hate from the newly-throned Omnipotence?
PROMETHEUS
  Be heedful—lest his will be wroth with thee!
OCEANUS
    Thy doom, Prometheus, cries to me Beware

PROMETHEUS
  Mount, make away, discretion at thy side!
OCEANUS
    Thy word is said to me in act to go:
  For lo, my hippogriff with waving wings
  Fans the smooth course of air, and fain is he
  To rest his limbs within his ocean stall.
             [Exit OCEANUS. CHORUS
  For the woe and the wreck and the doom,
    Prometheus I utter my sighs;
O'er my cheek flows the fountain of tears
    from tender, compassionate eyes.
For stern and abhorred is the sway
    of Zeus on his self-sought throne,
And ruthless the spear of his scorn,

to the gods of the days that are done.
And over the limitless earth
  goes up a disconsolate cry:
Ye were all so fair, and have fallen;
  so great and your might has gone by!
So wails with a mighty lament
  the voice of the mortals, who dwell
In the Eastland, the home of the holy,
  for thee and the fate that befel;
And they of the Colchian land, the
  maidens whose arm is for war;
And the Scythian bowmen, who roam
  by the lake of Maeotis afar;
And the blossom of battling hordes,
  that flowers upon Caucasus' height,
With clashing of lances that pierce,
  and with clamour of swords that smite.
Strange is thy sorrow! one only I know
  who has suffered thy pain—
Atlas the Titan, the god,
  in a ruthless, invincible chain!
He beareth for ever and ever
  the burden and poise of the sky,
The vault of the rolling heaven,
  and earth re-echoes his cry.
The depths of the sea are troubled;
  they mourn from their caverns profound,
And the darkest and innermost hell
  moans deep with a sorrowful sound;
And the rivers of waters, that flow
  from the fountains that spring without stain,
Are as one in the great lamentation,
  and moan for thy piteous pain.
PROMETHEUS
  Deem not that I in pride or wilful scorn
Restrain my speech; 'tis wistful memory
That rends my heart, when I behold myself
Abased to wretchedness. To these new gods
I and none other gave their lots of power
In full attainment; no more words hereof
I speak—the tale ye know. But listen now

Unto the rede of mortals and their woes,
And how their childish and unreasoning state
Was changed by me to consciousness and thought.
Yet not in blame of mortals will I speak,
But as in proof of service wrought to them.
For, in the outset, eyes they had and saw not;
And ears they had but heard not; age on age,
Like unsubstantial shapes in vision seen,
They groped at random in the world of sense,
Nor knew to link their building, brick with brick,
Nor how to turn its aspect to the sun,
Nor how to join the beams by carpentry,
In hollowed caves they dwelt, as emmets dwell,
Weak feathers for each blast, in sunless caves.
Nor had they certain forecast of the cold,
Nor of the advent of the flowery spring,
Nor of the fruitful summer. All they wrought,
Unreasoning they wrought, till I made clear
The laws of rising stars, and inference dim,
More hard to learn, of what their setting showed.
I taught to them withal that art of arts,
The lore of number, and the written word
That giveth sense to sound, the tool wherewith
The gift of memory was wrought in all,
And so came art and song. I too was first
To harness 'neath the yoke strong animals,
Obedient made to collar and to weight,
That they might bear whate'er of heaviest toil
Mortals endured before. For chariots too
I trained, and docile service of the rein,
Steeds, the delight of wealth and pomp and pride.
I too, none other, for seafarers wrought
Their ocean-roaming canvas-wingèd cars.
Such arts of craft did I, unhappy I,
Contrive for mortals: now, no feint I have
Whereby I may elude my present woe.
CHORUS
    A rueful doom is thine! distraught of soul,
And all astray, and like some sorry leech
Art thou, repining at thine own disease,
Unskilled, unknowing of the needful cure.

PROMETHEUS
    More wilt thou wonder when the rest thou hearest—
What arts for them, what methods I devised.
Foremost was this: if any man fell sick,
No aiding art he knew, no saving food,
No curing oil nor draught, but all in lack
Of remedies they dwindled, till I taught
The medicinal blending of soft drugs,
Whereby they ward each sickness from their side.
I ranged for them the methods manifold
Of the diviner's art; I first discerned
Which of night's visions hold a truth for day,
I read for them the lore of mystic sounds,
Inscrutable before; the omens seen
Which bless or ban a journey, and the flight
Of crook-clawed birds, did I make clear to man—
And how they soar upon the right, for weal,
How, on the left, for evil; how they dwell,
Each in its kind, and what their loves and hates,
And which can flock and roost in harmony.
From me, men learned what deep significance
Lay in the smoothness of the entrails set
For sacrifice, and which, of various hues,
Showed them a gift accepted of the gods;
They learned what streaked and varied comeliness
Of gall and liver told; I led them, too,
(By passing thro' the flame the thigh-bones, wrapt
In rolls of fat, and th' undivided chine),
Unto the mystic and perplexing lore
Of omens; and I cleared unto their eyes
The forecasts, dim and indistinct before,
Shown in the flickering aspect of a flame.
Of these, enough is said. The other boons,
Stored in the womb of earth, in aid of men—
Copper and iron, silver, gold withal—
Who dares affirm he found them ere I found?
None—well I know—save who would babble lies!
Know thou, in compass of a single phrase—
All arts, for mortals' use, Prometheus gave.
CHORUS
    Nay, aid not mortal men beyond their due,

Holding too light a reckoning of thyself
And of thine own distress: good hope have I
To see thee once again from fetters free
And matched with Zeus in parity of power.
PROMETHEUS
    Not yet nor thus hath Fate ordained the end—
Not until age-long pains and countless woes
Have bent and bowed me, shall my shackles fall;
Art strives too feebly against destiny.
CHORUS
    But what hand rules the helm of destiny?
PROMETHEUS
    The triform Fates, and Furies unforgiving.
CHORUS
    Then is the power of Zeus more weak than theirs?
PROMETHEUS
    He may not shun the fate ordained for him.

CHORUS
    What is ordained for him, save endless rule?
PROMETHEUS
    Seek not for answer: this thou may'st not learn.
CHORUS
    Surely thy silence hides some solemn thing.
PROMETHEUS
    Think on some other theme: 'tis not the hour,
This secret to unveil; in deepest dark
Be it concealed: by guarding it shall I
Escape at last from bonds, and scorn, and pain.
CHORUS
    O never may my weak and faint desire
    Strive against God most high—
Never be slack in service, never tire
    Of sacred loyalty;
Nor fail to wend unto the altar-side,
    Where with the blood of kine
Steams up the offering, by the quenchless tide
    Of Ocean, Sire divine!
Be this within my heart, indelible—
    Offend not with thy tongue!
Sweet, sweet it is, in cheering hopes to dwell,

Immortal, ever young,
In maiden gladness fostering evermore
   A soft content of soul!
But ah, I shudder at thine anguish sore—
   Thy doom thro' years that roll!
Thou could'st not cower to Zeus: a love too great
   Thou unto man hast given—
Too high of heart thou wert—ah, thankless fate!
   What aid, 'gainst wrath of Heaven,
Could mortal man afford? in vain thy gift
   To things so powerless!
Could'st thou not see? they are as dreams that drift;
   Their strength is feebleness
A purblind race, in hopeless fetters bound,
   They have no craft or skill,
That could o'erreach the ordinance profound
   of the eternal will.
Alas, Prometheus! on thy woe condign
   I looked, and learned this lore;
And a new strain floats to these lips of mine—
   Not the glad song of yore,
When by the lustral wave I sang to see
   My sister made thy bride,
Decked with thy gifts, thy loved Hesione,
   And clasped unto thy side.
                    [Enter IO, horned like a cow.]

IO
   Alack! what land, what folk are here?
Whom see I clenched in rocky fetters drear
Unto the stormy crag?
   for what thing done
Dost thou in agony atone?
Ah, tell me whither, well-a-day!
My feet have roamed their weary way?
Ah, but it maddens, the sting!
   it burns in my piteous side!
Ah, but the vision, the spectre,
   the earth-born, the myriad-eyed!
Avoid thee! Earth, hide him,
   thine offspring! he cometh—O aspect of ill!
Ghostly, and crafty of face,

and dead, but pursuing me still!
Ah, woe upon me, woe ineffable!
He steals upon my track, a hound of hell—
Where'er I stray, along the sands and brine,
Weary and foodless, come his creeping eyne!
    And ah, the ghostly sound—
The wax-stopped reed-flute's weird and drowsy drone!
Alack my wandering woes, that round and round
Lead me in many mazes, lost, foredone!
O child of Cronos! for what deed of wrong
Am I enthralled by thee in penance long?
Why by the stinging bruise, the thing of fear,
Dost thou torment me, heart and brain?
Nay, give me rather to the flames that sear,
    Or to some hidden grave,
Or to the rending jaws, the monsters of the main!
Nor grudge the boon for which I crave, O king!
Enough, enough of weary wandering,
    Pangs from which none can save!
    Hearken! in pity hold
Io, the ox-horned maid, thy love of old!
PROMETHEUS
    Hear Zeus or not, I hear and know thee well,
Daughter of Inachus; I know thee driven,
Stung by the gadfly, mazed with agony.
Ay, thou art she whose beauty fired the breast
Of Zeus with passion; she whom Hera's hate
Now harasses o'er leagues and leagues of land.
IO
    Alack, thou namest Inachus my sire!
Wottest thou of him? how, from lips of pain,
Comes to my woeful ears truth's very strain?
    How knowest thou the curse, the burning fire
The god-sent, piercing pest that stings and clings?
Ah me! in frenzied, foodless wanderings
Hither I come, and on me from on high
    Lies Hera's angry craft! Ah, men unblest!
Not one there is, not one, that is unblest as I.
    But thou—tell me the rest!
Utter the rede of woes to come for me;
Utter the aid, the cure, if aid or cure there be!

PROMETHEUS

Lo, clearly will I show forth all thy quest—
Not in dark speech, but with such simple phrase
As doth befit the utterance of a friend.
I am Prometheus, who gave fire to men.

IO

O daring, proven champion of man's race,
What sin, Prometheus, dost thou thus atone?

PROMETHEUS

One moment since, I told my woes and ceased.

IO

Then should I plead my suit to thee in vain?

PROMETHEUS

Nay, speak thy need; nought would I hide from thee.

IO

Pronounce who nailed thee to the rocky cleft.

PROMETHEUS

Zeus, by intent; Hephaestus, by his hand.

IO

For what wrongdoing do these pains atone?

PROMETHEUS

What I have said, is said; suffice it thee!

IO

Yet somewhat add; forewarn me in my woe
What time shall bring my wandering to its goal?

PROMETHEUS

Fore-knowledge is fore-sorrow; ask it not.

IO

Nay, hide not from me destiny's decree.

PROMETHEUS

I grudge thee not the gift which I withhold.

IO

Then wherefore tarry ere thou tell me all?

PROMETHEUS

Nothing I grudge, but would not rack thy soul.

IO

Be not compassionate beyond my wish.

PROMETHEUS

Well, thou art fain, and I will speak. Attend!

CHORUS

Nay—ere thou speak, hear me, bestow on me

A portion of the grace of granted prayers.
First let us learn how Io's frenzy came—
(She telling her disasters manifold)
Then of their sequel let her know from thee.
PROMETHEUS
    Well were it, Io, thus to do their will—
Right well! they are the sisters of thy sire.
'Tis worth the waste and effluence of time,
To tell, with tears of perfect moan, the doom
Of sorrows that have fallen, when 'tis sure
The listeners will greet the tale with tears.
IO
    I know not how I should mistrust your prayer;
Therefore the whole that ye desire of me
Ye now shall learn in one straightforward tale.
Yet, as it leaves my lips, I blush with shame
To tell that tempest of the spite of Heaven,
And all the wreck and ruin of my form,
And whence they swooped upon me, woe is me!
Long, long in visions of the night there came
Voices and forms into my maiden bower,
Alluring me with smoothly glozing words—
O maiden highly favoured of high Heaven,
Why cherish thy virginity so long?
Thine is it to win wedlock's noblest crown!
Know that Zeus' heart thro' thee is all aflame,
Pierced with desire as with a dart, and longs
To join in utmost rite of love with thee.
Therefore, O maiden, shun not with disdain
Th' embrace of Zeits, but hie thee forth straightway
To the lush growth of Lerna's meadow-land,
Where are the flocks and steadings of thy home,
And let Zeus' eye be eased of its desire.
Night after night, haunted by dreams like these,
Heartsick, I ventured at the last to tell
Unto my sire these visions of the dark.
Then sent he many a wight, on sacred quest,
To Delphi and to far Dodona's shrine,
Being fall fain to learn what deed or word
Would win him favour from the powers of heaven.
But they came back repeating oracles

Mystic, ambiguous, inscrutable,
Till, at the last, an utterance direct,
Obscure no more, was brought to Inachus—
A peremptory charge to fling me forth
Beyond my home and fatherland, a thing
Sent loose in banishment o'er all the world;
And—should he falter—Zeus should launch on him
A fire-eyed bolt, to shatter and consume
Himself and all his race to nothingness.
Bowing before such utterance from the shrine
Of Loxias, he drave me from our halls,
Barring the gates against me: loth he was
To do, as I to suffer, this despite:
But the strong curb of Zeus had overborne
His will to me-ward. As I parted thence,
In form and mind I grew dishumanized,
And horned as now ye see me, poison-stung
By the envenomed bitings of the brize,
I leapt and flung in frenzy, rushed away
To the bright waters of Cerchneia's stream
And Lerna's beach: but ever at my side,
A herdsman by his heifer, Argus moved,
Earth-born, malevolent of mood, and peered,
With myriad eyes, where'er my feet would roam.
But on him in a moment, unforeseen,
Came Fate, and sundered him from life; but I,
Still maddened by the gadfly's sting, the scourge
Of God's infliction, roam the weary world.
How I have fared, thou hearest: be there aught
Of what remains to bear, that thou canst tell,
Speak on! but let not thy compassion warm
Thy words to cheering falsehood. Worst of woes
Are words that break their promise to our hope!
CHORUS
   Woe! woe! avaunt—thou and thy tale of bane!
  O never, never dared I dream
Such horror of strange sounds should pierce mine ear;
Such loathly sights, such tortures hard to bear,
Outrage, pollution, agony supreme,
Wasting my heart with double edge of pain!
Ah Fate, ah Fate! I gaze on Io's dole,

And shudder to my soul!
PROMETHEUS
    Thou wailest all too soon, fulfilled of fear—
Tarry awhile, till thou have learned the whole.
CHORUS
    Say on, reveal it! suffering souls are fain
To know aright what yet remains to bear.
PROMETHEUS
    Lightly, with help of mine, did ye achieve
That which ye first desired: from Io's mouth
craved to hear, recounted by herself,
The story of her strivings. Listen now
To what shall follow, to what woefulness
The wrath of Hera must compel this maid.
                (To Io)
And thou, O child of Inachus, within
Thine inmost heart store up these words of mine,
That thou may'st learn thy wanderings and their goal.
First from this spot toward the sunrise turn,
And cross the steppe that knoweth not the plough:
Thus to the nomad Scythians shalt thou come,
Who dwell in wattled homes, not built on earth
But borne along on wains of sturdy wheel—
Equipped, themselves, with bows of mighty reach.
Pass them avoidingly, and leave their land,
And skirt the beaches where the tides make moan,
Till lo! upon the left hand thou shalt find
The Chalybes, stout craftsmen of the steel—
Beware of them! no gentleness is theirs,
No kindly welcome to a stranger's foot!
Thence to the Stream of Violence shalt thou come—
Like name, like nature; see thou cross it not,
('Tis fatal to the forder!) till thou come
Right to the very Caucasus, the peak
That overtops the world, and from its brows
The river pants in spray its wrathful stream.
Thence, o'er the pinnacles that court the stars,
Onward and southward thou must take thy way,
And reach the warlike horde of Amazons,
Maidens through hate of man; and gladly they
Will guide thy maiden feet. That host, in days

That are not yet, shall fix their home and dwell
At Themiscyra, on Thermodon's bank,
Nigh whereunto the grim projecting fang
Of Salmydessus' cape affronts the main,
The seaman's curse, to ships a stepmother!
Then at the jutting land, Cimmerian styled,
That screens the narrowing portal of the mere,
Thou shalt arrive; pass o'er it, brave at heart,
And ferry thee across Macotis' ford.
So shall there be great rumour evermore,
In ears of mortals, of thy passage strange;
And Bosporos shall be that channel's name,
Because the ox-horned thing did pass thereby.
So, from the wilds of Europe wander'd o'er,
To Asia's continent thou com'st at last.
                              (To the CHORUS)
And ye, what think ye? Seems he not, that lord
And tyrant of the gods, as tyrannous
Unto all other lives? A high god's lust
Constrained this mortal maid to roam the world!
                              (To Io)
Poor maid! a brutal wooer sure was thine!
For know that all which I have told thee now
Is scarce the prelude of thy woes to come.
IO
    Alas for me, alas!
PROMETHEUS
    Again thou criest, with a heifer's low.
  What wilt thou do, learning thy future woes?
CHORUS
    What, hast thou further sorrows for her ear?
PROMETHEUS
    Yea, a vext ocean of predestined pain.
IO
    What profit then is life to me? Ah, why
  Did I not cast me from this stubborn crag?
  So with one spring, one crash upon the ground,
  I had attained surcease from all my woes.
  Better it is to die one death outright
  Than linger out long life in misery.
PROMETHEUS

Ill would'st thou bear these agonies of mine—
Mine, with whose fate it standeth not to win
The goal of death, which were release from pain!
Now, there is set no limit to my woe
Till Zeus be hurled from his omnipotence.

IO

Zeus hurled from pride of place! Can such things be?

PROMETHEUS

Thou wert full fain, methinks, to see that sight!

IO

Even so—his overthrow who wrought my pain.

PROMETHEUS

Then may'st thou know thereof; such fall shall be.

IO

And who shall wrench the sceptre from his hand?

PROMETHEUS

By his own mindless counsels shall he fall.

IO

And how? unless the telling harm, say on!

PROMETHEUS

Wooing a bride, his ruin he shall win.

IO

Goddess, or mortal? tell me, if thou may'st.

PROMETHEUS

No matter which—more must not be revealed.

IO

Doth then a consort thrust him from his throne?

PROMETHEUS

The child she bears him shall o'ercome his sire.

IO

And hath he no avoidance of this doom?

PROMETHEUS

None, surely—till that I, released from bonds—

IO

Who can release thee, but by will of Zeus?

PROMETHEUS

Fate gives this duty to a child of thine!

IO

How? Shall a child of mine undo thy woes?

PROMETHEUS

Yea, of thy lineage, thirteen times removed.

IO
　Dark beyond guessing grows thine oracle.
PROMETHEUS
　Yea—seek not therefore to foreknow thy woes.
IO
　As thou didst proffer hope, withdraw it not.
PROMETHEUS
　Two tales I have—choose! for I grant thee one.
IO
　And which be they? reveal, and leave me choice.
PROMETHEUS
　　I grant it: shall I in all clearness show
　Thy future woes, or my deliverance?
CHORUS
　　Nay! of the two, vouchsafe her wish to her
　And mine to me, deigning a truth to each—
　To her, reveal her future wanderings—
　To me, thy future saviour, as I crave!
PROMETHEUS
　　I will not set myself to thwart your will
　Withholding aught of what ye crave to know.
　First to thee, Io, will I tell and trace
　Thy scared circuitous wandering mark it well,
　Deep in retentive tablets of the soul.
　When thou hast overpast the ferry's flow
　That sunders continent from continent,
　Straight to the eastward and the flaming face
　Of dawn, and highways trodden by the sun,
　Pass, till thou come unto the windy land
　Of daughters born to Boreas: beware
　Lest the strong spirit of the stormy blast
　Snatch thee aloft, and sweep thee to the void,
　On wings of raving wintry hurricane!
　Wend by the noisy tumult of the wave,
　Until thou reach the Gorgon-haunted plains
　Beside Cisthene. In that solitude
　Dwell Phorcys' daughters, beldames worn with time,
　Three, each swan-shapen, single-toothed, and all
　Peering thro' shared endowment of one eye;
　Never on them doth the sun shed his rays,
　Never falls radiance of the midnight moon.

But, hard by these, their sisters, clad with wings,
Serpentine-curled, dwell, loathed of mortal men,—
The Gorgons!—he of men who looks on them
Shall gasp away his life. Of such fell guard
I bid thee to beware. Now, mark my words
When I another sight of terror tell—
Beware the Gryphon pack, the hounds of Zeus,
As keen of fang as silent of their tongues!
Beware the one-eyed Arimaspian band
That tramp on horse-hoofs, dwelling by the ford
Of Pluto and the stream that flows with gold:
Keep thou aloof from these. To the world's end
Thou comest at the last, the dark-faced tribe
That dwell beside the sources of the sun,
Where springs the river, Aethiopian named.
Make thou thy way along his bank, until
Thou come unto the mighty downward slope
Where from the overland of Bybline hills
Nile pours his hallowed earth-refreshing wave.
He by his course shall guide thee to the realm
Named from himself, three-angled, water-girt;
There, Io, at the last, hath Fate ordained,
For thee and for thy race, the charge to found,
Far from thy native shore, a new abode.
Lo, I have said: if aught hereof appear
Hard to thy sense and inarticulate,
Question me o'er again, and soothly learn—
God wot, I have too much of leisure here!

CHORUS

   If there be aught beyond, or aught pass'd o'er,
Which thou canst utter, of her woe-worn maze,
Speak on! if all is said, then grant to us
  That which we asked, as thou rememberest.

PROMETHEUS

   She now hath learned, unto its utmost end,
Her pilgrimage; but yet, that she may know
That 'tis no futile fable she hath heard,
I will recount her history of toil
Ere she came hither; let it stand for proof
Of what I told, my forecast of the end.
So, then—to sum in brief the weary tale—

I turn me to thine earlier exile's close.
When to Molossia's lowland thou hadst come,
Nigh to Dodona's cliff and ridge sublime,
(Where is the shrine oracular and seat
Of Zeus, Thesprotian styled, and that strange thing
And marvel past belief, the prophet-oaks
That syllable his speech), thou by their tongues,
With clear acclaim and unequivocal,
Wert thus saluted—Hail, O bride of Zeus
That art to be—hast memory thereof?
Thence, stung anew with frenzy, thou didst hie
Along the shoreward track, to Rhea's lap,
The mighty main; then, stormily distraught,
Backward again and eastward. To all time,
Be well assured, that inlet of the sea
All mortal men shall call Ionian,
In memory that Io fared thereby.
Take this for proof and witness that my mind
Hath more in ken than ever sense hath shown.
(To the CHORUS)
That which remains, to you and her alike
I will relate, and, to my former words
Reverting, add this final prophecy.
(To Io)
There lieth, at the verge of land and sea,
Where Nilus issues thro' the silted sand,
A town, Canopus called: and there at length
Shall Zeus renew the reason in thy brain
With the mere touch and contact of his hand
Fraught now with fear no more: and thou shalt bear
A child, dark Epaphus—his very name
Memorial of Zeus' touch that gave him life.
And his shall be the foison and the fruit
Of all the land enriched by spreading Nile.
Thence the fifth generation of his seed
Back unto Argos, yet unwillingly,
Shall flee for refuge—fifty maidens they,
Loathing a wedlock with their next in blood,
More kin than kind, from their sire's brother sprung.
And on their track, astir with wild desire,
Like falcons fierce closing on doves that flee,

Shall speed the suitors, craving to achieve
A prey forbidden, a reluctant bride.
Yet power divine shall foil them, and forbid
Possession of the maids, whom Argive land
Shall hold protected, when unsleeping hate,
Horror, and watchful ambush of the night,
Have laid the suitors dead, by female hands.
For every maid shall smite a man to death,
Dyeing a dagger's edges in his throat—
Such bed of love befall mine enemies!
Yet in one bride shall yearning conquer hate,
Bidding her spare the bridegroom at her side,
Blunting the keen edge of her set resolve.
Thus of two scorns the former shall she choose,
The name of coward, not of murderess.
In Argos shall she bear, in after time,
A royal offspring. Long it were to tell
In clear succession all that thence shall be.
Take this for sooth—in lineage from her
A hero shall arise, an archer great,
And he shall be my saviour from these woes.
Such knowledge of the future Themis gave,
The ancient Titaness, to me her son.
But how, and by what skill, 'twere long to say,
And no whit will the knowledge profit thee.

IO

    O woe, O rending and convulsive pain,
Frenzy and agony, again, again
    Searing my heart and brain!
O dagger of the sting, unforged with fire
Yet burning, burning ever! O my heart,
Pulsing with horror, beating at my breast!
O rolling maddened eyes! away, apart,
    Raving with anguish dire,
I spring, by frenzy-fiends possest.
O wild and whirling words, that sweep in gloom
    Down to dark waves of doom!

                   [Exit IO.

CHORUS

    O well and sagely was it said—
    Yea, wise of heart was he who first

Gave forth in speech the thought he nursed—
In thine own order see thou wed!
   Let not the humble heart aspire
  To the gross home of wealth and pride;
  Nor be it to a hearth allied
That vaunts of many a noble sire.
   O Fates, of awful empery!
  Never may I by Zeus be wooed—
  Never give o'er my maidenhood
To any god that dwells on high.
   A shudder to my soul is sent,
  Beholding Io's doom forlorn—
  By Hera's malice put to scorn,
Roaming in mateless banishment.
   From wedlock's crown of fair desire
  I would not shrink—an idle fear!
  But may no god to me draw near
With shunless might and glance of fire!
   That were a strife wherein no chance
  Of conquest lies: from Zeus most high
  And his resolve, no subtlety
Could win me my deliverance.
PROMETHEUS
   And yet shall Zeus, for all his stubborn pride,
Be brought to low estate! aha, he schemes
Such wedlock as shall bring his doom on him,
Flung from his kingship to oblivion's lap!
Ay, then the curse his father Cronos spake
As he fell helpless from his agelong throne,
Shall be fulfilled unto the utterance!
No god but I can manifest to him
A rescue from such ruin as impends—
I know it, I, and how it may be foiled.
Go to, then, let him sit and blindly trust
His skyey rumblings, for security,
And wave his levin with its blast of flame!
All will avail him not, nor bar his fall
Down to dishonour vile, intolerable
So strong a wrestler is he moulding now
To his own proper downfall—yea, a shape
Portentous and unconquerably huge,

Who truly shall reveal a flame more strong
Than is the lightning, and a crash of sound
More loud than thunder, and shall dash to nought
Poseidon's trident-spear, the ocean-bane
That makes the firm earth quiver. Let Zeus strike
Once on this rock, he speedily shall learn
How far the fall from power to slavery!
CHORUS
  Beware! thy wish doth challenge Zeus himself.
PROMETHEUS
  I voice my wish and its fulfilment too.
CHORUS
  What, dare we look for one to conquer Zeus?
PROMETHEUS
  Ay—Zeus shall wear more painful bonds than mine
CHORUS
  Darest thou speak such taunts and tremble not?
PROMETHEUS
  Why should I fear, who am immortal too?
CHORUS
  Yet he might doom thee to worse agony.
PROMETHEUS
  Out on his dooming! I foreknow it all.
CHORUS
  Yet do the wise revere Necessity.
PROMETHEUS
    Ay, ay—do reverence, cringe and crouch to power
  Whene'er, where'er thou see it! But, for me,
  I reck of Zeus as something less than nought.
  Let him put forth his power, attest his sway,
  Howe'er he will—a momentary show,
  A little brief authority in heaven!
  Aha, I see out yonder one who comes,
  A bidden courier, truckling at Zeus' nod,
  A lacquey in his new lord's livery,
  Surely on some fantastic errand sped!
                              [Enter HERMES.
HERMES
  Thou, double-dyed in gall of bitterness,
  Trickster and sinner against gods, by giving
  The stolen fire to perishable men!

Attend—the Sire supreme doth bid thee tell
What is the wedlock which thou vauntest now,
Whereby he falleth from supremacy?
Speak forth the whole, make all thine utterance clear,
Have done with words inscrutable, nor cause
To me, Prometheus! any further toil
Or twofold journeying. Go to—thou seest
Zeus doth not soften at such words as thine!
PROMETHEUS

    Pompous, in sooth, thy word, and swoln with pride,
As doth befit the lacquey of thy lords!
O ye young gods! how, in your youthful sway,
Ye deem secure your citadels of sky,
Beyond the reach of sorrow or of fall!
Have I not seen two dynasties of gods
Already flung therefrom? and soon shall see
A third, that now in tyranny exults,
Shamed, ruined, in an hour! What sayest thou?
Crouch I and tremble at these stripling powers?
Small homage unto such from me, or none!
Betake thee hence, sweat back along thy road—
Look for no answer from me, get thee gone!
HERMES

    Think—it was such audacities of will
That drove thee erst to anchorage in woe!
PROMETHEUS

    Ay—but mark this: mine heritage of pain
I would not barter for thy servitude.
HERMES

    Better, forsooth, be bond-slave to a crag,
Than true-born herald unto Zeus the Sire!
PROMETHEUS

    Take thine own coin—taunts for a taunting slave!
HERMES

    Proud art thou in thy circumstance, methinks!
PROMETHEUS

    Proud? in such pride then be my foemen set,
And I to see—and of such foes art thou!
HERMES

    What, blam'st thou me too for thy sufferings?
PROMETHEUS

Mark a plain word—I loathe all gods that are,
Who reaped my kindness and repay with wrong.
HERMES
I hear no little madness in thy words.
PROMETHEUS
Madness be mine, if scorn of foes be mad.
HERMES
Past bearing were thy pride, in happiness.
PROMETHEUS
Ah me!
HERMES
Zeus knoweth nought of sorrow's cry!
PROMETHEUS
He shall! Time's lapse bringeth all lessons home.
HERMES
To thee it brings not yet discretion's curb.
PROMETHEUS
No—else I had not wrangled with a slave!
HERMES
Then thou concealest all that Zeus would learn?
PROMETHEUS
As though I owed him aught and should repay!
HERMES
Scornful thy word, as though I were a child—
PROMETHEUS
Child, ay—or whatsoe'er hath less of brain—
Thou, deeming thou canst wring my secret out!
No mangling torture, no, nor sleight of power
There is, by which he shall compel my speech,
Until these shaming bonds be loosed from me.
So, let him fling his blazing levin-bolt!
Let him with white and winged flakes of snow,
And rumbling earthquakes, whelm and shake the world!
For nought of this shall bend me to reveal
The power ordained to hurl him from his throne.
HERMES
Bethink thee if such words can mend thy lot
PROMETHEUS
All have I long foreseen, and all resolved.
HERMES
Perverse of will! constrain, constrain thy soul

To think more wisely in the grasp of doom!
PROMETHEUS
    Truce to vain words! as wisely wouldst thou strive
To warn a swelling wave: imagine not
That ever I before thy lord's resolve
Will shrink in womanish terror, and entreat,
As with soft suppliance of female hands,
The Power I scorn unto the utterance,
To loose me from the chains that bind me here—
A world's division 'twixt that thought and me!
HERMES
    So, I shall speak, whate'er I speak, in vain!
No prayer can melt or soften thy resolve;
But, as a colt new-harnessed champs the bit,
Thou strivest and art restive to the rein.
But all too feeble is the stratagem
In which thou art so confident: for know
That strong self-will is weak and less than nought
In one more proud than wise. Bethink thee now—
If these my words thou shouldest disregard—
What storm, what might as of a great third wave
Shall dash thy doom upon thee, past escape!
First shall the Sire, with thunder and the flame
Of lightning, rend the crags of this ravine,
And in the shattered mass o'erwhelm thy form,
Immured and morticed in a clasping rock.
Thence, after age on age of durance done,
Back to the daylight shall thou come, and there
The eagle-hound of Zeus, red-ravening, fell
With greed, shall tatter piecemeal all thy flesh
To shreds and ragged vestiges of form—
Yea, an unbidden guest, a day-long bane,
That feeds, and feeds—yea, he shall gorge his fill
On blackened fragments, from thy vitals gnawed.
Look for no respite from that agony
Until some other deity be found,
Ready to bear for thee the brunt of doom,
Choosing to pass into the lampless world
Of Hades and the murky depths of hell.
Hereat, advise thee! 'tis no feigned threat
Whereof I warn thee, but an o'er-true tale.

The lips of Zeus know nought of lying speech,
But wreak in action all their words foretell.
Therefore do thou look warily, and deem
Prudence a better saviour than self-will.
CHORUS
    Meseems that Hermes speaketh not amiss,
Bidding thee leave thy wilfulness and seek
The wary walking of a counselled mind.
  Give heed! to err through anger shames the wise.
PROMETHEUS
    All, all I knew, whate'er his tongue
In idle arrogance hath flung.
'Tis the world's way, the common lot—
Foe tortures foe and pities not.
Therefore I challenge him to dash
His bolt on me, his zigzag flash
  Of piercing, rending flame!
Now be the welkin stirred amain
With thunder-peal and hurricane,
And let the wild winds now displace
From its firm poise and rooted base
  The stubborn earthly frame!
The raging sea with stormy surge
Rise up and ravin and submerge
  Each high star-trodden way!
Me let him lift and dash to gloom
Of nether hell, in whirls of doom!
Yet—do he what extremes he may—
He cannot crush my life away!
HERMES
    Such are the counsels, such the strain,
Heard from wild lips and frenzied brain!
In word or thought, how fails his fate
Of madness wild and desperate?
                    (To the CHORUS)
But ye, who stand compassionate
Here at his side, depart in haste!
Lest of his penalty ye taste,
  And shattered brain and reason feel
The roaring, ruthless thunder-peal!
CHORUS

Out on thee! if thy heart be fain
I should obey thee, change thy strain!
Vile is thine hinted cowardice,
And loathed of me thy base advice,
　Weakly to shrink from pain!
Nay, at his side, whate'er befall,
I will abide, endure it all!
Among all things abhorr'd, accurst,
I hold betrayers for the worst!

HERMES

　Nay, ye are warned! remember well—
Nor cry, when meshed in nets of hell,
Ah cruel fate, ah Zeus unkind—
Thus, by a sentence undivined,
To dash us to the realms below!
It is no sudden, secret blow—
Nay, ye achieve your proper woe—
Warn'd and foreknowing shall ye go,
Through your own folly trapped and ta'en,
Into the net the Fates ordain—
The vast, illimitable pain!

　　　　　　　　[Thunder and lightning.

PROMETHEUS

　Hark! for no more in empty word,
But in sheer sooth, the world is stirred!
The massy earth doth heave and sway,
And thro' their dark and secret way
　The cavern'd thunders boom!
See, how they gleam athwart the sky,
　The lightnings, through the gloom!
And whirlwinds roll the dust on high,
And right and left the storm-clouds leap
To battle in the skyey deep,
In wildest uproar unconfined,
An universe of warring wind!
And falling sky and heaving sea
Are blent in one! on me, on me,
Nearer and ever yet more near,
Flaunting its pageantry of fear,
Drives down in might its destined road
The tempest of the wrath of God!

O holy Earth, O mother mine!
O Sky, that biddest speed along
Thy vault the common Light divine,—
  Be witness of my wrong!

         [The rocks are rent with fire and earthquake,
      and fall, burying PROMETHEUS in the ruins.

The Suppliant Maidens

Dramatis Personae:
DANAUS,
THE KING OF ARGOS,
HERALD OF AEGYPTUS.
Chorus of the Daughters of Danaus.
Attendants.

ARGUMENT
Io, the daughter of Inachus, King of Argos, was beloved of Zeus. But Hera
was jealous of that love, and by her ill will was Io given over to frenzy, and her
body took the semblance of a heifer: and Argus, a many-eyed herdsman, was
set by Hera to watch Io whithersoever she strayed. Yet, in despite of Argus,
did Zeus draw nigh unto her in the shape of a bull. And by the will of Zeus
and the craft of Hermes was Argus slain. Then Io was driven over far lands
and seas by her madness, and came at length to the land of Egypt. There was
she restored to herself by a touch of the hand of Zeus, and bare a child called
Epaphus. And from Epaphus sprang Libya, and from Libya, Belus; and from
Belus, Aegyptus and Danaus. And the sons of Aegyptus willed to take the
daughters of Danaus in marriage. But the maidens held such wedlock in
horror, and fled with their father over the sea to Argos; and the king and
citizens of Argos gave them shelter and protection from their pursuers.

Scene. —A sacred precinct near the gates of Argos: statue and shrines of
Zeus and other deities stand around.

CHORUS

ZEUS! Lord and guard of suppliant hands!
Look down benign on us who crave
Thine aid—whom winds and waters drave
From where, through drifting shifting sands,
Pours Nilus to the wave.
From where the green land, god-possest,
Closes and fronts the Syrian waste,
We flee as exiles, yet unbanned
By murder's sentence from our land;
But—since Aegyptus had decreed
His sons should wed his brother's seed,—

Ourselves we tore from bonds abhorred,
From wedlock not of heart but hand,
Nor brooked to call a kinsman lord!
And Danaus, our sire and guide,
The king of counsel, pond'ring well
The dice of fortune as they fell,
Out of two griefs the kindlier chose,
And bade us fly, with him beside,
Heedless what winds or waves arose,
And o'er the wide sea waters haste,
Until to Argos' shore at last
  Our wandering pinnace came—
Argos, the immemorial home
Of her from whom we boast to come—
Io, the ox-horned maiden, whom,
After long wandering, woe, and scathe,
Zeus with a touch, a mystic breath,
  Made mother of our name.
Therefore, of all the lands of earth,
On this most gladly step we forth,
And in our hands aloft we bear—
Sole weapon for a suppliant's wear—
The olive-shoot, with wool enwound!
  City, and land, and waters wan
Of Inachus, and gods most high,
And ye who, deep beneath the ground,
Bring vengeance weird on mortal man,
Powers of the grave, on you we cry!
And unto Zeus the Saviour, guard
Of mortals' holy purity!
Receive ye us—keep watch and ward
Above the suppliant maiden band!
Chaste be the heart of this your land
Towards the weak! but, ere the throng,
The wanton swarm, from Egypt sprung,
Leap forth upon the silted shore,
Thrust back their swift-rowed bark again,
Repel them, urge them to the main!
And there, 'mid storm and lightning's shine,
And scudding drift and thunder's roar,
Deep death be theirs, in stormy brine!

Before they foully grasp and win
Us, maiden-children of their kin,
And climb the couch by law denied,
And wrong each weak reluctant bride.
  And now on her I call,
    Mine ancestress, who far on Egypt's shore
    A young cow's semblance wore,—
A maiden once, by Hera's malice changed!
    And then on him withal,
Who, as amid the flowers the grazing creature
    ranged,
Was in her by a breath of Zeus conceived;
    And, as the hour of birth drew nigh,
By fate fulfilled, unto the light he came;
    And Epaphus for name,
Born from the touch of Zeus, the child received.
    On him, on him I cry,
    And him for patron hold—
  While in this grassy vale I stand,
    Where Io roamed of old!
And here, recounting all her toil and pain,
Signs will I show to those who rule the land
That I am child of hers; and all shall understand,
Hearing the doubtful tale of the dim past made plain.
      And, ere the end shall be,
Each man the truth of what I tell shall see.
      And if there dwell hard by
One skilled to read from bird-notes augury,
That man, when through his ears shall thrill our
    tearful wail,
  Shall deem he hears the voice, the plaintive tale
Of her, the piteous spouse of Tereus, lord of guile—
Whom the hawk harries yet, the mourning nightingale.
She, from her happy home and fair streams scared
    away,
  Wails wild and sad for haunts beloved erewhile.
  Yea, and for Itylus—ah, well-a-day!
  Slain by her own, his mother's hand,
Maddened by lustful wrong, the deed by Tereus
    planned.
Like her I wail and wail, in soft Ionian tones,

And as she wastes, even so
Wastes my soft cheek, once ripe with Nilus' suns
And all my heart dissolves in utter woe
   Sad flowers of grief I cull,
    Fleeing from kinsmen's love unmerciful—
Yea, from the clutching hands, the wanton crowd,
I sped across the waves, from Egypt's land of cloud
   Gods of the ancient cradle of my race,
  Hear me, just gods! With righteous grace
    On me, on me look down!
Grant not to youth its heart's unchaste desire,
But, swiftly spurning lust's unholy fire,
 Bless only love and willing wedlock's crown
 The war-worn fliers from the battle's wrack
 Find refuge at the hallowed altar-side,
    The sanctuary divine,—
 Ye gods! such refuge unto me provide—
   Such sanctuary be mine!
Though the deep will of Zeus be hard to track,
   Yet doth it flame and glance,
 A beacon in the dark, 'mid clouds of chance
    That wrap mankind
Yea, though the counsel fall, undone it shall not be,
Whate'er be shaped and fixed within Zeus' ruling mind—
Dark as a solemn grove, with sombre leafage shaded,
  His paths of purpose wind,
  A marvel to man's eye
  Smitten by him, from towering hopes degraded,
  Mortals lie low and still
Tireless and effortless, works forth its will
    The arm divine!
God from His holy seat, in calm of unarmed power,
Brings forth the deed, at its appointed hour!
  Let Him look down on mortal wantonness!
 Lo! how the youthful stock of Belus' line
   Craves for me, uncontrolled—
   With greed and madness bold—
   Urged on by passion's sunless stress—
And, cheated, learns too late the prey has 'scaped
   their hold!
 Ah, listen, listen to my grievous tale,

My sorrow's words, my shrill and tearful cries!
    Ah woe, ah woe!
  Loud with lament the accents use,
And from my living lips my own sad dirges flow!
    O Apian land of hill and dale,
Thou kennest yet, O land, this faltered foreign wail—
    Have mercy, hear my prayer!
 Lo, how again, again, I rend and tear
My woven raiment, and from off my hair
    Cast the Sidonian veil!
  Ah, but if fortune smile, if death be driven away,
Vowed rites, with eager haste, we to the gods will pay!
    Alas, alas again!
O wither drift the waves? and who shall loose the pain?
      O Apian land of hill and dale,
Thou kennest yet, O land, this faltered foreign wail!
    Have mercy, hear my prayer!
Lo, how again, again, I rend and tear
My woven raiment, and from off my hair
    Cast the Sidonian veil!
  The wafting oar, the bark with woven sail,
    From which the sea foamed back,
Sped me, unharmed of storms, along the breeze's track—
    Be it unblamed of me!
But ah, the end, the end of my emprise!
May He, the Father, with all-seeing eyes,
    Grant me that end to see!
Grant that henceforth unstained as heretofore
 I may escape the forced embrace
 Of those proud children of the race
    That sacred Io bore.
  And thou, O maiden-goddess chaste and pure—
    Queen of the inner fane,—
Look of thy grace on me, O Artemis,
 Thy willing suppliant—thine, thine it is,
Who from the lustful onslaught fled secure,
 To grant that I too without stain
The shelter of thy purity may gain!
  Grant that henceforth unstained as heretofore
 I may escape the forced embrace
 Of those proud children of the race

That sacred Io bore!
    Yet if this may not be,
  We, the dark race sun-smitten, we
  Will speed with suppliant wands
To Zeus who rules below, with hospitable hands
Who welcomes all the dead from all the lands:
Yea by our own hands strangled, we will go,
Spurned by Olympian gods, unto the gods below!
    Zeus, hear and save!
The searching, poisonous hate, that Io vexed and drave,
 Was of a goddess: well I know
 The bitter ire, the wrathful woe
  Of Hera, queen of heaven—
A storm, a storm her breath, whereby we yet are driven!
  Bethink thee, what dispraise
 Of Zeus himself mankind will raise,
If now he turn his face averted from our cries!
If now, dishonoured and alone,
The ox-horned maiden's race shall be undone,
Children of Epaphus, his own begotten son—
Zeus, listen from on high!—to thee our prayers arise.
    Zeus, hear and save!
The searching poisonous hate, that Io vexed and drave,
 Was of a goddess: well I know
 The bitter ire, the wrathful woe
  Of Hera, queen of heaven—
A storm, a storm her breath, whereby we yet are driven!

DANAUS

  Children, be wary—wary he with whom
Ye come, your trusty sire and steersman old:
And that same caution hold I here on land,
And bid you hoard my words, inscribing them
On memory's tablets. Lo, I see afar
Dust, voiceless herald of a host, arise;
And hark, within their grinding sockets ring
Axles of hurrying wheels! I see approach,
Borne in curved cars, by speeding horses drawn,
A speared and shielded band. The chiefs, perchance,
Of this their land are hitherward intent
To look on us, of whom they yet have heard
By messengers alone. But come who may,

And come he peaceful or in ravening wrath
Spurred on his path, 'twere best, in any case,
Damsels, to cling unto this altar-mound
Made sacred to their gods of festival,—
A shrine is stronger than a tower to save,
A shield that none may cleave. Step swift thereto,
And in your left hands hold with reverence
The white-crowned wands of suppliance, the sign
Beloved of Zeus, compassion's lord, and speak
To those that question you, words meek and low
And piteous, as beseems your stranger state,
Clearly avowing of this flight of yours
The bloodless cause; and on your utterance
See to it well that modesty attend;
From downcast eyes, from brows of pure control,
Let chastity look forth; nor, when ye speak,
Be voluble nor eager—they that dwell
Within this land are sternly swift to chide.
And be your words submissive: heed this well;
For weak ye are, outcasts on stranger lands,
And froward talk beseems not strengthless hands.
CHORUS
   O father, warily to us aware
Thy words are spoken, and thy wisdom's best
My mind shall hoard, with Zeus our sire to aid.
DANAUS
   Even so—with gracious aspect let him aid.
CHORUS
   Fain were I now to seat me by thy side.
DANAUS
   Now dally not, but put our thought in act.
CHORUS
   Zeus, pity our distress, or e'er we die.
DANAUS
   If so he will, your toils to joy will turn.

CHORUS
   Lo, on this shrine, the semblance of a bird
DANAUS
   Zeus' bird of dawn it is; invoke the sign.
CHORUS

Thus I invoke the saving rays of morn.
DANAUS
   Next, bright Apollo, exiled once from heaven.
CHORUS
   The exiled god will pity our exile.
DANAUS
   Yea, may he pity, giving grace and aid.
CHORUS
   Whom next invoke I, of these other gods?
DANAUS
   Lo, here a trident, symbol of a god.
CHORUS
   Who gave sea-safety; may he bless on land!
DANAUS
   This next is Hermes, carved in Grecian wise.
CHORUS
   Then let him herald help to freedom won.
DANAUS
   Lastly, adore this altar consecrate
To many lesser gods in one; then crouch
On holy ground, a flock of doves that flee,
Scared by no alien hawks, a kin not kind,
Hateful, and fain of love more hateful still.
Foul is the bird that rends another bird,
And foul the men who hale unwilling maids,
From sire unwilling, to the bridal bed.
Never on earth, nor in the lower world,
Shall lewdness such as theirs escape the ban:
There too, if men say right, a God there is
Who upon dead men turns their sin to doom,
To final doom. Take heed, draw hitherward,
That from this hap your safety ye may win.
                        [Enter the KING OF ARGOS.

THE KING OF ARGOS
   Speak—of what land are ye? No Grecian band
Is this to whom I speak, with Eastern robes
And wrappings richly dight: no Argive maid,
No woman in all Greece such garb doth wear.
This too gives marvel, how unto this land,
Unheralded, unfriended, without guide,

And without fear, ye came? yet wands I see,
True sign of suppliance, by you laid down
On shrines of these our gods of festival.
No land but Greece can read such signs aright.
Much else there is, conjecture well might guess,
But let words teach the man who stands to hear.
CHORUS
    True is the word thou spakest of my garb;
But speak I unto thee as citizen,
Or Hermes' wandbearer, or chieftain king?
THE KING OF ARGOS
    For that, take heart and answer without fear.
I am Pelasgus, ruler of this land,
Child of Palaichthon, whom the earth brought forth;
And, rightly named from me, the race who reap
This country's harvests are Pelasgian called.
And o'er the wide and westward-stretching land,
Through which the lucent wave of Strymon flows
I rule; Perrhaebia's land my boundary is
Northward, and Pindus' further slopes, that watch
Paeonia, and Dodona's mountain ridge.
West, east, the limit of the washing seas
Restrains my rule—the interspace is mine.
But this whereon we stand is Apian land,
Styled so of old from the great healer's name;
For Apis, coming from Naupactus' shore
Beyond the strait, child of Apollo's self
And like him seer and healer, cleansed this land
From man-devouring monsters, whom the earth,
Stained with pollution of old bloodshedding,
Brought forth in malice, beasts of ravening jaws,
A grisly throng of serpents manifold.
And healings of their hurt, by knife and charm,
Apis devised, unblamed of Argive men,
And in their prayers found honour, for reward.
—Lo, thou hast heard the tokens that I give:
Speak now thy race, and tell a forthright tale;
In sooth, this people loves not many words.
CHORUS
    Short is my word and clear. Of Argive race
We come, from her, the ox-horned maiden who

Erst bare the sacred child. My word shall give
Whate'er can 'stablish this my soothfast tale.
THE KING OF ARGOS
    O stranger maids, I may not trust this word,
That ye have share in this our Argive race.
No likeness of our country do ye bear,
But semblance as of Libyan womankind.
Even such a stock by Nilus' banks might grow;
Yea and the Cyprian stamp, in female forms,
Shows to the life, what males impressed the same.
And, furthermore, of roving Indian maids
Whose camping-grounds by Aethiopia lie,
And camels burdened even as mules, and bearing
Riders, as horses bear, mine ears have heard;
And tales of flesh-devouring mateless maids
Called Amazons: to these, if bows ye bare,
I most had deemed you like. Speak further yet,
That of your Argive birth the truth I learn.
CHORUS
    Here in this Argive land—so runs the tale—
Io was priestess once of Hera's fane.
THE KING OF ARGOS
    Yea, truth it is, and far this word prevails:
Is't said that Zeus with mortal mingled love?
CHORUS
    Ay, and that Hera that embrace surmised.
THE KING OF ARGOS
    How issued then this strife of those on high?
CHORUS
    By Hera's will, a heifer she became.
THE KING OF ARGOS
    Held Zeus aloof then from the horned beast?
CHORUS
    'Tis said, he loved, in semblance of a bull.
THE KING OF ARGOS
    And his stern consort, did she aught thereon?
CHORUS
    One myriad-eyed she set, the heifer's guard.
THE KING OF ARGOS
    How namest thou this herdsman many-eyed?
CHORUS

Argus, the child of Earth, whom Hermes slew.
THE KING OF ARGOS
Still did the goddess vex the beast ill-starred?
CHORUS
She wrought a gadfly with a goading sting.
THE KING OF ARGOS
Thus drave she Io hence, to roam afar?
CHORUS
Yea—this thy word coheres exact with mine.
THE KING OF ARGOS
Then to Canopus and to Memphis came she?
CHORUS
And by Zeus' hand was touched, and bare a child.
THE KING OF ARGOS
Who vaunts him the Zeus-mated creature's son?
CHORUS
Epaphus, named rightly from the saving touch.
THE KING OF ARGOS
And whom in turn did Epaphus beget?
CHORUS
Libya, with name of a wide land endowed.
THE KING OF ARGOS
And who from her was born unto the race?
CHORUS
Belus: from him two sons, my father one.
THE KING OF ARGOS
Speak now to me his name, this greybeard wise.

CHORUS
Revere the gods thus crowned, who steer the State.
THE KING OF ARGOS
Awe thrills me, seeing these shrines with leafage crowned.
CHORUS
  Yea, stern the wrath of Zeus, the suppliants' lord.
Child of Palaichthon, royal chief
  Of thy Pelasgians, hear!
Bow down thine heart to my relief—
  A fugitive, a suppliant, swift with fear,
A creature whom the wild wolves chase
O'er toppling crags; in piteous case
  Aloud, afar she lows,

Calling the herdsman's trusty arm to save her from her foes!
THE KING OF ARGOS
  Lo, with bowed heads beside our city shrines
Ye sit 'neath shade of new-plucked olive-boughs.
Our distant kin's resentment Heaven forefend!
Let not this hap, unhoped and unforeseen,
Bring war on us: for strife we covet not.
CHORUS
  Justice, the daughter of right-dealing Zeus,
Justice, the queen of suppliants, look down,
    That this our plight no ill may loose
    Upon your town!
  This word, even from the young, let age and wisdom learn:
  If thou to suppliants show grace,
    Thou shalt not lack Heaven's grace in turn,
So long as virtue's gifts on heavenly shrines have place.
THE KING OF ARGOS
  Not at my private hearth ye sit and sue;
And if the city bear a common stain,
Be it the common toil to cleanse the same:
Therefore no pledge, no promise will I give,
Ere counsel with the commonwealth be held.
CHORUS
  Nay, but the source of sway, the city's self, art thou,
  A power unjudged! thine, only thine,
    To rule the right of hearth and shrine!
  Before thy throne and sceptre all men bow!
  Thou, in all causes lord, beware the curse divine!
THE KING OF ARGOS
  May that curse fall upon mine enemies!
I cannot aid you without risk of scathe,
Nor scorn your prayers—unmerciful it were.
Perplexed, distraught I stand, and fear alike
The twofold chance, to do or not to do.
CHORUS
  Have heed of him who looketh from on high,
  The guard of woeful mortals, whosoe'er
    Unto their fellows cry,
  And find no pity, find no justice there.
  Abiding in his wrath, the suppliants' lord
Doth smite, unmoved by cries, unbent by prayerful word.

THE KING OF ARGOS

But if Aegyptus' children grasp you here,
Claiming, their country's right, to hold you theirs
As next of kin, who dares to counter this?
Plead ye your country's laws, if plead ye may,
That upon you they lay no lawful hand.

CHORUS

Let me not fall, O nevermore,
A prey into the young men's hand;
Rather than wed whom I abhor,
By pilot-stars I flee this land;
O king, take justice to thy side,
And with the righteous powers decide!

THE KING OF ARGOS

Hard is the cause—make me not judge thereof.
Already I have vowed it, to do nought
Save after counsel with my people ta'en,
King though I be; that ne'er in after time,
If ill fate chance, my people then may say—
In aid of strangers thou the state hast slain.

CHORUS

Zeus, lord of kinship, rules at will
The swaying balance, and surveys
Evil and good; to men of ill
Gives evil, and to good men praise.
And thou—since true those scales do sway—
Shall thou from justice shrink away?

THE KING OF ARGOS

A deep, a saving counsel here there needs—
An eye that like a diver to the depth
Of dark perplexity can pass and see,
Undizzied, unconfused. First must we care
That to the State and to ourselves this thing
Shall bring no ruin; next, that wrangling hands
Shall grasp you not as prey, nor we ourselves
Betray you thus embracing sacred shrines,
Nor make the avenging all-destroying god,
Who not in hell itself sets dead men free,
A grievous inmate, an abiding bane.—
Spake I not right, of saving counsel's need?

CHORUS

   Yea, counsel take and stand to aid
  At Justice' side and mine.
Betray not me, the timorous maid
  Whom far beyond the brine
A godless violence cast forth forlorn.
  O King, wilt thou behold—
Lord of this land, wilt thou behold me torn
  From altars manifold?
Bethink thee of the young men's wrath and lust,
  Hold off their evil pride;
Steel not thyself to see the suppliant thrust
  From hallowed statues' side,
Haled by the frontlet on my forehead bound,
  As steeds are led, and drawn
By hands that drag from shrine and altar-mound
  My vesture's fringed lawn.
Know thou that whether for Aegyptus' race
  Thou dost their wish fulfil,
Or for the gods and for each holy place—
  Be thy choice good or ill,
Blow is with blow requited, grace with grace
  Such is Zeus' righteous will.

THE KING OF ARGOS
   Yea, I have pondered: from the sea of doubt
Here drives at length the bark of thought ashore;
Landward with screw and windlass haled, and firm,
Clamped to her props, she lies. The need is stern;
With men or gods a mighty strife we strive
Perforce, and either hap in grief concludes.
For, if a house be sacked, new wealth for old
Not hard it is to win—if Zeus the lord
Of treasure favour—more than quits the loss,
Enough to pile the store of wealth full high;
Or if a tongue shoot forth untimely speech,
Bitter and strong to goad a man to wrath,
Soft words there be to soothe that wrath away:
But what device shall make the war of kin
Bloodless? that woe, the blood of many beasts,
And victims manifold to many gods,
Alone can cure. Right glad I were to shun
This strife, and am more fain of ignorance

Than of the wisdom of a woe endured.
The gods send better than my soul foretells!
CHORUS
   Of many cries for mercy, hear the end.
THE KING OF ARGOS
   Say on, then, for it shall not 'scape mine ear.
CHORUS
   Girdles we have, and bands that bind our robes.
THE KING OF ARGOS
   Even so; such things beseem a woman's wear.
CHORUS
   Know, then, with these a fair device there is—
THE KING OF ARGOS
   Speak, then: what utterance doth this foretell?
CHORUS
   Unless to us thou givest pledge secure—
THE KING OF ARGOS
   What can thy girdles' craft achieve for thee?
CHORUS
   Strange votive tablets shall these statues deck.
THE KING OF ARGOS
   Mysterious thy resolve—avow it clear.
CHORUS
   Swiftly to hang me on these sculptured gods!
THE KING OF ARGOS
   Thy word is as a lash to urge my heart.
CHORUS
   Thou seest truth, for I have cleared thine eye
THE KING OF ARGOS
   Yea, and woes manifold, invincible,
A crowd of ills, sweep on me torrent-like.
My bark goes forth upon a sea of troubles
Unfathomed, ill to traverse, harbourless.
For if my deed shall match not your demand,
Dire, beyond shot of speech, shall be the bane
Your death's pollution leaves unto this land.
Yet if against your kin, Aegyptus' race,
Before our gates I front the doom of war,
Will not the city's loss be sore? Shall men
For women's sake incarnadine the ground?
But yet the wrath of Zeus, the suppliants' lord

I needs must fear: most awful unto man
The terror of his anger. Thou, old man,
The father of these maidens, gather up
Within your arms these wands of suppliance,
And lay them at the altars manifold
Of all our country's gods, that all the town
Know, by this sign, that ye come here to sue.
Nor, in thy haste, do thou say aught of me.
Swift is this folk to censure those who rule;
But, if they see these signs of suppliance,
It well may chance that each will pity you,
And loathe the young men's violent pursuit;
And thus a fairer favour you may find:
For, to the helpless, each man's heart is kind.
DANAUS
    To us, beyond gifts manifold it is
To find a champion thus compassionate;
Yet send with me attendants, of thy folk,
Rightly to guide me, that I duly find
Each altar of your city's gods that stands
Before the fane, each dedicated shrine;
And that in safety through the city's ways
I may pass onwards: all unlike to yours
The outward semblance that I wear—the race
that Nilus rears is all dissimilar
  That of Inachus. Keep watch and ward
  Lest heedlessness bring death: full oft, I ween,
  Friend hath slain friend, not knowing whom he slew.
THE KING OF ARGOS
    Go at his side, attendants,—he saith well.
On to the city's consecrated shrines!
Nor be of many words to those ye meet,
The while this suppliant voyager ye lead.
        [Exit DANAUS with attendants.
CHORUS
    Let him go forward, thy command obeying.
But me how biddest, how assurest thou?
THE KING OF ARGOS
    Leave there the new-plucked boughs, thy sorrow's sign.
CHORUS
    Thus beckoned forth, at thy behest I leave them.

THE KING OF ARGOS
  Now to this level precinct turn thyself.
CHORUS
  Unconsecrate it is, and cannot shield me.
THE KING OF ARGOS
  We will not yield thee to those falcons' greed.
CHORUS
  What help? more fierce they are than serpents fell
THE KING OF ARGOS
  We spake thee fair—speak thou them fair in turn.
CHORUS
  What marvel that we loathe them, scared in soul?
THE KING OF ARGOS
  Awe towards a king should other fears transcend.
CHORUS
  Thus speak, thus act, and reassure my mind.
THE KING OF ARGOS
  Not long thy sire shall leave thee desolate.
  But I will call the country's indwellers,
  And with soft words th' assembly will persuade,
  And warn your sire what pleadings will avail.
  Therefore abide ye, and with prayer entreat
  The country's gods to compass your desire;
  The while I go, this matter to provide,
  Persuasion and fair fortune at my side.
                              [Exit the KING OF ARGOS.
CHORUS
    O King of Kings, among the blest
  Thou highest and thou happiest,
      Listen and grant our prayer,
    And, deeply loathing, thrust
  Away from us the young men's lust,
      And deeply drown
  In azure waters, down and ever down,
    Benches and rowers dark,
    The fatal and perfidious bark!
  Unto the maidens turn thy gracious care;
  Think yet again upon the tale of fame,
  How from the maiden loved of thee there sprung
  Mine ancient line, long since in many a legend sung!
    Remember, O remember, thou whose hand

Did Io by a touch to human shape reclaim.
For from this Argos erst our mother came
    Driven hence to Egypt's land,
Yet sprung of Zeus we were, and hence our birth we claim.
    And now have I roamed back
    Unto the ancient track
Where Io roamed and pastured among flowers,
    Watched o'er by Argus' eyes,
Through the lush grasses and the meadow bowers.
  Thence, by the gadfly maddened, forth she flies
  Unto far lands and alien peoples driven
  And, following fate, through paths of foam and surge,
  Sees, as she goes, the cleaving strait divide
    Greece, from the Eastland riven.
And swift through Asian borders doth she urge
Her course, o'er Phrygian mountains' sheep-clipt side;
Thence, where the Mysian realm of Teuthras lies
  Towards Lydian lowlands hies,
And o'er Cilician and Pamphylian hills
  And ever-flowing rills,
And thence to Aphrodite's fertile shore,
The land of garnered wheat and wealthy store
And thence, deep-stung by wild unrest,
By the winged fly that goaded her and drave,
Unto the fertile land, the god-possest,
    (Where, fed from far-off snows,
    Life-giving Nilus flows,
Urged on by Typho's strength, a fertilizing wave)
She roves, in harassed and dishonoured flight
Scathed by the blasting pangs of Hera's dread despite.
    And they within the land
    With terror shook and wanned,
So strange the sight they saw, and were afraid—
A wild twy-natured thing, half heifer and half maid.
Whose hand was laid at last on Io, thus forlorn,
  With many roamings worn?
Who bade the harassed maiden's peace return?
  Zeus, lord of time eterne.
Yea, by his breath divine, by his unscathing strength,
    She lays aside her bane,
And softened back to womanhood at length

Sheds human tears again.
Then, quickened with Zeus' veritable seed,
   A progeny she bare,
A stainless babe, a child of heavenly breed.
   Of life and fortune fair.
His is the life of life—so all men say,—
   His is the seed of Zeus.
Who else had power stern Hera's craft to stay,
   Her vengeful curse to loose?
     Yea, all from Zeus befell!
  And rightly wouldst thou tell
That we from Epaphus, his child, were born:
   Justly his deed was done;
   Unto what other one,
Of all the gods, should I for justice turn?
   From him our race did spring;
   Creator he and King,
Ancient of days and wisdom he, and might.
   As bark before the wind,
   So, wafted by his mind,
Moves every counsel, each device aright.
   Beneath no stronger hand
   Holds he a weak command,
No throne doth he abase him to adore;
   Swift as a word, his deed
   Acts out what stands decreed
In counsels of his heart, for evermore.
                  [Re-enter DANAUS.

DANAUS
   Take heart, my children: the land's heart is kind,
  And to full issue has their voting come.
CHORUS
   All hail, my sire; thy word brings utmost joy.
  Say, to what issue is the vote made sure,
  And how prevailed the people's crowding hands?
DANAUS
   With one assent the Argives spake their will,
  And, hearing, my old heart took youthful cheer,
  The very sky was thrilled when high in air
  The concourse raised right hands and swore their oath:—
  Free shall the maidens sojourn in this land.

Unharried, undespoiled by mortal wight:
No native hand, no hand of foreigner
Shall drag them hence; if any man use force—
Whoe'er of all our countrymen shall fail
To come unto their aid, let him go forth,
Beneath the people's curse, to banishment.
So did the king of this Pelasgian folk
Plead on behalf of us, and bade them heed
That never, in the after-time, this realm
Should feed to fulness the great enmity
Of Zeus, the suppliants' guard, against itself!
A twofold curse, for wronging stranger-guests
Who are akin withal, confrontingly
Should rise before this city and be shown
A ruthless monster, fed on human doom.
Such things the Argive people heard, and straight,
Without proclaim of herald, gave assent:
Yea, in full conclave, the Pelasgian folk
Heard suasive pleas, and Zeus through them resolved.

CHORUS

Arouse we now to chant our prayer
For fair return of service fair
  And Argos' kindly will.
Zeus, lord of guestright, look upon
The grace our stranger lips have won.
In right and truth, as they begun,
Guide them, with favouring hand, until
Thou dost their blameless wish fulfil!
    Now may the Zeus-born gods on high
    Hear us pour forth
  A votive prayer for Argos' clan!—
  Never may this Pelasgian earth,
Amid the fire-wrack, shrill the dismal cry
  On Ares, ravening lord of fight,
Who in an alien harvest mows down man!
  For lo, this land had pity on our plight,
And unto us were merciful and leal,
To us, the piteous flock, who at Zeus' altar kneel!
They scornèd not the pleas of maidenhood,
Nor with the young men's will hath their will stood.
    They knew right well.

Th' unearthly watching fiend invincible,
The foul avenger—let him not draw near!
For he, on roofs ill-starred,
Defiling and polluting, keeps a ghastly ward!
They knew his vengeance, and took holy heed
To us, the sister suppliants, who cry
  To Zeus, the lord of purity:
Therefore with altars pure they shall the gods revere.
    Thus, through the boughs that shade our lips, fly forth in air,
    Fly forth, O eager prayer!
  May never pestilence efface
    This city's race,
  Nor be the land with corpses strewed,
    Nor stained with civic blood!
  The stem of youth, unpluckt, to manhood come,
  Nor Ares rise from Aphrodité's bower,
The lord of death and bane, to waste our youthful flower.
    Long may the old
  Crowd to the altars kindled to consume
    Gifts rich and manifold—
  Offered to win from powers divine
  A benison on city and on shrine:
    Let all the sacred might adore
    Of Zeus most high, the lord
    Of guestright and the hospitable board,
Whose immemorial law doth rule Fate's scales aright:
    The garners of earth's store
    Be full for evermore,
And grace of Artemis make women's travail light;
  No devastating curse of fell disease
    This city seize;
  No clamour of the State arouse to war
    Ares, from whom afar
  Shrinketh the lute, by whom the dances fail—
    Ares, the lord of wail.
  Swarm far aloof from Argos' citizens
    All plague and pestilence,
  And may the Archer-God our children spare!
  May Zeus with foison and with fruitfulness
    The land's each season bless,
  And, quickened with Heaven's bounty manifold,

Teem grazing flock and fold.
  Beside the altars of Heaven's hallowing
    Loud let the minstrels sing,
And from pure lips float forth the harp-led strain in air!
  And let the people's voice, the power
  That sways the State, in danger's hour
    Be wary, wise for all;
  Nor honour in dishonour hold,
  But—ere the voice of war be bold—
  Let them to stranger peoples grant
  Fair and unbloody covenant—
    Justice and peace withal;
  And to the Argive powers divine
  The sacrifice of laurelled kine,
    By rite ancestral, pay.
  Among three words of power and awe,
  Stands this, the third, the mighty law—
  Your gods, your fathers deified,
  Ye shall adore. Let this abide
    For ever and for aye.
DANAUS
    Dear children, well and wisely have ye prayed;
I bid you now not shudder, though ye hear
New and alarming tidings from your sire.
From this high place beside the suppliants' shrine
The bark of our pursuers I behold,
By divers tokens recognized too well.
Lo, the spread canvas and the hides that screen
The gunwale; lo, the prow, with painted eyes
That seem her onward pathway to descry,
Heeding too well the rudder at the stern
That rules her, coming for no friendly end.
And look, the seamen—all too plain their race—
Their dark limbs gleam from out their snow-white garb;
Plain too the other barks, a fleet that comes
All swift to aid the purpose of the first,
That now, with furled sail and with pulse of oars
Which smite the wave together, comes aland.
But ye, be calm, and, schooled not scared by fear,
Confront this chance, be mindful of your trust
In these protecting gods. And I will hence,

And champions who shall plead your cause aright
Will bring unto your side. There come perchance
Heralds or envoys, eager to lay hand
And drag you captive hence; yet fear them not;
Foiled shall they be. Yet well it were for you
(If, ere with aid I come, I tarry long),
Not by one step this sanctuary to leave.
Farewell, fear nought: soon shall the hour be born
When he that scorns the gods shall rue his scorn
CHORUS
 Ah but I shudder, father!—ah, even now,
Even as I speak, the swift-winged ships draw nigh!
 I shudder, I shiver, I perish with fear:
 Overseas though I fled,
Yet nought it avails; my pursuers are near!
DANAUS
 Children, take heart; they who decreed to aid
Thy cause will arm for battle, well I ween.
CHORUS
 But desperate is Aegyptus' ravening race,
With fight unsated; thou too know'st it well.
 In their wrath they o'ertake us; the prow is deep-dark
 In the which they have sped,
And dark is the bench and the crew of the bark!
DANAUS
 Yea but a crew as stout they here shall find,
And arms well steeled beneath a noon-day sun.
CHORUS
 Ah yet, O father, leave us not forlorn!
Alone, a maid is nought, a strengthless arm.
With guile they Pursue me, with counsel malign,
 And unholy their soul;
And as ravens they seize me, unheeding the shrine!
DANAUS
 Fair will befall us, children, in this chance,
If thus in wrath they wrong the gods and you.
CHORUS
 Alas, nor tridents nor the sanctity
Of shrines will drive them, O my sire, from us!
 Unholy and daring and cursed is their ire,
 Nor own they control

Of the gods, but like jackals they glut their desire!

DANAUS
    Ay, but Come wolf, flee jackal, saith the saw;
Nor can the flax-plant overbear the corn.
CHORUS
    Lustful, accursèd, monstrous is their will
As of beasts ravening—'ware we of their power!
DANAUS
    Look you, not swiftly puts a fleet to sea,
Nor swiftly to its moorings; long it is
Or e'er the saving cables to the shore
Are borne, and long or e'er the steersmen cry,
The good ship swings at anchor—all is well.
Longest of all, the task to come aland
Where haven there is none, when sunset fades
In night. To pilot wise, the adage saith,
Night is a day of wakefulness and pain.
Therefore no force of weaponed men, as yet
Scatheless can come ashore, before the bank
Lie at her anchorage securely moored.
Bethink thee therefore, nor in panic leave
The shrine of gods whose succour thou hast won
I go for aid—men shall not blame me long,
Old, but with youth at heart and on my tongue
                         [Exit DANAUS.
CHORUS
    O land of hill and dale, O holy land,
What shall befall us? whither shall we flee,
From Apian land to some dark lair of earth?
    O would that in vapour of smoke I might rise to the
      clouds of the sky,
That as dust which flits up without wings I might pass
    and evanish and die!
I dare not, I dare not abide: my heart yearns, eager
    to fly;
And dark is the cast of my thought; I shudder and
    tremble for fear.
My father looked forth and beheld: I die of the sight
    that draws near.
And for me be the strangling cord, the halter made

ready by Fate,
Before to my body draws nigh the man of my horror
   and hate.
Nay, ere I will own him as lord, as handmaid to
   Hades I go!
And oh, that aloft in the sky, where the dark clouds
   are frozen to snow,
A refuge for me might be found, or a mountain-top
   smooth and too high
   For the foot of the goat, where the vulture sits lonely,
   and none may descry
The pinnacle veiled in the cloud,
   the highest and sheerest of all,
Ere to wedlock that rendeth my heart,
   and love that is loveless, I fall!
Yea, a prey to the dogs and the birds of the mount
   will I give me to be,—
From wailing and curse and pollution it is death,
   only death, sets me free:
Let death come upon me before
   to the ravisher's bed I am thrust;
What champion, what saviour but death can I find,
   or what refuge from lust?
I will utter my shriek of entreaty,
   a prayer that shrills up to the sky,
That calleth the gods to compassion,
   a tuneful, a pitiful cry,
That is loud to invoke the releaser.
   O father, look down on the fight;
Look down in thy wrath on the wronger,
   with eyes that are eager for right.
Zeus, thou that art lord of the world,
   whose kingdom is strong over all,
Have mercy on us! At thine altar for refuge
   and safety we call.
For the race of Aegyptus is fierce,
   with greed and with malice afire;
They cry as the questing hounds,
   they sweep with the speed of desire.
But thine is the balance of fate,
   thou rulest the wavering scale,

And without thee no mortal emprise
   shall have strength to achieve or prevail.
     Alack, alack! the ravisher—
He leaps from boat to beach, he draweth near!
  Away, thou plunderer accurst!
   Death seize thee first,
Or e'er thou touch me—off! God, hear our cry,
   Our maiden agony!
Ah, ah, the touch, the prelude of my shame.
   Alas, my maiden fame!
  O sister, sister, to the altar cling,
   For he that seizeth me,
Grim is his wrath and stern, by land as on the sea.
   Guard us, O king!
        [Enter the HERALD OF AEGYPTUS]
HERALD OF AEGYPTUS
  Hence to my barge—step swiftly, tarry not.
CHORUS
   Alack, he rends—he rends my hair! O wound on
   wound!
  Help! my lopped head will fall, my blood gush o'er
   the ground!
HERALD OF AEGYPTUS
  Aboard, ye cursèd—with a new curse, go!
CHORUS
    Would God that on the wand'ring brine
  Thou and this braggart tongue of thine
  Had sunk beneath the main—
  Thy mast and planks, made fast in vain!
  Thee would I drive aboard once more,
A slayer and a dastard, from the shore!
HERALD OF AEGYPTUS
   Be still, thou vain demented soul;
  My force thy craving shall control.
  Away, aboard! What, clingest to the shrine?
  Away! this city's gods I hold not for divine

CHORUS
    Aid me, ye gods, that never, never
   I may again behold
   The mighty, the life-giving river,

Nilus, the quickener of field and fold!
   Alack, O sire, unto the shrine I cling—
  Shrine of this land from which mine ancient line did spring!
HERALD OF AEGYPTUS
    Shrines, shrines, forsooth!—the ship, the ship be shrine!
  Aboard, perforce and will-ye nill-ye, go!
    Or e'er from hands of mine
  Ye suffer torments worse and blow on blow.
CHORUS
      Alack, God grant those hands may strive in vain
      With the salt-streaming wave,
    When 'gainst the wide-blown blasts thy bark shall strain
  To round Sarpedon's cape, the sandbank's treach'rous grave.
HERALD OF AEGYPTUS
    Shrill ye and shriek unto what gods ye may,
  Ye shall not leap from out Aegyptus' bark,
  How bitterly soe'er ye wail your woe.
CHORUS
    Alack, alack my wrong!
  Stern is thy voice, thy vaunting loud and strong.
  Thy sire, the mighty Nilus, drive thee hence
  Turning to death and doom thy greedy violence!
HERALD OF AEGYPTUS
    Swift to the vessel of the double prow,
  Go quickly! let none linger, else this hand
  Ruthless will hale you by your tresses hence.
CHORUS
    Alack, O father! from the shrine
  Not aid but agony is mine.
  As a spider he creeps and he clutches his prey,
  And he hales me away.
  A spectre of darkness, of darkness. Alas and alas! well-a-day!
  O Earth, O my mother! O Zeus, thou king of the earth, and her child!
  Turn back, we pray thee, from us his clamour and threatenings wild!

HERALD OF AEGYPTUS
    Peace! I fear not this country's deities.
  They fostered not my childhood nor mine age.
CHORUS
    Like a snake that is human he comes,
    he shudders and crawls to my side;

As an adder that biteth the foot,
  his clutch on my flesh doth abide.
O Earth, O my mother! O Zeus, thou king of the earth,
  and her child!
Turn back, we pray thee, from us his clamour
  and threatenings wild!
HERALD OF AEGYPTUS
  Swift each unto the ship; repine no more,
Or my hand shall not spare to rend your robe.
CHORUS
  O chiefs, O leaders, aid me, or I yield!
HERALD OF AEGYPTUS
  Peace! if ye have not ears to hear my words,
Lo, by these tresses must I hale you hence.
CHORUS
  Undone we are, O king! all hope is gone.
HERALD OF AEGYPTUS
  Ay, kings enow ye shall behold anon,
Aegyptus' sons—Ye shall not want for kings.
                [Enter the KING OF ARGOS.
THE KING OF ARGOS
  Sirrah, what dost thou? in what arrogance
Darest thou thus insult Pelasgia's realm?
Deemest thou this a woman-hearted town?
Thou art too full of thy barbarian scorn
For us of Grecian blood, and, erring thus,
Thou dost bewray thyself a fool in all!
HERALD OF AEGYPTUS
  Say thou wherein my deeds transgress my right.
THE KING OF ARGOS
  First, that thou play'st a stranger's part amiss.
HERALD OF AEGYPTUS
  Wherein? I do but search and claim mine own.
THE KING OF ARGOS
  To whom of our guest-champions hast appealed?
HERALD OF AEGYPTUS
  To Hermes, herald's champion, lord of search.
THE KING OF ARGOS
  Yea, to a god—yet dost thou wrong the gods!
HERALD OF AEGYPTUS
  The gods that rule by Nilus I revere.

THE KING OF ARGOS

Hear I aright? our Argive gods are nought?

HERALD OF AEGYPTUS

The prey is mine, unless force rend it from me.

THE KING OF ARGOS

At thine own peril touch them—'ware, and soon!

HERALD OF AEGYPTUS

I hear thy speech, no hospitable word.

THE KING OF ARGOS

I am no host for sacrilegious hands.

HERALD OF AEGYPTUS

I will go tell this to Aegyptus' sons.

THE KING OF ARGOS

Tell it! my pride will ponder not thy word.

HERALD OF AEGYPTUS

Yet, that I have my message clear to say
(For it behooves that heralds' words be clear,
Be they or ill or good), how art thou named?
By whom despoilèd of this sister-band
Of maidens pass I homeward?—speak and say!
For lo, henceforth in Ares' court we stand,
Who judges not by witness but by war:
No pledge of silver now can bring the cause
To issue: ere this thing end, there must be
Corpse piled on corpse and many lives gasped forth.

THE KING OF ARGOS

What skills it that I tell my name to thee?
Thou and thy mates shall learn it ere the end.
Know that if words unstained by violence
Can change these maidens' choice, then mayest thou,
With full consent of theirs, conduct them hence.
But thus the city with one voice ordained—
No force shall bear away the maiden band.
Firmly this word upon the temple wall
Is by a rivet clenched, and shall abide:
Not upon wax inscribed and delible,
Nor upon parchment sealed and stored away.—
Lo, thou hast heard our free mouths speak their will:
Out from our presence—tarry not, but go!

HERALD OF AEGYPTUS

Methinks we stand on some new edge of war:

Be strength and triumph on the young men's side!
THE KING OF ARGOS
    Nay but here also shall ye find young men,
Unsodden with the juices oozed from grain.
                  [Exit HERALD OF AEGYPTUS
But ye, O maids, with your attendants true,
Pass hence with trust into the fencèd town,
Ringed with a wide confine of guarding towers.
Therein are many dwellings for such guests
As the State honours; there myself am housed
Within a palace neither scant nor strait.
There dwell ye, if ye will to lodge at ease
In halls well-thronged: yet, if your soul prefer,
Tarry secluded in a separate home.
Choose ye and cull, from these our proffered gifts,
Whiche'er is best and sweetest to your will:
And I and all these citizens whose vote
Stands thus decreed, will your protectors be.
Look not to find elsewhere more loyal guard.
CHORUS
    O godlike chief, God grant my prayer:
Fair blessings on thy proffers fair,
Lord of Pelasgia's race!
Yet, of thy grace, unto our side
Send thou the man of courage tried,
Of counsel deep and prudent thought,—
Be Danaus to his children brought;
For his it is to guide us well
And warn where it behoves to dwell—
What place shall guard and shelter us
From malice and tongues slanderous:
Swift always are the lips of blame
A stranger-maiden to defame—
But Fortune give us grace!
THE KING OF ARGOS
    A stainless fame, a welcome kind
From all this people shall ye find:
Dwell therefore, damsels, loved of us,
Within our walls, as Danaus
Allots to each, in order due,
Her dower of attendants true.

[Re-enter DANAUS. DANAUS

High thanks, my children, unto Argos con,
And to this folk, as to Olympian gods,
Give offerings meet of sacrifice and wine;
For saviours are they in good sooth to you.
From me they heard, and bitter was their wrath,
How those your kinsmen strove to work you wrong,
And how of us were thwarted: then to me
This company of spearmen did they grant,
That honoured I might walk, nor unaware
Die by some secret thrust and on this land
Bring down the curse of death, that dieth not.
Such boons they gave me: it behoves me pay
A deeper reverence from a soul sincere.
Ye, to the many words of wariness
Spoken by me your father, add this word,
That, tried by time, our unknown company
Be held for honest: over-swift are tongues
To slander strangers, over-light is speech
To bring pollution on a stranger's name.
Therefore I rede you, bring no shame on me
Now when man's eye beholds your maiden prime.
Lovely is beauty's ripening harvest-field,
But ill to guard; and men and beasts, I wot,
And birds and creeping things make prey of it.
And when the fruit is ripe for love, the voice
Of Aphrodite bruiteth it abroad,
The while she guards the yet unripened growth.
On the fair richness of a maiden's bloom
Each passer looks, o'ercome with strong desire,
With eyes that waft the wistful dart of love.
Then be not such our hap, whose livelong toil
Did make our pinnace plough the mighty main:
Nor bring we shame upon ourselves, and joy
Unto my foes. Behold, a twofold home—
One of the king's and one the people's gift—
Unbought, 'tis yours to hold,—a gracious boon.
Go—but remember ye your sire's behest,
And hold your life less dear than chastity.
CHORUS
    The gods above grant that all else be well.

But fear not thou, O sire, lest aught befall
Of ill unto our ripened maidenhood.
So long as Heaven have no new ill devised,
From its chaste path my spirit shall not swerve.
SEMI-CHORUS

Pass and adore ye the Blessed, the gods of the city
who dwell
Around Erasinus, the gush of the swift immemorial
tide.
SEMI-CHORUS

Chant ye, O maidens; aloud let the praise of
Pelasgia swell;
Hymn we no longer the shores where Nilus to ocean
doth glide.
SEMI-CHORUS

Sing we the bounteous streams that ripple and gush
through the city;
Quickening flow they and fertile, the soft new life of
the plain.
SEMI-CHORUS

Artemis, maiden most pure, look on us with grace
and with pity—
Save us from forced embraces: such love hath no
crown but a pain.

SEMI-CHORUS

Yet not in scorn we chant, but in honour of
Aphrodite;
She truly and Hera alone have power with Zeus and
control.
Holy the deeds of her rite, her craft is secret and
mighty,
And high is her honour on earth, and subtle her
sway of the soul.
SEMI-CHORUS

Yea, and her child is Desire: in the train of his
mother he goeth—
Yea and Persuasion soft-lipped, whom none can deny
or repel:
Cometh Harmonia too, on whom Aphrodite bestoweth
The whispering parley, the paths of the rapture that

lovers love well.
SEMI-CHORUS
    Ah, but I tremble and quake lest again they should
    sail to reclaim!
  Alas for the sorrow to come, the blood and the
    carnage of war.
  Ah, by whose will was it done that o'er the wide
    ocean they came,
  Guided by favouring winds, and wafted by sail and
    by oar?
SEMI-CHORUS
    Peace! for what Fate hath ordained will surely not
    tarry but come;
  Wide is the counsel of Zeus, by no man escaped or
    withstood:
  Only I Pray that whate'er, in the end, of this wedlock
    he doom,
  We as many a maiden of old, may win from the ill
    to the good.
SEMI-CHORUS
    Great Zeus, this wedlock turn from me—
  Me from the kinsman bridegroom guard!

SEMI-CHORUS
  Come what come may, 'tis Fate's decree.
SEMI-CHORUS
  Soft is thy word—the doom is hard.
SEMI-CHORUS
  Thou know'st not what the Fates provide.
SEMI-CHORUS
    How should I scan Zeus' mighty will,
  The depth of counsel undescried?
SEMI-CHORUS
  Pray thou no word of omen ill.
SEMI-CHORUS
  What timely warning wouldst thou teach?
SEMI-CHORUS
  Beware, nor slight the gods in speech.
SEMI-CHORUS
    Zeus, hold from my body the wedlock detested, the
    bridegroom abhorred!

It was thou, it was thou didst release
  Mine ancestress Io from sorrow: thine healing it
     was that restored,
  The touch of thine hand gave her peace.
SEMI-CHORUS
     Be thy will for the cause of the maidens! of two ills,
     the lesser I pray—
  The exile that leaveth me pure.
  May thy justice have heed to my cause, my prayers
     to thy mercy find way!
  For the hands of thy saving are sure.
                     [Exeunt omnes.

The Seven Against Thebes

Dramatis Personae:
ETEOCLES.
A SPY.
CHORUS OF CADMEAN MAIDENS.
ANTIGONE.
ISMENE.
A HERALD.

ETEOCLES
    Clansmen of Cadmus, at the signal given
By time and season must the ruler speak
Who sets the course and steers the ship of State
With hand upon the tiller, and with eye
Watchful against the treachery of sleep.
For if all go aright, thank Heaven, men say,
But if adversely—which may God forefend!—
One name on many lips, from street to street,
Would bear the bruit and rumour of the time,
Down with Eteocles!—a clamorous curse,
A dirge of ruin. May averting Zeus
Make good his title here, in Cadmus' hold!
You it beseems now boys unripened yet
To lusty manhood, men gone past the prime
And increase of the full begetting seed,
And those whom youth and manhood well combined
Array for action—all to rise in aid
Of city, shrines, and altars of all powers
Who guard our land; that ne'er, to end of time,
Be blotted out the sacred service due
To our sweet mother-land and to her brood.
For she it was who to their guest-right called
Your waxing youth, was patient of the toil,
And cherished you on the land's gracious lap,
Alike to plant the hearth and bear the shield
In loyal service, for an hour like this.
Mark now! until to-day, luck rules our scale;

For we, though long beleaguered, in the main
Have with our sallies struck the foemen hard.
But now the seer, the feeder of the birds,
(Whose art unerring and prophetic skill
Of ear and mind divines their utterance
Without the lore of fire interpreted)
Foretelleth, by the mastery of his art,
That now an onset of Achaea's host
Is by a council of the night designed
To fall in double strength upon our walls.
Up and away, then, to the battlements,
The gates, the bulwarks! don your panoplies,
Array you at the breast-work, take your stand
On floorings of the towers, and with good heart
Stand firm for sudden sallies at the gates,
Nor hold too heinous a respect for hordes
Sent on you from afar: some god will guard!
I too, for shrewd espial of their camp,
Have sent forth scouts, and confidence is mine
They will not fail nor tremble at their task,
And, with their news, I fear no foeman's guile.

                         [Enter A SPY.

THE SPY

   Eteocles, high king of Cadmus' folk,
I stand here with news certified and sure
From Argos' camp, things by myself descried.
Seven warriors yonder, doughty chiefs of might,
Into the crimsoned concave of a shield
Have shed a bull's blood, and, with hands immersed
Into the gore of sacrifice, have sworn
By Ares, lord of fight, and by thy name,
Blood-lapping Terror, Let our oath be heard—
Either to raze the walls, make void the hold
Of Cadmus—strive his children as they may—
Or, dying here, to make the foemen's land
With blood impasted. Then, as memory's gift
Unto their parents at the far-off home,
Chaplets they hung upon Adrastus' car,
With eyes tear-dropping, but no word of moan.
For their steeled spirit glowed with high resolve,
As lions pant, with battle in their eyes.

For them, no weak alarm delays the clear
Issues of death or life! I parted thence
Even as they cast the lots, how each should lead,
Against which gate, his serried company.
Rank then thy bravest, with what speed thou may'st,
Hard by the gates, to dash on them, for now,
Full-armed, the onward ranks of Argos come!
The dust whirls up, and from their panting steeds
White foamy flakes like snow bedew the plain.
Thou therefore, chieftain! like a steersman skilled,
Enshield the city's bulwarks, ere the blast
Of war comes darting on them! hark, the roar
Of the great landstorm with its waves of men!
Take Fortune by the forelock! for the rest,
By yonder dawn-light will I scan the field
Clear and aright, and surety of my word
Shall keep thee scatheless of the coming storm.

ETEOCLES

O Zeus and Earth and city-guarding gods,
And thou, my father's Curse, of baneful might,
Spare ye at least this town, nor root it up,
By violence of the foemen, stock and stem!
For here, from home and hearth, rings Hellas' tongue.
Forbid that e'er the yoke of slavery
Should bow this land of freedom, Cadmus' hold!
Be ye her help! your cause I plead with mine—
A city saved doth honour to her gods!

[Exit ETEOCLES, etc. Enter the CHORUS OF MAIDENS.

CHORUS

I wail in the stress of my terror,
    and shrill is my cry of despair.
The foemen roll forth from their camp
    as a billow, and onward they bear!
Their horsemen are swift in the forefront,
    the dust rises up to the sky,
A signal, though speechless, of doom,
    a herald more clear than a cry!
Hoof-trampled, the land of my love
    bears onward the din to mine ears.
As a torrent descending a mountain,
    it thunders and echoes and nears!

The doom is unloosened and cometh!
　　O kings and O queens of high Heaven,
Prevail that it fall not upon us:
　　the sign for their onset is given—
They stream to the walls from without,
　　white-shielded and keen for the fray.
They storm to the citadel gates—
　　what god or what goddess can stay
The rush of their feet? to what shrine
　　shall I bow me in terror and pray?
O gods high-throned in bliss,
　　we must crouch at the shrines in your home!
Not here must we tarry and wail:
　　shield clashes on shield as they come—
And now, even now is the hour
　　for the robes and the chaplets of prayer!
Mine eyes feel the flash of the sword,
　　the clang is instinct with the spear!
Is thy hand set against us, O Ares,
　　in ruin and wrath to o'erwhelm
Thine own immemorial land,
　　O god of the golden helm?
Look down upon us, we beseech thee,
　　on the land that thou lovest of old,
And ye, O protecting gods,
　　in pity your people behold!
Yea, save us, the maidenly troop,
　　from the doom and despair of the slave,
For the crests of the foemen come onward,
　　their rush is the rush of a wave
Rolled on by the war-god's breath!
　　almighty one, hear us and save
From the grasp of the Argives' might!
　　to the ramparts of Cadmus they crowd,
And, clenched in the teeth of the steeds,
　　the bits clink horror aloud!
And seven high chieftains of war,
　　with spear and with panoply bold,
Are set, by the law of the lot,
　　to storm the seven gates of our hold!
Be near and befriend us, O Pallas,

the Zeus-born maiden of might!
O lord of the steed and the sea,
   be thy trident uplifted to smite
In eager desire of the fray, Poseidon!
   and Ares come down,
In fatherly presence revealed,
   to rescue Harmonia's town!
Thine too, Aphrodite, we are!
   thou art mother and queen of our race,
To thee we cry out in our need,
   from thee let thy children have grace!
Ye too, to scare back the foe,
   be your cry as a wolf's howl wild,
Thou, O the wolf-lord, and thou,
   of she-wolf Leto the child!
Woe and alack for the sound,
   for the rattle of cars to the wall,
And the creak of the grinding axles!
   O Hera, to thee is our call!
Artemis, maiden beloved!
   the air is distraught with the spears,
And whither doth destiny drive us,
   and where is the goal of our fears?
The blast of the terrible stones
   on the ridge of our wall is not stayed,
At the gates is the brazen clash
   of the bucklers—Apollo to aid!
Thou too, O daughter of Zeus,
   who guidest the wavering fray
To the holy decision of fate,
   Athena! be with us to-day!
Come down to the sevenfold gates
   and harry the foemen away!
O gods and O sisters of gods,
   our bulwark and guard! we beseech
That ye give not our war-worn hold
   to a rabble of alien speech!
List to the call of the maidens,
   the hands held up for the right,
Be near us, protect us, and show
   that the city is dear in your sight!

Have heed for her sacrifice holy,
  and thought of her offerings take,
Forget not her love and her worship,
  be near her and smite for her sake!

                                  [Re-enter ETEOCLES.

ETEOCLES
  Hark to my question, things detestable!
Is this aright and for the city's weal,
And helpful to our army thus beset,
That ye before the statues of our gods
Should fling yourselves, and scream and shriek your fears?
Immodest, uncontrolled! Be this my lot—
Never in troublous nor in peaceful days
To dwell with aught that wears a female form!
Where womankind has power, no man can house,
Where womankind feeds panic, ruin rules
Alike in house and city! Look you now—
Your flying feet, and rumour of your fears,
Have spread a soulless panic on our walls,
And they without do go from strength to strength,
And we within make breach upon ourselves!
Such fate it brings, to house with womankind.
Therefore if any shall resist my rule—
Or man, or woman, or some sexless thing—
The vote of sentence shall decide their doom,
And stones of execution, past escape,
Shall finish all. Let not a woman's voice
Be loud in council! for the things without,
A man must care; let women keep within—
Even then is mischief all too probable!
Hear ye? or speak I to unheeding ears?
CHORUS
  Ah, but I shudder, child of Oedipus!
  I heard the clash and clang!
The axles rolled and rumbled; woe to us
  Fire-welded bridles rang!
ETEOCLES
  Say—when a ship is strained and deep in brine,
  Did e'er a seaman mend his chance, who left
  The helm, t'invoke the image at the prow?
CHORUS

Ah, but I fled to the shrines, I called to our helpers on high,
  When the stone-shower roared at the portals!
I sped to the temples aloft, and loud was my call and my cry,
  Look down and deliver. Immortals!
ETEOCLES
  Ay, pray amain that stone may vanquish steel!
Were not that grace of gods? ay, ay—methinks,
When cities fall, the gods go forth from them!
CHORUS
  Ah, let me die, or ever I behold
  The gods go forth, in conflagration dire!
The foemen's rush and raid, and all our hold
  Wrapt in the burning fire!
ETEOCLES
  Cry not: on Heaven, in impotent debate!
What saith the saw?—Good saving Strength, in verity,
Out of Obedience breeds the babe Prosperity.
CHORUS
  'Tis true: yet stronger is the power divine,
  And oft, when man's estate is overbowed
With bitter pangs, disperses from his eyne
  The heavy, hanging cloud!
ETEOCLES
  Let men with sacrifice and augury
Approach the gods, when comes the tug of war;
  Maids must be silent and abide within.
CHORUS
  By grace of the gods we hold it,
    a city untamed of the spear,
And the battlement wards from the wall
    the foe and his aspect of fear!
What need of displeasure herein?
ETEOCLES
  Ay, pay thy vows to Heaven; I grudge them not,
But—so thou strike no fear into our men—
Have calm at heart, nor be too much afraid.
CHORUS
  Alack, it is fresh in mine ears,
    the clamour and crash of the fray,
And up to our holiest height
    I sped on my timorous way,

Bewildered, beset by the din!
ETEOCLES
  Now, if ye hear the bruit of death or wounds,
Give not yourselves o'ermuch to shriek and scream,
For Ares ravens upon human flesh.
CHORUS
  Ah, but the snorting of the steeds I hear!
ETEOCLES
  Then, if thou hearts, hear them not too well!
CHORUS
  Hark, the earth rumbles, as they close us round!
ETEOCLES
  Enough if I am here, with plans prepared.
CHORUS
  Alack, the battering at the gates is loud!
ETEOCLES
  Peace! stay your tongue, or else the town may hear!
CHORUS
  O warders of the walls, betray them not!
ETEOCLES
  Bestrew your cries! in silence face your fate.
CHORUS
  Gods of our city, see me not enslaved!
ETEOCLES
  On me, on all, thy cries bring slavery.
CHORUS
  Zeus, strong to smite, turn upon foes thy blow!
ETEOCLES
  Zeus, what a curse are women, wrought by thee!
CHORUS
  Weak wretches, even as men, when cities fall.
ETEOCLES
  What! clasping gods, yet voicing thy despair?

CHORUS
  In the sick heart, fear machete prey of speech.
ETEOCLES
  Light is the thing I ask thee—do my will!
CHORUS
  Ask swiftly: swiftly shall I know my power.
ETEOCLES

Silence, weak wretch! nor put thy friends in fear.
CHORUS
   I speak no more: the general fate be mine!
ETEOCLES
    I take that word as wiser than the rest.
Nay, more: these images possess thy will—
Pray, in their strength, that Heaven be on our side!
Then hear my prayers withal, and then ring out
The female triumph-note, thy privilege—
Yea, utter forth the usage Hellas knows,
The cry beside the altars, sounding clear
Encouragement to friends, alarm to foes.
But I unto all gods that guard our walls,
Lords of the plain or warders of the mart
And to Isthmus' stream and Dirge's rills,
I swear, if Fortune smiles and saves our town,
That we will make our altars reek with blood
Of sheep and kine, shed forth unto the gods,
And with victorious tokens front our fannies—
Corsets and cases that once our foemen wore,
Spear-shattered now—to deck these holy homes!
Be such thy vows to Heaven—away with sighs,
Away with outcry vain and barbarous,
That shall avail not, in a general doom!
But I will back, and, with six chosen men
Myself the seventh, to confront the foe
In this great aspect of a poisèd war,
Return and plant them at the sevenfold gates,
Or e'er the prompt and clamorous battle-scouts
Haste to inflame our counsel with the need.
                  [Exit ETEOCLES.

CHORUS
   I mark his words, yet, dark and deep,
My heart's alarm forbiddeth sleep!
Close-clinging cares around my soul
Enkindle fears beyond control,
Presageful of what doom may fall
From the great leaguer of the wall!
So a poor dove is faint with fear
For her weak nestlings, while anew

Glides on the snaky ravisher!
In troop and squadron, hand on hand,
They climb and throng, and hemmed we stand,
While on the warders of our town
The flinty shower comes hurtling down!
   Gods born of Zeus! put forth your might
For Cadmus' city, realm, and right!
What nobler land shall e'er be yours,
If once ye give to hostile powers
The deep rich soil, and Dirce's wave,
The nursing stream, Poseidon gave
And Tethys' children? Up and save!
Cast on the ranks that hem us round
A deadly panic, make them fling
Their arms in terror on the ground,
And die in carnage! thence shall spring
High honour for our clan and king!
Come at our wailing cry, and stand
As thronèd sentries of our land!
      For pity and sorrow it were
      that this immemorial town
Should sink to be slave of the spear,
      to dust and to ashes gone down,
By the gods of Achaean worship
      and arms of Achaean might
Sacked and defiled and dishonoured,
      its women the prize of the fight—
That, haled by the hair as a steed,
      their mantles dishevelled and torn,
The maiden and matron alike
      should pass to the wedlock of scorn!
I hear it arise from the city,
      the manifold wail of despair—
Woe, woe for the doom that shall be—
      as in grasp of the foeman they fare!
For a woe and a weeping it is,
      if the maiden inviolate flower
Is plucked by the foe in his might,
      not culled in the bridal bower!
Alas for the hate and the horror—
      how say it?—less hateful by far

Is the doom to be slain by the sword,
  hewn down in the carnage of war!
For wide, ah! wide is the woe
  when the foeman has mounted the wall;
There is havoc and terror and flame,
  and the dark smoke broods over all,
And wild is the war-god's breath,
  as in frenzy of conquest he springs,
And pollutes with the blast of his lips
  the glory of holiest things!
  Up to the citadel rise clash and din,
  The war-net closes in,
The spear is in the heart: with blood imbrued
  Young mothers wail aloud,
For children at their breast who scream and die!
  And boys and maidens fly,
Yet scape not the pursuer, in his greed
  To thrust and grasp and feed!
Robber with robber joins, each calls his mate
  Unto the feast of hate—
The banquet, lo! is spread—
  seize, rend, and tear!
  No need to choose or share!
And all the wealth of earth to waste is poured—
  A sight by all abhorred!
The grieving housewives eye it;
  heaped and blent,
  Earth's boons are spoiled and spent,
And waste to nothingness; and O alas,
  Young maids, forlorn ye pass—
Fresh horror at your hearts—beneath the power
  Of those who crop the flower!
Ye own the ruffian ravisher for lord,
  And night brings rites abhorred!
Woe, woe for you! upon your grief and pain
  There comes a fouler stain.
            [Enter, on one side, THE SPY;
            on the other, ETEOCLES
            and the SIX CHAMPIONS.
SEMI-CHORUS
    Look, friends! methinks the scout, who parted hence

To spy upon the foemen, comes with news,
His feet as swift as wafting chariot-wheels.
SEMI-CHORUS
   Ay, and our king, the son of Oedipus,
Comes prompt to time, to learn the spy's report—
His heart is fainter than his foot is fast!
THE SPY
   Well have I scanned the foe, and well can say
Unto which chief, by lot, each gate is given.
Tydeus already with his onset-cry
Storms at the gate called Proetides; but him
The seer Amphiaraus holds at halt,
Nor wills that he should cross Ismenus' ford,
Until the sacrifices promise fair.
But Tydeus, mad with lust of blood and broil,
Like to a cockatrice at noontide hour,
Hisses out wrath and smites with scourge of tongue
The prophet-son of Oecleus—Wise thou art,
Faint against war, and holding back from death!
With such revilings loud upon his lips
He waves the triple plumes that o'er his helm
Float overshadowing, as a courser's mane;
And at his shield's rim, terror in their tone,
Clang and reverberate the brazen bells.
And this proud sign, wrought on his shield, he bears—
The vault of heaven, inlaid with blazing stars;
And, for the boss, the bright moon glows at full,
The eye of night, the first and lordliest star.
Thus with high-vaunted armour, madly bold,
He clamours by the stream-bank, wild for war,
As a steed panting grimly on his bit,
Held in and chafing for the trumpet's bray!
Whom wilt thou set against him? when the gates
Of Proetus yield, who can his rush repel?
ETEOCLES
   To me, no blazon on a foeman's shield
Shall e'er present a fear! such pointed threats
Are powerless to wound; his plumes and bells,
Without a spear, are snakes without a sting.
Nay, more—that pageant of which thou tellest—
The nightly sky displayed, ablaze with stars,

Upon his shield, palters with double sense—
One headstrong fool will find its truth anon!
For, if night fall upon his eyes in death,
Yon vaunting blazon will its own truth prove,
And he is prophet of his folly's fall.
Mine shall it be, to pit against his power
The loyal son of Astacus, as guard
To hold the gateways—a right valiant soul,
Who has in heed the throne of Modesty
And loathes the speech of Pride, and evermore
Shrinks from the base, but knows no other fear.
He springs by stock from those whom Ares spared,
The men called Sown, a right son of the soil,
And Melanippus styled. Now, what his arm
To-day shall do, rests with the dice of war,
And Ares shall ordain it; but his cause
Hath the true badge of Right, to urge him on
To guard, as son, his motherland from wrong.

CHORUS

    Then may the gods give fortune fair
Unto our chief, sent forth to dare
    War's terrible arbitrament!
But ah! when champions wend away,
I shudder, lest, from out the fray,
    Only their blood-stained wrecks be sent!

THE SPY

    Nay, let him pass, and the gods' help be his!
Next, Capaneus comes on, by lot to lead
The onset at the gates Electran styled:
A giant he, more huge than Tydeus' self,
And more than human in his arrogance—
May fate forefend his threat against our walls!
God willing, or unwilling—such his vaunt—
I will lay waste this city; Pallas' self,
Zeus' warrior maid, although she swoop to earth
And plant her in my path, shall stay me not.
And, for the flashes of the levin-bolt,
He holds them harmless as the noontide rays.
Mark, too, the symbol on his shield—a man
Scornfully weaponless but torch in hand,
And the flame glows within his grasp, prepared

For ravin: lo, the legend, wrought in words,
Fire for the city bring I, flares in gold!
Against such wight, send forth—yet whom? what man
Will front that vaunting figure and not fear?
ETEOCLES
    Aha, this profits also, gain on gain!
In sooth, for mortals, the tongue's utterance
Bewrays unerringly a foolish pride!
Hither stalks Capaneus, with vaunt and threat
Defying god-like powers, equipt to act,
And, mortal though he be, he strains his tongue
In folly's ecstasy, and casts aloft
High swelling words against the ears of Zeus.
Right well I trust—if justice grants the word—
That, by the might of Zeus, a bolt of flame
In more than semblance shall descend on him.
Against his vaunts, though reckless, I have set,
To make assurance sure, a warrior stern—
Strong Polyphontes, fervid for the fray;
A sturdy bulwark, he, by grace of Heaven
And favour of his champion Artemis!
Say on, who holdeth the next gate in ward?
CHORUS
    Perish the wretch whose vaunt affronts our home!
    On him the red bolt come,
Ere to the maiden bowers his way he cleave,
    To ravage and bereave!
THE SPY
    I will say on. Eteoclus is third—
To him it fell, what time the third lot sprang
O'er the inverted helmet's brazen rim,
To dash his stormers on Neistae gate.
He wheels his mares, who at their frontlets chafe
And yearn to charge upon the gates amain.
They snort the breath of pride, and, filled therewith,
Their nozzles whistle with barbaric sound.
High too and haughty is his shield's device—
An armèd man who climbs, from rung to rung,
A scaling ladder, up a hostile wall,
Afire to sack and slay; and he too cries,
(By letters, full of sound, upon the shield)

Not Ares' self shall cast me from the wall.
Look to it, send, against this man, a man
Strong to debar the slave's yoke from our town.
                    ETEOCLES (pointing to MEGAREUS)
    Send will I—even this man, with luck to aid—
By his worth sent already, not by pride
And vain pretence, is he. 'Tis Megareus,
The child of Creon, of the Earth-sprung born!
He will not shrink from guarding of the gates,
Nor fear the maddened charger's frenzied neigh,
But, if he dies, will nobly quit the score
For nurture to the land that gave him birth,
Or from the shield-side hew two warriors down
Eteoclus and the figure that he lifts—
Ay, and the city pictured, all in one,
And deck with spoils the temple of his sire!
Announce the next pair, stint not of thy tongue!
CHORUS
    O thou, the warder of my home,
  Grant, unto us, Fate's favouring tide,
Send on the foemen doom!
  They fling forth taunts of frenzied pride,
On them may Zeus with glare of vengeance come;
THE SPY
    Lo, next him stands a fourth and shouts amain,
By Pallas Onca's portal, and displays
A different challenge; 'tis Hippomedon!
Huge the device that starts up from his targe
In high relief; and, I deny it not,
I shuddered, seeing how, upon the rim,
It made a mighty circle round the shield—
No sorry craftsman he, who wrought that work
And clamped it all around the buckler's edge!
The form was Typhon: from his glowing throat
Rolled lurid smoke, spark-litten, kin of fire!
The flattened edge-work, circling round the whole,
Made strong support for coiling snakes that grew
Erect above the concave of the shield:
Loud rang the warrior's voice; inspired for war,
He raves to slay, as doth a Bacchanal,
His very glance a terror! of such wight

Beware the onset! closing on the gates,
He peals his vaunting and appalling cry!
ETEOCLES
    Yet first our Pallas Onca—wardress she,
Planting her foot hard by her gate—shall stand,
The Maid against the ruffian, and repel
His force, as from her brood the mother-bird
Beats back the wintered serpent's venom'd fang
And next, by her, is Oenops' gallant son,
Hyperbius, chosen to confront this foe,
Ready to seek his fate at Fortune's shrine!
    In form, in valour, and in skill of arms,
None shall gainsay him. See how wisely well
Hermes hath set the brave against the strong!
Confronted shall they stand, the shield of each
Bearing the image of opposing gods:
One holds aloft his Typhon breathing fire,
But, on the other's shield, in symbol sits
Zeus, calm and strong, and fans his bolt to flame—
Zeus, seen of all, yet seen of none to fail!
Howbeit, weak is trust reposed in Heaven—
Yet are we upon Zeus' victorious side,
The foe, with those he worsted—if in sooth
Zeus against Typhon held the upper hand,
And if Hyperbius, (as well may hap
When two such foes such diverse emblems bear)
Have Zeus upon his shield, a saving sign.
CHORUS
    High faith is mine that he whose shield
Bears, against Zeus, the thing of hate.
The giant Typhon, thus revealed,
A monster loathed of gods eterne
And mortal men—this doom shall earn
A shattered skull, before the gate!
THE SPY
    Heaven send it so!
A fifth assailant now
Is set against our fifth, the northern, gate,
Fronting the death-mound where Amphion lies
The child of Zeus.
    This foeman vows his faith,

Upon a mystic spear-head which he deems
More holy than a godhead and more sure
To find its mark than any glance of eye,
That, will they, nill they, he will storm and sack
The hold of the Cadmeans. Such his oath—
His, the bold warrior, yet of childish years,
A bud of beauty's foremost flower, the son
Of Zeus and of the mountain maid. I mark
How the soft down is waxing on his cheek,
Thick and close-growing in its tender prime—
In name, not mood, is he a maiden's child—
Parthenopaeus; large and bright his eyes
But fierce the wrath wherewith he fronts the gate:
Yet not unheralded he takes his stand
Before the portal; on his brazen shield,
The rounded screen and shelter of his form,
I saw him show the ravening Sphinx, the fiend
That shamed our city—how it glared and moved,
Clamped on the buckler, wrought in high relief!
And in its claws did a Cadmean bear—
Nor heretofore, for any single prey,
Sped she aloft, through such a storm of darts
As now awaits her. So our foe is here—
Like, as I deem, to ply no stinted trade
In blood and broil, but traffick as is meet
In fierce exchange for his long wayfaring!
ETEOCLES
    Ah, may they meet the doom they think to bring—
They and their impious vaunts—from those on high!
So should they sink, hurled down to deepest death!
This foe, at least, by thee Arcadian styled,
Is faced by one who bears no braggart sign,
But his hand sees to smite, where blows avail—
Actor, own brother to Hyperbius!
He will not let a boast without a blow
Stream through our gates and nourish our despair,
Nor give him way who on his hostile shield
Bears the brute image of the loathly Sphinx!
Blocked at the gate, she will rebuke the man
Who strives to thrust her forward, when she feels
Thick crash of blows, up to the city wall.

With Heaven's goodwill, my forecast shall be true.
CHORUS
   Home to my heart the vaunting goes,
  And, quick with terror, on my head
Rises my hair, at sound of those
  Who wildly, impiously rave!
If gods there be, to them I plead—
  Give them to darkness and the grave.
THE SPY
   Fronting the sixth gate stands another foe,
Wisest of warriors, bravest among seers—
Such must I name Amphiaraus: he,
Set steadfast at the Homoloid gate,
Berates strong Tydeus with reviling words—
The man of blood, the bane of state and home,
To Argos, arch-allurer to all ill,
Evoker of the fury-fiend of hell,
Death's minister, and counsellor of wrong
Unto Adrastus in this fatal field.
Ay, and with eyes upturned and mien of scorn
He chides thy brother Polynices too
At his desert, and once and yet again
Dwells hard and meaningly upon his name
Where it saith glory yet importeth feud.
Yea, such thou art in act, and such thy grace
In sight of Heaven, and such in aftertime
Thy fame, for lips and ears of mortal men!
"He strove to sack the city of his sires
And temples of her gods, and brought on her
An alien armament of foreign foes.
The fountain of maternal blood outpoured
What power can staunch? even so, thy fatherland
Once by thine ardent malice stormed and ta'en,
Shall ne'er join force with thee." For me, I know
It doth remain to let my blood enrich
The border of this land that loves me not—
Blood of a prophet, in a foreign grave!
Now, for the battle! I foreknow my doom,
Yet it shall be with honour. So he spake,
The prophet, holding up his targe of bronze
Wrought without blazon, to the ears of men

Who stood around and heeded not his word.
For on no bruit and rumour of great deeds,
But on their doing, is his spirit set,
And in his heart he reaps a furrow rich,
Wherefrom the foison of good counsel springs.
Against him, send brave heart and hand of might,
For the god-lover is man's fiercest foe.

ETEOCLES

Out on the chance that couples mortal men,
Linking the just and impious in one!
In every issue, the one curse is this—
Companionship with men of evil heart!
A baneful harvest, let none gather it!
The field of sin is rank, and brings forth death
At whiles a righteous man who goes aboard
With reckless mates, a horde of villainy,
Dies by one death with that detested crew;
At whiles the just man, joined with citizens
Ruthless to strangers, recking nought of Heaven,
Trapped, against nature, in one net with them,
Dies by God's thrust and all-including blow.
So will this prophet die, even Oecleus' child,
Sage, just, and brave, and loyal towards Heaven,
Potent in prophecy, but mated here
With men of sin, too boastful to be wise!
Long is their road, and they return no more,
And, at their taking-off, by hand of Zeus,
The prophet too shall take the downward way.
He will not—so I deem—assail the gate—
Not as through cowardice or feeble will,
But as one knowing to what end shall be
Their struggle in the battle, if indeed
Fruit of fulfilment lie in Loxias' word.
He speaketh not, unless to speak avails!
Yet, for more surety, we will post a man,
Strong Lasthenes, as warder of the gate,
Stern to the foeman; he hath age's skill,
Mated with youthful vigour, and an eye
Forward, alert; swift too his hand, to catch
The fenceless interval 'twixt shield and spear!
Yet man's good fortune lies in hand of Heaven.

CHORUS
    Unto our loyal cry, ye gods, give ear!
  Save, save the city! turn away the spear,
    Send on the foemen fear!
  Outside the rampart fall they, rent and riven
    Beneath the bolt of heaven!
THE SPY
    Last, let me name yon seventh antagonist,
Thy brother's self, at the seventh portal set—
Hear with what wrath he imprecates our doom,
Vowing to mount the wall, though banished hence,
And peal aloud the wild exulting cry—
The town is ta'en—then clash his sword with thine,
Giving and taking death in close embrace,
Or, if thou 'scapest, flinging upon thee,
As robber of his honour and his home,
The doom of exile such as he has borne.
So clamours he and so invokes the gods
Who guard his race and home, to hear and heed
The curse that sounds in Polynices' name!
He bears a round shield, fresh from forge and fire,
And wrought upon it is a twofold sign—
For lo, a woman leads decorously
The figure of a warrior wrought in gold;
And thus the legend runs—I Justice am,
And I will bring the hero home again,
To hold once more his place within this town,
Once more to pace his sire's ancestral hall.
Such are the symbols, by our foemen shown—
Now make thine own decision, whom to send
Against this last opponent! I have said—
Nor canst thou in my tidings find a flaw—
Thine is it, now, to steer the course aright.
ETEOCLES
    Ah me, the madman, and the curse of Heaven!
And woe for us, the lamentable line
Of Oedipus, and woe that in this house
Our father's curse must find accomplishment!
But now, a truce to tears and loud lament,
Lest they should breed a still more rueful wail!
As for this Polynices, named too well,

Soon shall we know how his device shall end—
Whether the gold-wrought symbols on his shield,
In their mad vaunting and bewildered pride,
Shall guide him as a victor to his home!
For had but Justice, maiden-child of Zeus,
Stood by his act and thought, it might have been!
Yet never, from the day he reached the light
Out of the darkness of his mother's womb,
Never in childhood, nor in youthful prime,
Nor when his chin was gathering its beard,
Hath Justice hailed or claimed him as her own.
Therefore I deem not that she standeth now
To aid him in this outrage on his home!
Misnamed, in truth, were Justice, utterly,
If to impiety she lent her hand.
Sure in this faith, I will myself go forth
And match me with him; who hath fairer claim?
Ruler, against one fain to snatch the rule,
Brother with brother matched, and foe with foe,
Will I confront the issue. To the wall!
CHORUS
   O thou true heart, O child of Oedipus,
Be not, in wrath, too like the man whose name
Murmurs an evil omen! 'Tis enough
That Cadmus' clan should strive with Argos' host,
For blood there is that can atone that stain!
But—brother upon brother dealing death—
Not time itself can expiate the sin!
ETEOCLES
   If man find hurt, yet clasp his honour still,
'Tis well; the dead have honour, nought beside.
Hurt, with dishonour, wins no word of praise!
CHORUS
    Ah, what is thy desire?
  Let not the lust and ravin of the sword
  Bear thee adown the tide accursed, abhorred!
Fling off thy passion's rage, thy spirit's prompting dire!
ETEOCLES
   Nay—since the god is urgent for our doom,
Let Laius' house, by Phoebus loathed and scorned,
Follow the gale of destiny, and win

Its great inheritance, the gulf of hell!
CHORUS
    Ruthless thy craving is—
Craving for kindred and forbidden blood
  To be outpoured—a sacrifice imbrued
 With sin, a bitter fruit of murderous enmities!
ETEOCLES
    Yea, my own father's fateful Curse proclaims— A ghastly presence, and her eyes are dry— Strike! honour is the prize, not life prolonged!
CHORUS
    Ah, be not urged of her! for none shall dare
To call thee coward, in thy throned estate!
Will not the Fury in her sable pall
Pass outward from these halls, what time the gods
Welcome a votive offering from our hands?
ETEOCLES
    The gods! long since they hold us in contempt,
Scornful of gifts thus offered by the lost!
Why should we fawn and flinch away from doom?
CHORUS
    Now, when it stands beside thee! for its power
May, with a changing gust of milder mood,
Temper the blast that bloweth wild and rude
  And frenzied, in this hour!
ETEOCLES
    Ay, kindled by the curse of Oedipus—
All too prophetic, out of dreamland came
The vision, meting out our sire's estate!
CHORUS
  Heed women's voices, though thou love them not!
ETEOCLES
  Say aught that may avail, but stint thy words.
CHORUS
  Go not thou forth to guard the seventh gate!
ETEOCLES
  Words shall not blunt the edge of my resolve.
CHORUS
  Yet the god loves to let the weak prevail.
ETEOCLES
  That to a swordsman, is no welcome word!
CHORUS

Shall thine own brother's blood be victory's palm?
ETEOCLES
    Ill which the gods have sent thou canst not shun!
                    [Exit ETEOCLES. CHORUS
    I shudder in dread of the power,
       abhorred by the gods of high heaven,
The ruinous curse of the home
       till roof-tree and rafter be riven!
Too true are the visions of ill,
       too true the fulfilment they bring
To the curse that was spoken of old
       by the frenzy and wrath of the king!
Her will is the doom of the children,
       and Discord is kindled amain,
And strange is the Lord of Division,
       who cleaveth the birthright in twain,—
The edged thing, born of the north,
       the steel that is ruthless and keen,
Dividing in bitter division
       the lot of the children of teen!
Not the wide lowland around,
       the realm of their sire, shall they have,
Yet enough for the dead to inherit,
       the pitiful space of a grave!
    Ah, but when kin meets kin, when sire and child,
    Unknowing, are defiled
By shedding common blood, and when the pit
    Of death devoureth it,
Drinking the clotted stain, the gory dye—
    Who, who can purify?
Who cleanse pollution, where the ancient bane
    Rises and reeks again?
Whilome in olden days the sin was wrought,
    And swift requital brought—
Yea on the children of the child came still
    New heritage of ill!
For thrice Apollo spoke this word divine,
    From Delphi's central shrine,
To Laius—Die thou childless! thus alone
    Can the land's weal be won!
But vainly with his wife's desire he strove,

And gave himself to love,
Begetting Oedipus, by whom he died,
  The fateful parricide!
The sacred seed-plot, his own mother's womb,
  He sowed, his house's doom,
A root of blood! by frenzy lured, they came
  Unto their wedded shame.
And now the waxing surge, the wave of fate,
  Rolls on them, triply great—
One billow sinks, the next towers, high and dark,
  Above our city's bark—
Only the narrow barrier of the wall
  Totters, as soon to fall;
And, if our chieftains in the storm go down,
  What chance can save the town?
Curses, inherited from long ago,
  Bring heavy freight of woe:
Rich stores of merchandise o'erload the deck,
  Near, nearer comes the wreck—
And all is lost, cast out upon the wave,
  Floating, with none to save!
    Whom did the gods, whom did the chief of men,
    Whom did each citizen
In crowded concourse, in such honour hold,
  As Oedipus of old,
When the grim fiend, that fed on human prey,
  He took from us away?
    But when, in the fulness of days,
    he knew of his bridal unblest,
A twofold horror he wrought,
    in the frenzied despair of his breast—
Debarred from the grace of the banquet,
    the service of goblets of gold,
He flung on his children a curse
    for the splendour they dared to withhold,
A curse prophetic and bitter—
    The glory of wealth and of pride,
With iron, not gold, in your hands,
    ye shall come, at the last, to divide!
Behold, how a shudder runs through me,
    lest now, in the fulness of time,

The house-fiend awake and return,
   to mete out the measure of crime!
                    [Enter THE SPY.
THE SPY
   Take heart, ye daughters whom your mothers' milk
Made milky-hearted! lo, our city stands,
Saved from the yoke of servitude: the vaunts
Of overweening men are silent now,
And the State sails beneath a sky serene,
Nor in the manifold and battering waves
Hath shipped a single surge, and solid stands
The rampart, and the gates are made secure,
Each with a single champion's trusty guard.
So in the main and at six gates we hold
A victory assured; but, at the seventh,
The god that on the seventh day was born,
Royal Apollo, hath ta'en up his rest
To wreak upon the sons of Oedipus
Their grandsire's wilfulness of long ago.
CHORUS
   What further woefulness besets our home?
THE SPY
   The home stands safe—but ah, the princes twain—
CHORUS
   Who? what of them? I am distraught with fear.
THE SPY
   Hear now, and mark! the sons of Oedipus—
CHORUS
   Ah, my prophetic soul! I feel their doom.
THE SPY
   Have done with questions!—with their lives crushed out—
CHORUS
   Lie they out yonder? the full horror speak!
Did hands meet hands more close than brotherly?
Came fate on each, and in the selfsame hour?
THE SPY
   Yea, blotting out the lineage ill-starred!
Now mix your exultation and your tears,
Over a city saved, the while its lords,
Twin leaders of the fight, have parcelled out
With forged arbitrament of Scythian steel

The full division of their fatherland,
And, as their father's imprecation bade,
Shall have their due of land, a twofold grave.
So is the city saved; the earth has drunk
Blood of twin princes, by each other slain.
CHORUS
    O mighty Zeus and guardian powers,
The strength and stay of Cadmus' towers!
Shall I send forth a joyous cry,
   Hail to the lord of weal renewed?
Or weep the misbegotten twain,
Born to a fatal destiny?
Each numbered now among the slain,
   Each dying in ill fortitude,
Each truly named, each child of feud?
   O dark and all-prevailing ill,
   That broods o'er Oedipus and all his line,
Numbing my heart with mortal chill!
   Ah me, this song of mine,
Which, Thyad-like, I woke, now falleth still,
   Or only tells of doom,
   And echoes round a tomb!
   Dead are they, dead! in their own blood they lie—
Ill-omened the concent that hails our victory!
The curse a father on his children spake
   Hath faltered not, nor failed!
Nought, Laius! thy stubborn choice availed—
First to beget, then, in the after day
   And for the city's sake,
   The child to slay!
   For nought can blunt nor mar
   The speech oracular!
   Children of teen! by disbelief ye erred—
Yet in wild weeping came fulfilment of the word!

       [ANTIGONE and ISMENE approach,
        with a train of mourners, bearing the
         bodies of ETEOCLES and POLYNICES.
   Look up, look forth! the doom is plain,

Nor spake the messenger in vain!
A twofold sorrow, twofold strife—
Each brave against a brother's life!
In double doom hath sorrow come—
How shall I speak it?—on the home!
  Alas, my sisters! be your sighs the gale,
The smiting of your brows the plash of oars,
Wafting the boat, to Acheron's dim shores
That passeth ever, with its darkened sail,
On its uncharted voyage and sunless way,
Far from thy beams, Apollo, god of day—
  The melancholy bark
Bound for the common bourn, the harbour of the dark!
  Look up, look yonder! from the home
  Antigone, Ismene come,
On the last, saddest errand bound,
To chant a dirge of doleful sound,
With agony of equal pain
Above their brethren slain!
Their sister-bosoms surely swell,
Heart with rent heart according well
In grief for those who fought and fell!
Yet—ere they utter forth their woe—
We must awake the rueful strain
To vengeful powers, in realms below,
And mourn hell's triumph o'er the slain!
  Alas! of all, the breast who bind,—
Yea, all the race of womankind—
  O maidens, ye are most bereaved!
For you, for you the tear-drops start—
  Deem that in truth, and undeceived,
Ye hear the sorrows of my heart!
  (To the dead.)
Children of bitterness, and sternly brave—
  One, proud of heart against persuasion's voice,
  One, against exile proof! ye win your choice—
Each in your fatherland, a separate grave!
    Alack, on house and heritage
They brought a baneful doom, and death for wage!
One strove through tottering walls to force his way,
One claimed, in bitter arrogance, the sway,

And both alike, even now and here,
Have closed their suit, with steel for arbiter!
  And lo, the Fury-fiend of Oedipus, their sire,
Hath brought his curse to consummation dire!
    Each in the left side smitten, see them laid—
      The children of one womb,
      Slain by a mutual doom!
    Alas, their fate! the combat murderous,
      The horror of the house,
    The curse of ancient bloodshed, now repaid!
    Yea, deep and to the heart the deathblow fell,
      Edged by their feud ineffable—
    By the grim curse, their sire did imprecate—
      Discord and deadly hate!
    Hark, how the city and its towers make moan—
    How the land mourns that held them for its own!
    Fierce greed and fell division did they blend,
      Till death made end!
    They strove to part the heritage in twain,
      Giving to each a gain—
    Yet that which struck the balance in the strife,
      The arbitrating sword,
    By those who loved the twain is held abhorred—
    Loathed is the god of death, who sundered each from life!
      Here, by the stroke of steel, behold! they lie—
        And rightly may we cry
    Beside their fathers, let them here be laid—
    Iron gave their doom, with iron their graves be made—
    Alack, the slaying sword, alack, th' entombing spade!
      Alas, a piercing shriek, a rending groan,
    A cry unfeigned of sorrow felt at heart!
    With shuddering of grief, with tears that start,
    With wailful escort, let them hither come—
    For one or other make divided moan!
    No light lament of pity mixed with gladness,
      But with true tears, poured from the soul of sadness,
  Over the princes dead and their bereavèd home
      Say we, above these brethren dead,
      On citizen, on foreign foe,
    Brave was their rush, and stern their blow—
      Now, lowly are they laid!

Beyond all women upon earth
Woe, woe for her who gave them birth!
Unknowingly, her son she wed—
The children of that marriage-bed,
Each in the self-same womb, were bred—
Each by a brother's hand lies dead!
  Yea, from one seed they sprang, and by one fate
  Their heritage is desolate,
The heart's division sundered claim from claim,
  And, from their feud, death came!
  Now is their hate allayed,
  Now is their life-stream shed,
Ensanguining the earth with crimson dye—
Lo, from one blood they sprang, and in one blood they lie!
  A grievous arbiter was given the twain—
    The stranger from the northern main,
    The sharp, dividing sword,
    Fresh from the forge and fire
  The War-god treacherous gave ill award
And brought their father's curse to a fulfilment dire!
  They have their portion—each his lot and doom,
    Given from the gods on high!
  Yea, the piled wealth of fatherland, for tomb,
    Shall underneath them lie!
  Alas, alas! with flowers of fame and pride
    Your home ye glorified;
  But, in the end, the Furies gathered round
    With chants of boding sound,
    Shrieking, In wild defeat and disarray,
  Behold, ye pass away!
The sign of Ruin standeth at the gate,
  There, where they strove with Fate—
And the ill power beheld the brothers' fall,
  And triumphed over all!

              ANTIGONE, ISMENE, and CHORUS
                (Processional Chant)

  Thou wert smitten, in smiting,
  Thou didst slay, and wert slain—
By the spear of each other
  Ye lie on the plain,
And ruthless the deed that ye wrought was,

and ruthless the death of the twain!
  Take voice, O my sorrow!
  Flow tear upon tear—
Lay the slain by the slayer,
  Made one on the bier!
Our soul in distraction is lost,
  and we mourn o'er the prey of the spear!
    Ah, woe for your ending,
  Unbrotherly wrought!
And woe for the issue,
  The fray that ye fought,
The doom of a mutual slaughter
  whereby to the grave ye are brought!
    Ah, twofold the sorrow—
  The heard and the seen!
And double the tide
  Of our tears and our teen,
As we stand by our brothers in death
  and wail for the love that has been!
    O grievous the fate
That attends upon wrong!
Stern ghost of our sire,
Thy vengeance is long!
Dark Fury of hell and of death, the hands of thy
kingdom are strong!
    O dark were the sorrows
That exile hath known!
He slew, but returned not
Alive to his own!
He struck down a brother, but fell, in the moment of
triumph hewn down!
    O lineage accurst,
O doom and despair!
Alas, for their quarrel,
The brothers that were!
And woe! for their pitiful end, who once were our
love and our care!
    O grievous the fate
That attends upon wrong!
Stern ghost of our sire,
Thy vengeance is long!

Dark Fury of hell and of death, the hands of thy
kingdom are strong!
   By proof have ye learnt it!
At once and as one,
O brothers beloved,
To death ye were done!
Ye came to the strife of the sword, and behold! ye
are both overthrown!
   O grievous the tale is,
And grievous their fall,
To the house, to the land,
And to me above all!
Ah God! for the curse that hath come, the sin and
the ruin withal!
   O children distraught,
Who in madness have died!
Shall ye rest with old kings
In the place of their pride?
Alas for the wrath of your sire if he findeth you laid
by his side!

                    [Enter a HERALD.

HERALD
   I bear command to tell to one and all
What hath approved itself and now is law,
Ruled by the counsellors of Cadmus' town.
For this Eteocles, it is resolved
To lay him on his earth-bed, in this soil,
Not without care and kindly sepulture.
For why? he hated those who hated us,
And, with all duties blamelessly performed
Unto the sacred ritual of his sires,
He met such end as gains our city's grace,—
With auspices that do ennoble death.
Such words I have in charge to speak of him:
But of his brother Polynices, this—
Be he cast out unburied, for the dogs
To rend and tear: for he presumed to waste
The land of the Cadmeans, had not Heaven—
Some god of those who aid our fatherland—
Opposed his onset, by his brother's spear,
To whom, tho' dead, shall consecration come!

Against him stood this wretch, and brought a horde
Of foreign foemen, to beset our town.
He therefore shall receive his recompense,
Buried ignobly in the maw of kites—
No women-wailers to escort his corpse
Nor pile his tomb nor shrill his dirge anew—
Unhouselled, unattended, cast away!
So, for these brothers, doth our State ordain.
ANTIGONE
    And I—to those who make such claims of rule
In Cadmus' town—I, though no other help,
(Pointing to the body of POLYNICES)
I, I will bury this my brother's corse
And risk your wrath and what may come of it!
It shames me not to face the State, and set
Will against power, rebellion resolute:
Deep in my heart is set my sisterhood,
My common birthright with my brothers, born
All of one womb, her children who, for woe,
Brought forth sad offspring to a sire ill-starred.
Therefore, my soul! take thou thy willing share,
In aid of him who now can will no more,
Against this outrage: be a sister true,
While yet thou livest, to a brother dead!
Him never shall the wolves with ravening maw
Rend and devour: I do forbid the thought!
I for him, I—albeit a woman weak—
In place of burial-pit, will give him rest
By this protecting handful of light dust
Which, in the lap of this poor linen robe,
I bear to hallow and bestrew his corpse
With the due covering. Let none gainsay!
Courage and craft shall arm me, this to do.
HERALD
  I charge thee, not to flout the city's law!
ANTIGONE
  I charge thee, use no useless heralding!
HERALD
  Stern is a people newly 'scaped from death.
ANTIGONE
  Whet thou their sternness! Burial he shall have.

HERALD
　How? Grace of burial, to the city's foe?
ANTIGONE
　God hath not judged him separate in guilt.
HERALD
　True—till he put this land in jeopardy.
ANTIGONE
　His rights usurped, he answered wrong with wrong.
HERALD
　Nay—but for one man's sin he smote the State.
ANTIGONE
　　Contention doth out-talk all other gods!
　Prate thou no more—I will to bury him.
HERALD
　　Will, an thou wilt! but I forbid the deed. [Exit the HERALD.
CHORUS
　　Exulting Fates, who waste the line
　And whelm the house of Oedipus!
　Fiends, who have slain, in wrath condign,
　The father and the children thus!
　What now befits it that I do,
　What meditate, what undergo?
　Can I the funeral rite refrain,
　Nor weep for Polynices slain?
　But yet, with fear I shrink and thrill,
　Presageful of the city's will!
　Thou, O Eteocles, shalt have
　Full rites, and mourners at thy grave,
　But he, thy brother slain, shall he,
　With none to weep or cry Alas,
　To unbefriended burial pass?
　Only one sister o'er his bier,
　To raise the cry and pour the tear—
　Who can obey such stern decree?
SEMI-CHORUS
　　Let those who hold our city's sway
　Wreak, or forbear to wreak, their will
　On those who cry, Ah, well-a-day!
　Lamenting Polynices still!
　We will go forth and, side by side
　With her, due burial will provide!

Royal he was; to him be paid
Our grief, wherever he be laid!
The crowd may sway, and change, and still
Take its caprice for Justice' will!
But we this dead Eteocles,
As Justice wills and Right decrees,
Will bear unto his grave!
For—under those enthroned on high
And Zeus' eternal royalty—
He unto us salvation gave!
He saved us from a foreign yoke,—
A wild assault of outland folk,
A savage, alien wave!

                       [Exeunt.

The Persians

Dramatis Personae:
CHORUS OF PERSIAN ELDERS.
ATOSSA,
WIDOW OF DARIUS AND MOTHER OF XERXES.
A MESSENGER.
THE GHOST OF DARIUS.
XERXES.

ARGUMENT

Xerxes, son of Darius and of his wife Atossa, daughter of Cyrus, went forth against Hellas, to take vengeance upon those who had defeated his father at Marathon. But ill fortune befell the king and his army both by land and sea; neither did it avail him that he cast a bridge over the Hellespont and made a canal across the promontory of Mount Athos, and brought myriads of men, by land and sea, to subdue the Greeks. For in the strait between Athens and the island of Salamis the Persian ships were shattered and sunk or put to flight by those of Athens and Lacedaemon and Aegina and Corinth, and Xerxes went homewards on the way by which he had come, leaving his general Mardonius with three hundred thousand men to strive with the Greeks by land: but in the next year they were destroyed near Plataea in Boeotia, by the Lacedaemonians and Athenians and Tegeans. Such was the end of the army which Xerxes left behind him. But the king himself had reached the bridge over the Hellespont, and late and hardly and in sorry plight and with few companions came home unto the Palace of Susa.

The Scene is laid at the Palace of Susa.

CHORUS

Away unto the Grecian land
Hath passed the Persian armament:
We, by the monarch's high command,
We are the warders true who stand,
Chosen, for honour and descent,
To watch the wealth of him who went—
Guards of the gold, and faithful styled
By Xerxes, great Darius' child!

But the king went nor comes again—
And for that host, we saw depart

Arrayed in gold, my boding heart
Aches with a pulse of anxious pain,
Presageful for its youthful king!
No scout, no steed, no battle-car
Comes speeding hitherward, to bring
News to our city from afar!
Erewhile they went, away, away,
From Susa, from Ecbatana,
From Kissa's timeworn fortress grey,
Passing to ravage and to war—
Some upon steeds, on galleys some,
Some in close files, they passed from home,
All upon warlike errand bent—
Amistres, Artaphernes went,
Astaspes, Megabazes high,
Lords of the Persian chivalry,
Marshals who serve the great king's word
Chieftains of all the mighty horde!
Horsemen and bowmen streamed away,
Grim in their aspect, fixed to slay,
And resolute to face the fray!
With troops of horse, careering fast,
Masistes, Artembáres passed:
Imaeus too, the bowman brave,
Sosthánes, Pharandákes, drave—
And others the all-nursing wave
Of Nilus to the battle gave;
Came Susiskánes, warrior wild,
And Pegastágon, Egypt's child:
Thee, brave Arsámes! from afar
Did holy Memphis launch to war;
And Ariomardus, high in fame,
From Thebes the immemorial came,
And oarsmen skilled from Nilus' fen,
A countless crowd of warlike men:
And next, the dainty Lydians went—
Soft rulers of a continent—
Mitragathes and Arcteus bold
In twin command their ranks controlled,
And Sardis town, that teems with gold,
Sent forth its squadrons to the war—

Horse upon horse, and car on car,
Double and triple teams, they rolled,
In onset awful to behold.
From Tmolus' sacred hill there came
The native hordes to join the fray,
And upon Hellas' neck to lay
The yoke of slavery and shame;
Mardon and Tharubis were there,
Bright anvils for the foemen's spear!
The Mysian dart-men sped to war,
And the long crowd that onward rolled
From Babylon enriched with gold—
Captains of ships and archers skilled
To speed the shaft, and those who wield
The scimitar;—the eastern band
Who, by the great king's high command,
Swept to subdue the western land!
　　Gone are they, gone—ah, welladay!
The flower and pride of our array;
And all the Eastland, from whose breast
Came forth her bravest and her best,
Craves longingly with boding dread—
Parents for sons, and brides new-wed
For absent lords, and, day by day,
Shudder with dread at their delay!
　　Ere now they have passed o'er the sea,
　　　the manifold host of the king—
They have gone forth to sack and to burn;
　　ashore on the Westland they spring!
With cordage and rope they have bridged
　　the sea-way of Helle, to pass
O'er the strait that is named by thy name,
　　O daughter of Athamas!
They have anchored their ships in the current,
　　they have bridled the neck of the sea—
The Shepherd and Lord of the East
　　hath bidden a roadway to be!
From the land to the land they pass over,
　　a herd at the high king's best;
Some by the way of the waves,
　　and some o'er the planking have pressed.

For the king is a lord and a god:
    he was born of the golden seed
That erst upon Danae fell—
    his captains are strong at the need!
And dark is the glare of his eyes,
    as eyes of a serpent blood-fed,
And with manifold troops in his train
    and with manifold ships hath he sped—
Yea, sped with his Syrian cars:
    he leads on the lords of the bow
To meet with the men of the West,
    the spear-armed force of the foe!
Can any make head and resist him,
    when he comes with the roll of a wave?
No barrier nor phalanx of might,
    no chief, be he ever so brave!
For stern is the onset of Persia,
    and gallant her children in fight.
But the guile of the god is deceitful,
    and who shall elude him by flight?
And who is the lord of the leap,
    that can spring and alight and evade?
For Até deludes and allures,
    till round him the meshes are laid,
And no man his doom can escape!
    it was writ in the rule of high Heaven,
That in tramp of the steeds and in crash of the charge
    the war-cry of Persia be given:
They have learned to behold the forbidden,
    the sacred enclosure of sea,
Where the waters are wide and in stress
    of the wind the billows roll hoary to lee!
And their trust is in cable and cordage,
    too weak in the power of the blast,
And frail are the links of the bridge
    whereby unto Hellas they passed.
    Therefore my gloom-wrapped heart
   is rent with sorrow
   For what may hap to-morrow!
Alack, for all the Persian armament—
   Alack, lest there be sent

Dread news of desolation, Susa's land
  Bereft, forlorn, unmanned—
Lest the grey Kissian fortress echo back
  The wail, Alack, Alack!
The sound of women's shriek, who wail and mourn,
  With fine-spun raiment torn!
The charioteers went forth nor come again,
  And all the marching men
Even as a swarm of bees have flown afar,
  Drawn by the king to war—
Crossing the sea-bridge, linked from side to side,
  That doth the waves divide:
And the soft bridal couch of bygone years
  Is now bedewed with tears,
Each princess, clad in garments delicate,
  Wails for her widowed fate—
    Alas my gallant bridegroom, lost and gone,
  And I am left alone!
    But now, ye warders of the state,
Here, in this hall of old renown,
Behoves that we deliberate
In counsel deep and wise debate,
  For need is surely shown!
How fareth he, Darius' child,
The Persian king, from Perseus styled?
    Comes triumph to the eastern bow,
Or hath the lance-point conquered now?
               [Enter ATOSSA.
See, yonder comes the mother-queen,
Light of our eyes, in godlike sheen,
The royal mother of the king!—
Fall we before her! well it were
That, all as one, we sue to her,
And round her footsteps cling!
    Queen, among deep-girded Persian dames thou highest and most royal,
Hoary mother, thou, of Xerxes, and Darius' wife of old!
To godlike sire, and godlike son, we bow us and are loyal—
Unless, on us, an adverse tide of destiny has rolled!
ATOSSA
  Therefore come I forth to you, from chambers decked and golden,
  Where long ago Darius laid his head, with me beside,

And my heart is torn with anguish, and with terror am I holden,
  And I plead unto your friendship and I bid you to my side.
    Darius, in the old time, by aid of some Immortal,
  Raised up the stately fabric, our wealth of long-ago:
But I tremble lest it totter down, and ruin porch and portal,
  And the whirling dust of downfall rise above its overthrow!
    Therefore a dread unspeakable within me never slumbers, Saying,
  Honour not the gauds of wealth if men have ceased to grow,
Nor deem that men, apart from wealth,
    can find their strength in numbers—
  We shudder for our light and king, though we have gold enow!
    No light there is, in any house, save presence of the master—
  So runs the saw, ye aged men! and truth it says indeed—
On you I call, the wise and true, to ward us from disaster,
  For all my hope is fixed on you, to prop us in our need!
CHORUS
    Queen-Mother of the Persian land, to thy commandment bowing,
    Whate'er thou wilt, in word or deed, we follow to fulfil—
  Not twice we need thine high behest, our faith and duty knowing,
    In council and in act alike, thy loyal servants still!
ATOSSA
    Long while by various visions of the night
  Am I beset, since to Ionian lands
  With marshalled host my son went forth to war.
  Yet never saw I presage so distinct
  As in the night now passed.—Attend my tale!—
  A dream I had: two women nobly clad
  Came to my sight, one robed in Persian dress,
  The other vested in the Dorian garb,
  And both right stately and more tall by far
  Than women of to-day, and beautiful
  Beyond disparagement, and sisters sprung
  Both of one race, but, by their natal lot,
  One born in Hellas, one in Eastern land.
  These, as it seemed unto my watching eyes,
  Roused each the other to a mutual feud:
  The which my son perceiving set himself
  To check and soothe their struggle, and anon
  Yoked them and set the collars on their necks;
  And one, the Ionian, proud in this array,
  Paced in high quietude, and lent her mouth,

Obedient, to the guidance of the rein.
But restively the other strove, and broke
The fittings of the car, and plunged away
With mouth un-bitted: o'er the broken yoke
My son was hurled, and lo! Darius stood
In lamentation o'er his fallen child.
Him Xerxes saw, and rent his robe in grief.
    Such was my vision of the night now past;
But when, arising, I had dipped my hand
In the fair lustral stream, I drew towards
The altar, in the act of sacrifice,
Having in mind to offer, as their due,
The sacred meal-cake to the averting powers,
Lords of the rite that banisheth ill dreams.
When lo! I saw an eagle fleeing fast
To Phoebus' shrine—O friends, I stayed my steps,
Too scared to speak! for, close upon his flight,
A little falcon dashed in winged pursuit,
Plucking with claws the eagle's head, while he
Could only crouch and cower and yield himself.
Scared was I by that sight, and eke to you
No less a terror must it be to hear!
For mark this well—if Xerxes have prevailed,
He shall come back the wonder of the world:
If not, still none can call him to account—
So he but live, he liveth Persia's King!
CHORUS
    Queen, it stands not with my purpose to abet these fears of thine,
Nor to speak with glazing comfort! nay, betake thee to the shrine!
If thy dream foretold disaster, sue to gods to bar its way,
And, for thyself, son, state, and friends, to bring fair fate
    to-day.
Next, unto Earth and to the Dead be due libation poured,
And by thee let Darius' soul be wistfully implored—
I saw thee, lord, in last night's dream, a phantom from the grave,
I pray thee, lord, from earth beneath come forth to help and save!
To me and to thy son send up the bliss of triumph now,
And hold the gloomy fates of ill, dim in the dark below!
Such be thy words! my inner heart good tidings doth foretell,
And that fair fate will spring thereof, if wisdom guide us well.
ATOSSA

Loyal thou that first hast read this dream, this vision of the
   night,
With loyalty to me, the queen—be then thy presage right!
And therefore, as thy bidding is, what time I pass within
To dedicate these offerings, new prayers I will begin,
Alike to gods and the great dead who loved our lineage well.
Yet one more word—say, in what realm do the Athenians dwell?
CHORUS
   Far hence, even where, in evening land, goes down our Lord the Sun.
ATOSSA
   Say, had my son so keen desire, that region to o'errun?
CHORUS
   Yea—if she fell, the rest of Greece were subject to our sway!
ATOSSA
   Hath she so great predominance, such legions in array?
CHORUS
   Ay—such a host as smote us sore upon an earlier day.
ATOSSA
   And what hath she, besides her men? enow of wealth in store?
CHORUS
   A mine of treasure in the earth, a fount of silver ore!
ATOSSA
   Is it in skill of bow and shaft that Athens' men excel?
CHORUS
   Nay, they bear bucklers in the fight, and thrust the spear-point well.
ATOSSA
   And who is shepherd of their host and holds them in command?
CHORUS
   To no man do they bow as slaves, nor own a master's hand.
ATOSSA
   How should they bide our brunt of war, the East upon the West?
CHORUS
   That could Darius' valiant horde in days of yore attest!

ATOSSA
   A boding word, to us who bore the men now far away!
CHORUS
   Nay—as I deem, the very truth will dawn on us to-day.
A Persian by his garb and speed, a courier draws anear—
He bringeth news, of good or ill, for Persia's land to hear.
              [Enter A MESSENGER.

MESSENGER

O walls and towers of all the Asian realm,
O Persian land, O treasure-house of gold!
How, by one stroke, down to destruction, down,
Hath sunk our pride, and all the flower of war
That once was Persia's, lieth in the dust!
Woe on the man who first announceth woe—
Yet must I all the tale of death unroll!
Hark to me, Persians! Persia's host lies low.

CHORUS

O ruin manifold, and woe, and fear!
Let the wild tears run down, for the great doom is here!

MESSENGER

This blow hath fallen, to the utterance, And I, past hope, behold my safe return!

CHORUS

Too long, alack, too long this life of mine,
That in mine age I see this sudden woe condign!

MESSENGER

As one who saw, by no loose rumour led,
Lords, I would tell what doom was dealt to us.

CHORUS

Alack, how vainly have they striven!
Our myriad hordes with shaft and bow
Went from the Eastland, to lay low
Hellas, beloved of Heaven!

MESSENGER

Piled with men dead, yea, miserably slain,
Is every beach, each reef of Salamis!

CHORUS

Thou sayest sooth—ah well-a-day!
Battered amid the waves, and torn,
On surges hither, thither, borne,
Dead bodies, bloodstained and forlorn,
In their long cloaks they toss and stray!

MESSENGER

Their bows availed not! all have perished, all,
By charging galleys crushed and whelmed in death.

CHORUS

Shriek out your sorrow's wistful wail!
To their untimely doom they went;

Ill strove they, and to no avail,
  And minished is their armament!
MESSENGER
    Out on thee, hateful name of Salamis,
Out upon Athens, mournful memory!
CHORUS
    Woe upon this day's evil fame!
  Thou, Athens, art our murderess;
Alack, full many a Persian dame
  Is left forlorn and husbandless!
ATOSSA
    Mute have I been awhile, and overwrought
At this great sorrow, for it passeth speech,
And passeth all desire to ask of it.
Yet if the gods send evils, men must bear.
                  (To the MESSENGER)
Unroll the record! stand composed and tell,
Although thy heart be groaning inwardly,
Who hath escaped, and, of our leaders, whom
Have we to weep? what chieftains in the van
Stood, sank, and died and left us leaderless?
MESSENGER
    Xerxes himself survives and sees the day.
ATOSSA
    Then to my line thy word renews the dawn
And golden dayspring after gloom of night!
MESSENGER
    But the brave marshal of ten thousand horse,
Artembares, is tossed and flung in death
Along the rugged rocks Silenian.
And Dadaces no longer leads his troop,
But, smitten by the spear, from off the prow
Hath lightly leaped to death; and Tenagon,
In true descent a Bactrian nobly born,
Drifts by the sea-lashed reefs of Salamis,
The isle of Ajax. Gone Lilaeus too,
Gone are Arsames and Argestes! all,
Around the islet where the sea-doves breed,
Dashed their defeated heads on iron rocks;
Arcteus, who dwelt beside the founts of Nile,
Adeues, Pheresseues, and with them

Pharnuchus, from one galley's deck went down.
Matallus, too, of Chrysa, lord and king
Of myriad hordes, who led unto the fight
Three times ten thousand swarthy cavaliers,
Fell, with his swarthy and abundant beard
Incarnadined to red, a crimson stain
Outrivalling the purple of the sea!
There Magian Arabus and Artames
Of Bactra perished—taking up, alike,
In yonder stony land their long sojourn.
Amistris too, and he whose strenuous spear
Was foremost in the fight, Amphistreus fell,
And gallant Ariomardus, by whose death
Broods sorrow upon Sardis: Mysia mourns
For Seisames, and Tharubis lies low—
Commander, he, of five times fifty ships,
Born in Lyrnessus: his heroic form
Is low in death, ungraced with sepulchre.
Dead too is he, the lord of courage high,
Cilicia's marshal, brave Syennesis,
Than whom none dealt more carnage on the foe,
Nor perished by a more heroic end.
So fell the brave: so speak I of their doom,
Summing in brief the fate of myriads!
ATOSSA
    Ah well-a-day! these crowning woes I hear,
The shame of Persia and her shrieks of dole!
But yet renew the tale, repeat thy words,
Tell o'er the count of those Hellenic ships,
And how they ventured with their beakèd prows
To charge upon the Persian armament.
MESSENGER
    Know, if mere count of ships could win the day,
The Persians had prevailed. The Greeks, in sooth,
Had but three hundred galleys at the most,
And other ten, select and separate.
But—I am witness—Xerxes held command
Of full a thousand keels, and, those apart,
Two hundred more, and seven, for speed renowned!—
So stands the reckoning, and who shall dare
To say we Persians had the lesser host?

ATOSSA

Nay, we were worsted by an unseen power
Who swayed the balance downward to our doom!

MESSENGER

In ward of heaven doth Pallas' city stand.

ATOSSA

How then? is Athens yet inviolate?

MESSENGER

While her men live, her bulwark standeth firm!

ATOSSA

Say, how began the struggle of the ships?
Who first joined issue? did the Greeks attack,
Or Xerxes, in his numbers confident?

MESSENGER

O queen, our whole disaster thus befell,
Through intervention of some fiend or fate—
I know not what—that had ill will to us.
From the Athenian host some Greek came o'er,
To thy son Xerxes whispering this tale—
Once let the gloom of night have gathered in,
The Greeks will tarry not, but swiftly spring
Each to his galley-bench, in furtive flight,
Softly contriving safety for their life.
Thy son believed the word and missed the craft
Of that Greek foeman, and the spite of Heaven,
And straight to all his captains gave this charge—
As soon as sunlight warms the ground no more,
And gloom enwraps the sanctuary of sky,
Range we our fleet in triple serried lines
To bar the passage from the seething strait,
This way and that: let other ships surround
The isle of Ajax, with this warning word—
That if the Greeks their jeopardy should scape
By wary craft, and win their ships a road.
Each Persian captain shall his failure pay
By forfeit of his head. So spake the king,
Inspired at heart with over-confidence,
Unwitting of the gods' predestined will.
Thereon our crews, with no disordered haste,
Did service to his bidding and purveyed
The meal of afternoon: each rower then

Over the fitted rowlock looped his oar.
Then, when the splendour of the sun had set,
And night drew on, each master of the oar
And each armed warrior straightway went aboard.
Forward the long ships moved, rank cheering rank,
Each forward set upon its ordered course.
And all night long the captains of the fleet
Kept their crews moving up and down the strait.
So the night waned, and not one Grecian ship
Made effort to elude and slip away.
But as dawn came and with her coursers white
Shone in fair radiance over all the earth,
First from the Grecian fleet rang out a cry,
A song of onset! and the island crags
Re-echoed to the shrill exulting sound.
Then on us Eastern men amazement fell
And fear in place of hope; for what we heard
Was not a call to flight! the Greeks rang out
Their holy, resolute, exulting chant,
Like men come forth to dare and do and die
Their trumpets pealed, and fire was in that sound,
And with the dash of simultaneous oars
Replying to the war-chant, on they came,
Smiting the swirling brine, and in a trice
They flashed upon the vision of the foe!
The right wing first in orderly advance
Came on, a steady column; following then,
The rest of their array moved out and on,
And to our ears there came a burst of sound,
A clamour manifold.—On, sons of Greece!
On, for your country's freedom! strike to save
Wives, children, temples of ancestral gods,
Graves of your fathers! now is all at stake.
Then from our side swelled up the mingled din
Of Persian tongues, and time brooked no delay—
Ship into ship drave hard its brazen beak
With speed of thought, a shattering blow! and first
One Grecian bark plunged straight, and sheared away
Bowsprit and stem of a Phoenician ship.
And then each galley on some other's prow
Came crashing in. Awhile our stream of ships

Held onward, till within the narrowing creek
Our jostling vessels were together driven,
And none could aid another: each on each
Drave hard their brazen beaks, or brake away
The oar-banks of each other, stem to stern,
While the Greek galleys, with no lack of skill,
Hemmed them and battered in their sides, and soon
The hulls rolled over, and the sea was hid,
Crowded with wrecks and butchery of men.
No beach nor reef but was with corpses strewn,
And every keel of our barbarian host
Hurried to flee, in utter disarray.
Thereon the foe closed in upon the wrecks
And hacked and hewed, with oars and splintered planks,
As fishermen hack tunnies or a cast
Of netted dolphins, and the briny sea
Rang with the screams and shrieks of dying men,
Until the night's dark aspect hid the scene.
Had I a ten days' time to sum that count
Of carnage, 'twere too little! know this well—
One day ne'er saw such myriad forms of death!

ATOSSA
    Woe on us, woe! disaster's mighty sea
Hath burst on us and all the Persian realm!
MESSENGER
    Be well assured, the tale is but begun—
The further agony that on us fell
Doth twice outweigh the sufferings I have told!
ATOSSA
    Nay, what disaster could be worse than this?
Say on! what woe upon the army came,
Swaying the scale to a yet further fall?
MESSENGER
    The very flower and crown of Persia's race,
Gallant of soul and glorious in descent,
And highest held in trust before the king,
Lies shamefully and miserably slain.
ATOSSA
    Alas for me and for this ruin, friends!
Dead, sayest thou? by what fate overthrown?

MESSENGER
    An islet is there, fronting Salamis—
Strait, and with evil anchorage: thereon
Pan treads the measure of the dance he loves
Along the sea-beach. Thither the king sent
His noblest, that, whene'er the Grecian foe
Should 'scape, with shattered ships, unto the isle,
We might make easy prey of fugitives
And slay them there, and from the washing tides
Rescue our friends. It fell out otherwise
Than he divined, for when, by aid of Heaven,
The Hellenes held the victory on the sea,
Their sailors then and there begirt themselves
With brazen mail and bounded from their ships,
And then enringed the islet, point by point,
So that our Persians in bewilderment
Knew not which way to turn. On every side,
Battered with stones, they fell, while arrows flew
From many a string, and smote them to the death.
Then, at the last, with simultaneous rush
The foe came bursting on us, hacked and hewed
To fragments all that miserable band,
Till not a soul of them was left alive.
Then Xerxes saw disaster's depth, and shrieked,
From where he sat on high, surveying all—
A lofty eminence, beside the brine,
Whence all his armament lay clear in view.
His robe he rent, with loud and bitter wail,
And to his land-force swiftly gave command
And fled, with shame beside him! Now, lament
That second woe, upon the first imposed!
ATOSSA
    Out on thee, Fortune! thou hast foiled the hope
And power of Persia: to this bitter end
My son went forth to wreak his great revenge
On famous Athens! all too few they seemed,
Our men who died upon the Fennel-field!
Vengeance for them my son had mind to take,
And drew on his own head these whelming woes.
But thou, say on! the ships that 'scaped from wreck—
Where didst thou leave them? make thy story clear.

MESSENGER
    The captains of the ships that still survived
Fled in disorder, scudding down the wind,
The while our land-force on Boeotian soil
Fell into ruin, some beside the springs
Dropping before they drank, and some outworn,
Pursued, and panting all their life away.
The rest of us our way to Phocis won,
And thence to Doris and the Melian gulf,
Where with soft stream Spercheus laves the soil.
Thence to the northward did Phthiotis' plain,
And some Thessalian fortress, lend us aid,
For famine-pinched we were, and many died
Of drought and hunger's twofold present scourge.
Thence to Magnesia came we, and the land
Where Macedonians dwell, and crossed the ford
Of Axius, and Bolbe's reedy fen,
And mount Pangaeus, in Edonian land.
There, in the very night we came, the god
Brought winter ere its time, from bank to bank
Freezing the holy Strymon's tide. Each man
Who heretofore held lightly of the gods,
Now crouched and proffered prayer to Earth and Heaven!
Then, after many orisons performed,
The army ventured on the frozen ford:
Yet only those who crossed before the sun
Shed its warm rays, won to the farther side.
For soon the fervour of the glowing orb
Did with its keen rays pierce the ice-bound stream,
And men sank through and thrust each other down—
Best was his lot whose breath was stifled first!
But all who struggled through and gained the bank,
Toilfully wending through the land of Thrace
Have made their way, a sorry, scanted few,
Unto this homeland. Let the city now
Lament and yearn for all the loved and lost.
My tale is truth, yet much untold remains
Of ills that Heaven hath hurled upon our land.
CHORUS
    Spirit of Fate, too heavy were thy feet,
Those ill to match! that sprang on Persia's realm.

ATOSSA

   Woe for the host, to wrack and ruin hurled!
O warning of the night, prophetic dream!
Thou didst foreshadow clearly all the doom,
While ye, old men, made light of woman's fears!
Ah well—yet, as your divination ruled
The meaning of the sign, I hold it good,
First, that I put up prayer unto the gods,
And, after that, forth from my palace bring
The sacrificial cake, the offering due
To Earth and to the spirits of the dead.
Too well I know it is a timeless rite
Over a finished thing that cannot change!
But yet—I know not—there may come of it
Alleviation for the after time.
You it beseems, in view of what hath happed,
T' advise with loyal hearts our loyal guards:
And to my son—if, ere my coming forth,
He should draw hitherward—give comfort meet,
Escort him to the palace in all state,
Lest to these woes he add another woe!
                        [Exit ATOSSA.

CHORUS

   Zeus, lord and king! to death and nought
Our countless host by thee is brought.
Deep in the gloom of death, to-day,
Lie Susa and Ecbatana:
How many a maid in sorrow stands
And rends her tire with tender hands!
How tears run down, in common pain
And woeful mourning for the slain!
O delicate in dole and grief,
Ye Persian women! past relief
Is now your sorrow! to the war
Your loved ones went and come no more!
Gone from you is your joy and pride—
Severed the bridegroom from the bride—
The wedded couch luxurious
Is widowed now, and all the house
Pines ever with insatiate sighs,
And we stand here and bid arise,

For those who forth in ardour went
And come not back, the loud lament!
  Land of the East, thou mournest for the host,
Bereft of all thy sons, alas the day!
For them whom Xerxes led hath Xerxes lost—
Xerxes who wrecked the fleet, and flung our hopes away!
  How came it that Darius once controlled,
And without scathe, the army of the bow,
Loved by the folk of Susa, wise and bold?
Now is the land-force lost, the shipmen sunk below!
  Ah for the ships that bore them, woe is me!
Bore them to death and doom! the crashing prows
Of fierce Ionian oarsmen swept the sea,
And death was in their wake, and shipwreck murderous!
  Late, late and hardly—if true tales they tell—
Did Xerxes flee along the wintry way
And snows of Thrace—but ah, the first who fell
Lie by the rocks or float upon Cychrea's bay!
    Mourn, each and all! waft heavenward your cry,
    Stung to the soul, bereaved, disconsolate!
  Wail out your anguish, till it pierce the sky,
In shrieks of deep despair, ill-omened, desperate!
    The dead are drifting, yea, are gnawed upon
    By voiceless children of the stainless sea,
  Or battered by the surge! we mourn and groan
For husbands gone to death, for childless agony!
    Alas the aged men, who mourn to-day
    The ruinous sorrows that the gods ordain!
  O'er the wide Asian land, the Persian sway
Can force no tribute now, and can no rule sustain.
    Yea, men will crouch no more to fallen power
    And kingship overthrown! the whole land o'er,
  Men speak the thing they will, and from this hour
The folk whom Xerxes ruled obey his word no more.
    The yoke of force is broken from the neck—
    The isle of Ajax and th' encircling wave
  Reek with a bloody crop of death and wreck
Of Persia's fallen power, that none can lift nor save!
          [Re-enter ATOSSA, in mourning robes.
ATOSSA
    Friends, whosoe'er is versed in human ills,

Knoweth right well that when a wave of woe
Comes on a man, he sees in all things fear;
While, in flood-tide of fortune, 'tis his mood
To take that fortune as unchangeable,
Wafting him ever forward. Mark me now—
The gods' thwart purpose doth confront mine eyes,
And all is terror to me; in mine ears
There sounds a cry, but not of triumph now—
So am I scared at heart by woe so great.
Therefore I wend forth from the house anew,
Borne in no car of state, nor robed in pride
As heretofore, but bringing, for the sire
Who did beget my son, libations meet
For holy rites that shall appease the dead—
The sweet white milk, drawn from a spotless cow,
The oozing drop of golden honey, culled
By the flower-haunting bee, and therewithal
Pure draughts of water from a virgin spring;
And lo! besides, the stainless effluence,
Born of the wild vine's bosom, shining store
Treasured to age, this bright and luscious wine.
And eke the fragrant fruit upon the bough
Of the grey olive-tree, which lives its life
In sprouting leafage, and the twining flowers,
Bright children of the earth's fertility.
But you, O friends! above these offerings poured
To reconcile the dead, ring out your dirge
To summon up Darius from the shades,
Himself a shade; and I will pour these draughts,
Which earth shall drink, unto the gods of hell.
CHORUS
    Queen, by the Persian land adored,
By thee be this libation poured,
Passing to those who hold command
Of dead men in the spirit-land!
And we will sue, in solemn chant,
That gods who do escort the dead
In nether realms, our prayer may grant—
  Back to us be Darius led!
    O Earth, and Hermes, and the king
Of Hades, our Darius bring!

For if, beyond the prayers we prayed,
He knoweth aught of help or aid,
He, he alone, in realms below,
Can speak the limit of our woe!
   Doth he hear me, the king we adored, who is god
      among gods of the dead?
   Doth he hear me send out in my sorrow the pitiful,
      manifold cry,
The sobbing lament and appeal? is the voice of my
      suffering sped
   To the realm of the shades? doth he hear me and
      pity my sorrowful sigh?
O Earth, and ye Lords of the dead! release ye that
      spirit of might,
Who in Susa the palace was born! let him rise up
      once more to the light!
      There is none like him, none of all
That e'er were laid in Persian sepulchres!
   Borne forth he was to honoured burial,
A royal heart! and followed by our tears.
   God of the dead, O give him back to us,
Darius, ruler glorious!
   He never wasted us with reckless war—
God, counsellor, and king, beneath a happy star!
   Ancient of days and king, awake and come—
      Rise o'er the mounded tomb!
Rise, plant thy foot, with saffron sandal shod
   Father to us, and god!
Rise with thy diadem, O sire benign,
   Upon thy brow!
List to the strange new sorrows of thy line,
   Sire of a woeful son!
      A mist of fate and hell is round us now,
And all the city's flower to death is done!
Alas, we wept thee once, and weep again!
O Lord of lords, by recklessness twofold
The land is wasted of its men,
And down to death are rolled
Wreckage of sail and oar,
Ships that are ships no more,
And bodies of the slain!

[The GHOST OF DARIUS rises.

GHOST OF DARIUS

    Ye aged Persians, truest of the true,
Coevals of the youth that once was mine,
What troubleth now our city? harken, how
It moans and beats the breast and rends the plain!
And I, beholding how my consort stood
Beside my tomb, was moved with awe, and took
The gift of her libation graciously.
But ye are weeping by my sepulchre,
And, shrilling forth a sad, evoking cry,
Summon me mournfully, Arise, arise.
No light thing is it, to come back from death,
For, in good sooth, the gods of nether gloom
Are quick to seize but late and loth to free!
Yet among them I dwell as one in power—
And lo, I come! now speak, and speed your words,
Lest I be blamed for tarrying overlong!
What new disaster broods o'er Persia's realm?

CHORUS

    With awe on thee I gaze,
And, standing face to face,
I tremble as I did in olden days!

GHOST OF DARIUS

    Nay, but as I rose to earth again, obedient to your call,
Prithee, tarry not in parley! be one word enough for all—
Speak and gaze on me unshrinking, neither let my face appal!

CHORUS

    I tremble to reveal,
Yet tremble to conceal
Things hard for friends to feel!

GHOST OF DARIUS

    Nay, but if the old-time terror on your spirit keeps its hold,
Speak thou, O royal lady who didst couch with me of old!
Stay thy weeping and lamenting and to me reveal the truth—
Speak! for man is born to sorrow; yea, the proverb sayeth sooth!
'Tis the doom of mortal beings, if they live to see old age,
To suffer bale, by land and sea, through war and tempest's rage.

ATOSSA

    O thou whose blissful fate on earth all mortal weal excelled—
Who, while the sunlight touched thine eyes, the lord of all wert

held!
A god to Persian men thou wert, in bliss and pride and fame—
I hold thee blest too in thy death, or e'er the ruin came!
Alas, Darius! one brief word must tell thee all the tale—
The Persian power is in the dust, gone down in blood and bale!

GHOST OF DARIUS
    Speak—by what chance? did man rebel, or pestilence descend?
ATOSSA
    Neither! by Athens' fatal shores our army met its end.
GHOST OF DARIUS
    Which of my children led our host to Athens? speak and say.
ATOSSA
    The froward Xerxes, leaving all our realm to disarray.
GHOST OF DARIUS
    Was it with army or with fleet on folly's quest he went?
ATOSSA
    With both alike, a twofold front of double armament.
GHOST OF DARIUS
    And how then did so large a host on foot pass o'er the sea?
ATOSSA
    He bridged the ford of Helle's strait by artful carpentry.
GHOST OF DARIUS
    How? could his craft avail to span the torrent of that tide?
ATOSSA
    'Tis sooth I say—some unknown power did fatal help provide!
GHOST OF DARIUS
    Alas, that power in malice came, to his bewilderment!
ATOSSA
    Alas, we see the end of all, the ruin on us sent.
GHOST OF DARIUS
    Speak, tell me how they fared therein, that thus ye mourn and weep?
ATOSSA
    Disaster to the army came, through ruin on the deep!
GHOST OF DARIUS
    Is all undone? hath all the folk gone down before the foe?
ATOSSA
    Yea, hark to Susa's mourning cry for warriors laid low!
GHOST OF DARIUS
    Alas for all our gallant aids, our Persia's help and pride!
ATOSSA

Ay! old with young, the Bactrian force hath perished at our side!
GHOST OF DARIUS
   Alas, my son! what gallant youths hath he sent down to death!

ATOSSA
   Alone, or with a scanty guard—for so the rumour saith—
GHOST OF DARIUS
   He came—but how, and to what end? doth aught of hope remain?
ATOSSA
   With joy he reached the bridge that spanned the Hellespontine main.
GHOST OF DARIUS
   How? is he safe, in Persian land? speak soothly, yea or nay!
ATOSSA
   Clear and more clear the rumour comes, for no man to gainsay.
GHOST OF DARIUS
     Woe for the oracle fulfilled, the presage of the war
Launched on my son, by will of Zeus! I deemed our doom afar
In lap of time; but, if a king push forward to his fate,
The god himself allures to death that man infatuate!
So now the very fount of woe streams out on those I loved,
And mine own son, unwisely bold, the truth hereof hath proved!
He sought to shackle and control the Hellespontine wave,
That rushes from the Bosphorus, with fetters of a slave!—
To curb and bridge, with welded links, the streaming water-way,
And guide across the passage broad his manifold array!
Ah, folly void of counsel! he deemed that mortal wight
Could thwart the will of Heaven itself and curb Poseidon's might!
Was it not madness? much I fear lest all my wealth and store
Pass from my treasure-house, to be the snatcher's prize once more!
ATOSSA
     Such is the lesson, ah, too late! to eager Xerxes taught—
Trusting random counsellors and hare-brained men of nought,
Who said Darius mighty wealth and fame to us did bring,
But thou art nought, a blunted spear, a palace-keeping king!
Unto those sorry counsellors a ready ear he lent,
And led away to Hellas' shore his fated armament.
GHOST OF DARIUS
     Therefore through them hath come calamity
Most huge and past forgetting; nor of old
Did ever such extermination fall
Upon the city Susa. Long ago

Zeus in his power this privilege bestowed,
That with a guiding sceptre one sole man
Should rule this Asian land of flock and herd.
Over the folk a Mede, Astyages,
Did grasp the power: then Cyaxares ruled
In his sire's place, and held the sway aright,
Steering his state with watchful wariness.
Third in succession, Cyrus, blest of Heaven,
Held rule and 'stablished peace for all his clan:
Lydian and Phrygian won he to his sway,
And wide Ionia to his yoke constrained,
For the god favoured his discretion sage.
Fourth in the dynasty was Cyrus' son,
And fifth was Mardus, scandal of his land
And ancient lineage. Him Artaphrenes,
Hardy of heart, within his palace slew,
Aided by loyal plotters, set for this.
And I too gained the lot for which I craved,
And oftentimes led out a goodly host,
Yet never brought disaster such as this
Upon the city. But my son is young
And reckless in his youth, and heedeth not
The warnings of my mouth. Mark this, my friends,
Born with my birth, coeval with mine age—
Not all we kings who held successive rule
Have wrought, combined, such ruin as my son!
CHORUS
    How then, O King Darius? whitherward
Dost thou direct thy warning? from this plight
How can we Persians fare towards hope again?
GHOST OF DARIUS
    By nevermore assailing Grecian lands,
Even tho' our Median force be double theirs—
For the land's self protects its denizens.
CHORUS
    How meanest thou? by what defensive power?
GHOST OF DARIUS
    She wastes by famine a too countless foe.
CHORUS
    But we will bring a host more skilled than huge.

GHOST OF DARIUS
 Why, e'en that army, camped in Hellas still,
Shall never win again to home and weal!
CHORUS
 How say'st thou? will not all the Asian host
Pass back from Europe over Helle's ford?
GHOST OF DARIUS
 Nay—scarce a tithe of all those myriads,
If man may trust the oracles of Heaven
When he beholds the things already wrought,
Not false with true, but true with no word false
If what I trow be truth, my son has left
A chosen rear-guard of our host, in whom
He trusts, now, with a random confidence!
They tarry where Asopus laves the ground
With rills that softly bless Boeotia's plain—
There is it fated for them to endure
The very crown of misery and doom,
Requital for their god-forgetting pride!
For why? they raided Hellas, had the heart
To wrong the images of holy gods,
And give the shrines and temples to the flame!
Defaced and dashed from sight the altars fell,
And each god's image, from its pedestal
Thrust and flung down, in dim confusion lies!
Therefore, for outrage vile, a doom as dark
They suffer, and yet more shall undergo—
They touch no bottom in the swamp of doom,
But round them rises, bubbling up, the ooze!
So deep shall lie the gory clotted mass
Of corpses by the Dorian spear transfixed
Upon Plataea's field! yea, piles of slain
To the third generation shall attest
By silent eloquence to those that see—
Let not a mortal vaunt him overmuch.
For pride grows rankly, and to ripeness brings
The curse of fate, and reaps, for harvest, tears!
Therefore when ye behold, for deeds like these,
Such stern requital paid, remember then
Athens and Hellas. Let no mortal wight,
Holding too lightly of his present weal

And passionate for more, cast down and spill
The mighty cup of his prosperity!
Doubt not that over-proud and haughty souls
Zeus lours in wrath, exacting the account.
Therefore, with wary warning, school my son,
Though he be lessoned by the gods already,
To curb the vaunting that affronts high Heaven!
And thou, O venerable Mother-queen,
Beloved of Xerxes, to the palace pass
And take therefrom such raiment as befits
Thy son, and go to meet him: for his garb
In this extremity of grief hangs rent
Around his body, woefully unstitched,
Mere tattered fragments of once royal robes!
Go thou to him, speak soft and soothing words—
Thee, and none other, will he bear to hear,
As well I know. But I must pass away
From earth above, unto the nether gloom;
Therefore, old men, take my farewell, and clasp,
Even amid the ruin of this time,
Unto your souls the pleasure of the day,
For dead men have no profit of their gold!

                  [The GHOST OF DARIUS sinks.

CHORUS

    Alas, I thrill with pain for Persia's woes—
Many fulfilled, and others hard at hand!

ATOSSA

    O spirit of the race, what sorrows crowd
Upon me! and this anguish stings me worst,
That round my royal son's dishonoured form
Hang rags and tatters, degradation deep!
I will away, and, bringing from within
A seemly royal robe, will straightway strive
To meet and greet my son: foul scorn it were
To leave our dearest in his hour of shame.

                      [Exit ATOSSA.

CHORUS

    Ah glorious and goodly they were,
      the life and the lot that we gained,
  The cities we held in our hand

when the monarch invincible reigned,
The king that was good to his realm,
    sufficing, fulfilled of his sway,
A lord that was peer of the gods,
    the pride of the bygone day!
Then could we show to the skies
    great hosts and a glorious name,
And laws that were stable in might;
    as towers they guarded our fame!
There without woe or disaster
    we came from the foe and the fight,
In triumph, enriched with the spoil,
    to the land and the city's delight.
What towns ere the Halys he passed!
    what towns ere he came to the West,
To the main and the isles of the Strymon,
    and the Thracian region possess'd!
And those that stand back from the main,
    enringed by their fortified wall,
Gave o'er to Darius, the king,
    the sceptre and sway over all!
Those too by the channel of Helle,
    where southward it broadens and glides,
By the inlets, Propontis! of thee,
    and the strait of the Pontic tides,
And the isles that lie fronting our sea-board,
    and the Eastland looks on each one,
Lesbo and Chios and Paros,
    and Samos with olive-trees grown,
And Naxos, and Myconos' rock,
    and Tenos with Andros hard by,
And isles that in midmost Aegean,
    aloof from the continent, lie—
And Lemnos and Icaros' hold—
    all these to his sceptre were bowed,
And Cnidos and neighbouring Rhodes,
    and Soli, and Paphos the proud,
And Cyprian Salamis, name-child of her
    who hath wrought us this wrong!
Yea, and all the Ionian tract,
    where the Greek-born inhabitants throng,

And the cities are teeming with gold—
   Darius was lord of them all,
And, great by his wisdom, he ruled,
   and ever there came to his call,
In stalwart array and unfailing,
   the warrior chiefs of our land,
And mingled allies from the tribes
   who bowed to his conquering hand!
But now there are none to gainsay
   that the gods are against us; we lie
Subdued in the havoc of wreck,
   and whelmed by the wrath of the sky!

                [Enter XERXES in disarray.

XERXES
   Alas the day, that I should fall
Into this grimmest fate of all,
  This ruin doubly unforeseen!
On Persia's land what power of Fate
Descends, what louring gloom of hate?
  How shall I bear my teen?
My limbs are loosened where they stand,
When I behold this aged band—
Oh God! I would that I too, I,
  Among the men who went to die,
Were whelmed in earth by Fate's command!

CHORUS
   Ah welladay, my King! ah woe
For all our heroes' overthrow—
  For all the gallant host's array,
  For Persia's honour, pass'd away,
  For glory and heroic sway
  Mown down by Fortune's hand to-day!
Hark, how the kingdom makes its moan,
For youthful valour lost and gone,
By Xerxes shattered and undone!
  He, he hath crammed the maw of hell
  With bowmen brave, who nobly fell,
Their country's mighty armament,
Ten thousand heroes deathward sent!
  Alas, for all the valiant band,
  O king and lord! thine Asian land

Down, down upon its knee is bent!
XERXES
    Alas, a lamentable sound,
A cry of ruth! for I am found
A curse to land and lineage,
With none my sorrow to assuage!
CHORUS
    Alas, a death-song desolate
I send forth, for thy home-coming!
A scream, a dirge for woe and fate,
    Such as the Asian mourners sing,
A sorry and ill-omened tale
Of tears and shrieks and Eastern wail!
XERXES
    Ay, launch the woeful sorrow's cry,
The harsh, discordant melody,
For lo, the power, we held for sure,
Hath turned to my discomfiture!
CHORUS
    Yea, dirges, dirges manifold
Will I send forth, for warriors bold,
For the sea-sorrow of our host!
The city mourns, and I must wail
With plashing tears our sorrow's tale,
Lamenting for the loved and lost!
XERXES
    Alas, the god of war, who sways
The scales of fight in diverse ways,
Gives glory to Ionia!
Ionian ships, in fenced array,
Have reaped their harvest in the bay,
A darkling harvest-field of Fate,
A sea, a shore, of doom and hate!
CHORUS
    Cry out, and learn the tale of woe!
Where are thy comrades? where the band
Who stood beside thee, hand in hand,
    A little while ago?
Where now hath Pharandákes gone,
Where Psammis, and where Pelagon?
Where now is brave Agdabatas,

And Susas too, and Datamas?
Hath Susiscanes past away,
The chieftain of Ecbatana?
XERXES
   I left them, mangled castaways,
  Flung from their Tyrian deck, and tossed
On Salaminian water-ways,
  From surging tides to rocky coast!
CHORUS
   Alack, and is Pharnuchus slain,
And Ariomardus, brave in vain?
Where is Seualces' heart of fire?
Lilaeus, child of noble sire?
Are Tharubis and Memphis sped?
Hystaechmas, Artembáres dead?
And where is brave Masistes, where?
Sum up death's count, that I may hear!
XERXES
   Alas, alas, they came, their eyes surveyed
Ancestral Athens on that fatal day.
Then with a rending struggle were they laid
Upon the land, and gasped their life away!
CHORUS
   And Batanochus' child, Alpistus great,
  Surnamed the Eye of State—
Saw you and left you him who once of old
Ten thousand thousand fighting-men enrolled?
His sire was child of Sesamas, and he
From Megabates sprang. Ah, woe is me,
  Thou king of evil fate!
Hast thou lost Parthus, lost Oebares great?
  Alas, the sorrow! blow succeedeth blow
On Persia's pride; thou tellest woe on woe!
XERXES
   Bitter indeed the pang for comrades slain,
  The brave and bold! thou strikest to my soul
Pain, pain beyond forgetting, hateful pain.
  My inner spirit sobs and sighs with dole!
CHORUS
   Another yet we yearn to see,
And see not! ah, thy chivalry,

Xanthis, thou chief of Mardian men
Countless! and thou, Anchares bright,
And ye, whose cars controlled the fight,
Arsaces and Diaixis wight,
Kegdadatas, Lythimnas dear,
And Tolmus, greedy of the spear!
I stand bereft! not in thy train
Come they, as erst! ah, ne'er again
Shall they return unto our eyes,
Car-borne, 'neath silken canopies!
XERXES
  Yea, gone are they who mustered once the host!
CHORUS
  Yea, yea, forgotten, lost!
XERXES
  Alas, the woe and cost!
CHORUS
    Alas, ye heavenly powers!
  Ye wrought a sorrow past belief,
    A woe, of woes the chief!
  With aspect stern, upon us Ate looms!
XERXES
  Smitten are we—time tells no heavier blow!
CHORUS
  Smitten! the doom is plain!
XERXES
  Curse upon curse and pang on pang we know!
CHORUS
    With the Ionian power
  We clashed, in evil hour!
  Woe falls on Persia's race, yea, woe again, again!
XERXES
  Yea, smitten am I, and my host is all to ruin hurled!
CHORUS
  Yea verily—in mighty wreck hath sunk the Persian world!
  XERXES (holding up a torn robe and a quiver)
  See you this tattered rag of pride?
CHORUS
  I see it, welladay!
XERXES
  See you this quiver?

CHORUS

Say, hath aught survived and 'scaped the fray?

XERXES

A store for darts it was, erewhile!

CHORUS

Remain but two or three!

XERXES

No aid is left!

CHORUS

Ionian folk such darts, unfearing, see!

XERXES

Right resolute they are! I saw disaster unforeseen.

CHORUS

Ah, speakest thou of wreck, of flight, of carnage that hath been?

XERXES

Yea, and my royal robe I rent, in terror at their fall!

CHORUS

Alas, alas!

XERXES

Yea, thrice alas!

CHORUS

For all have perished, all!

XERXES

Ah woe to us, ah joy to them who stood against our pride

CHORUS

And all our strength is minished and sundered from our side!

XERXES

No escort have I!

CHORUS

Nay, thy friends are whelmed beneath the tide!

XERXES

Wail, wail the miserable doom, and to the palace hie!

CHORUS

Alas, alas, and woe again!

XERXES

Shriek, smite the breast, as I!

CHORUS

An evil gift, a sad exchange, of tears poured out in vain!

XERXES

Shrill out your simultaneous wail!

CHORUS
Alas the woe and pain!
XERXES
O, bitter is this adverse fate!
CHORUS
I voice the moan with thee!
XERXES
Smite, smite thy bosom, groan aloud for my calamity!
CHORUS
I mourn and am dissolved in tears!
XERXES
Cry, beat thy breast amain!
CHORUS
O king, my heart is in thy woe!
XERXES
Shriek, wail, and shriek again!
CHORUS
O agony!
XERXES
A blackening blow—
CHORUS
A grievous stripe shall fall

XERXES
Yea, beat anew thy breast, ring out the doleful Mysian call!
CHORUS
An agony, an agony!
XERXES
Pluck out thy whitening beard!
CHORUS
By handfuls, ay, by handfuls, with dismal tear-drops smeared!
XERXES
Sob out thine aching sorrow!
CHORUS
I will thine best obey.
XERXES
With thine hands rend thy mantle's fold—
CHORUS
Alas, woe worth the day!
XERXES
With thine own fingers tear thy locks, bewail the army's weird!

CHORUS

By handfuls, yea, by handfuls, with tears of dole besmeared!

XERXES

Now let thine eyes find overflow—

CHORUS

I wend in wail and pain!

XERXES

Cry out for me an answering moan—

CHORUS

Alas, alas again!

XERXES

Shriek with a cry of agony, and lead the doleful train!

CHORUS

Alas, alas, the Persian land is woeful now to tread!

XERXES

Cry out and mourn! the city now doth wail above the dead!

CHORUS

I sob and moan!

XERXES

I bid ye now be delicate in grief

CHORUS

Alas, the Persian land is sad and knoweth not relief!

XERXES

Alas, the triple banks of oars and those who died thereby!

CHORUS

Pass! I will lead you, bring you home, with many a broken sigh! [Exeunt

Ingram Content Group UK Ltd.
Milton Keynes UK
UKHW010705130623
423332UK00003B/63